# Photography and Archaeology

# exposures

EXPOSURES is a series of books on photography designed to explore the rich history of the medium from thematic perspectives. Each title presents a striking collection of approximately 80 images and an engaging, accessible text that offers intriguing insights into a specific theme or subject.

Series editors: Mark Haworth-Booth and Peter Hamilton

Also published

*Photography and Spirit* John Harvey
*Photography and Australia* Helen Ennis
*Photography and Cinema* David Campany
*Photography and Literature* François Brunet
*Photography and Flight* Denis Cosgrove and William L. Fox
*Photography and Africa* Erin Haney
*Photography and Italy* Maria Antonella Pelizzari
*Photography and Death* Audrey Linkman
*Photography and Science* Kelley Wilder
*Photography and the USA* Mick Gidley
*Photography and Egypt* Maria Golia
*Photography and Anthropology* Chris Pinney
*Photography and Japan* Karen Fraser

# Photography and Archaeology

Frederick N. Bohrer

reaktion books

*To the memory of David Jacobs*

Published by Reaktion Books Ltd
33 Great Sutton Street
London EC1V 0DX
www.reaktionbooks.co.uk

First published 2011



Printed and bound in China

British Library Cataloguing in Publication Data
Bohrer, Frederick Nathaniel, 1956–
Photography and archaeology. – (Exposures)
1. Photography in archaeology.
2. Photography in archaeology – History.
I. Title II. Series
778.9'9301-dc22

ISBN 978 1 86189 870 8

# Contents

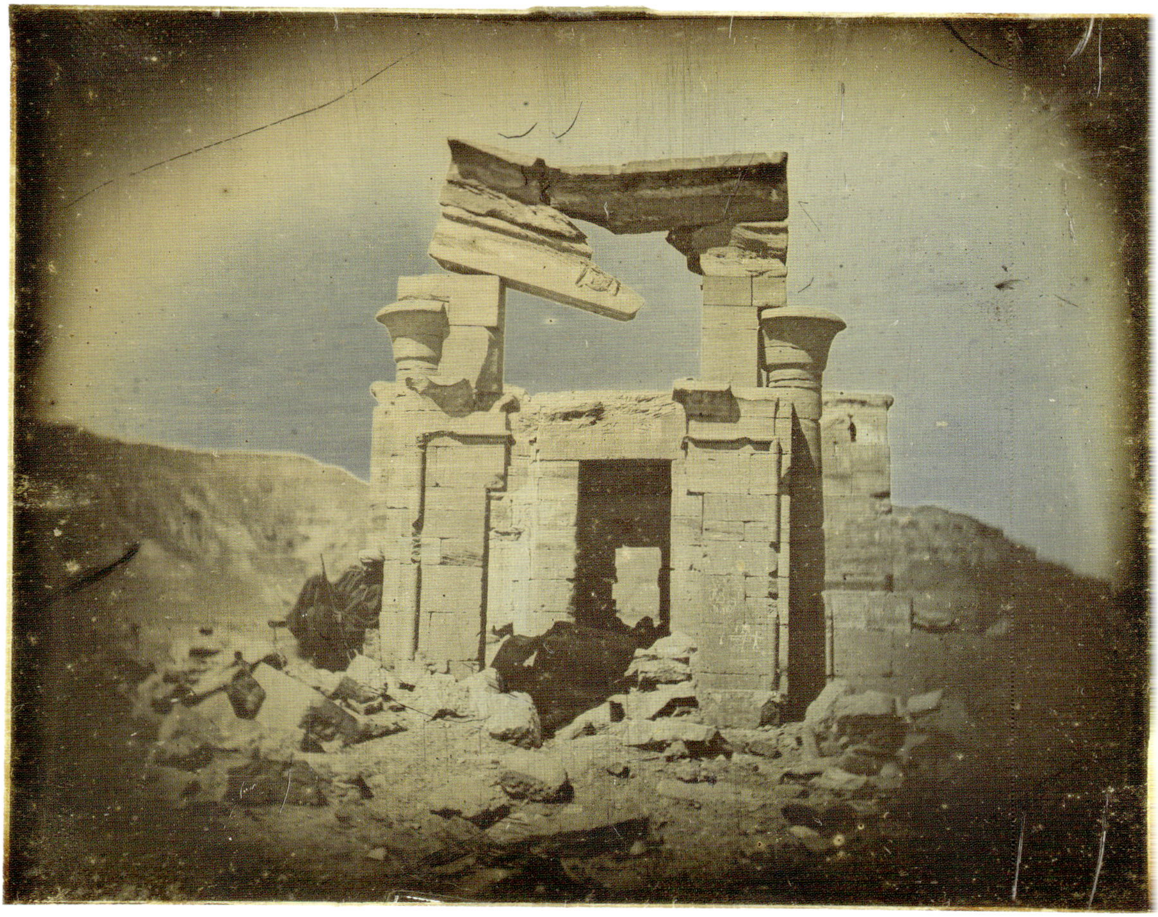

# Introduction: The Image as Object

> All the arts are based on the presence of man, only photography derives an advantage from his absence.
>
> André Bazin[1]

We don't see the past so much as look for it. The past is, after all, past. Seeing, at least in the literal sense, involves what is present to experience. Looking for the past, the very job of the archaeologist, is necessarily a unique sort of looking, focused on what is always beyond the experience he or she can be certain about. How is it possible at all? Looking at things archaeologically is looking for absence as much as presence, for traces of what is no longer, which must be inferred to be comprehensible, turning a disordered array of architectural fragments or potsherds or rubbish or tiles or coins or human remains into the remnant of once-living habitation and culture.

Archaeology's focus on the tangible, using it as a way to get beneath what is present, is not just aided but somehow fundamentally enabled by photography. Photography offers the possibility of an effortlessly archaeological way of seeing, eliding present into past while remaining tethered in objectivity. Everything in a photograph is always from the past. Unlike the saturating sense of artifice and individuality that André Bazin associated with media such as painting or sculpture, which he calls presence, the photograph appears more cold-bloodedly objective: the photographer's human presence, and artist's tendency to subjectivity, held in check by his mechanical apparatus. The distancing involved in both taking and looking at a photograph has often been remarked upon

1 Joseph-Philibert Girault de Prangey, 'Small Temple, Djèbel Selsêleh, Egypt', 1842–3, daguerreotype.

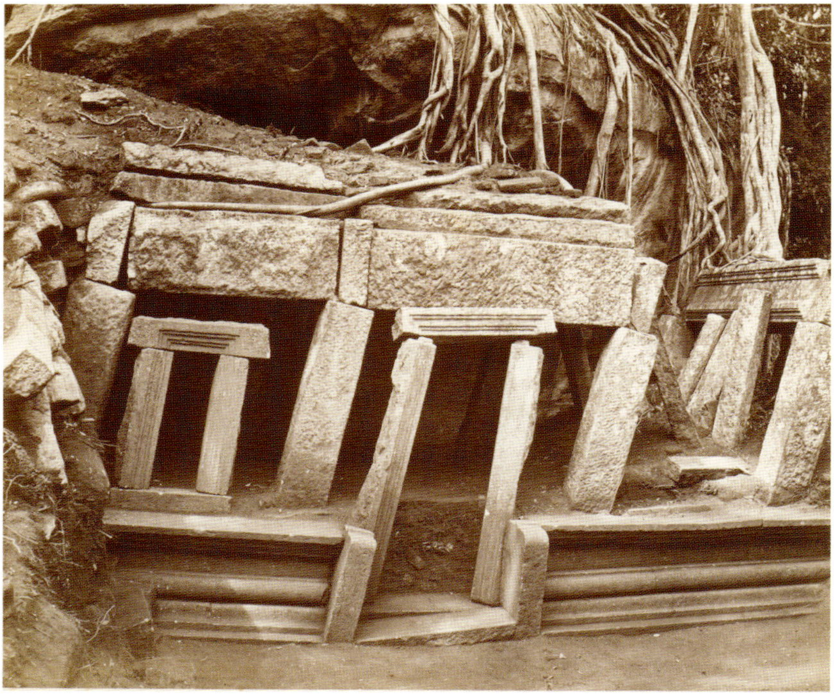

2 Joseph Lawton, 'Newly discovered ruins at the *Kaludiya Pokuna* (Bathing Pool), Mihintale, Sri Lanka', 1870–71, albumen silver print.

by theorists of photography, notably Roland Barthes, who stated decades ago that 'the tense of the photograph is the aorist' so that 'the same century invented History and Photography'.[2]

That century, the nineteenth, also invented archaeology. Archaeological photography pairs the technology of picturing absence with the science of deciphering absence and recuperating from it. For historian Kitty Hauser, 'The archaeological imagination refuses to acknowledge, quite, the loss of anything.'[3] The photographic imagination does something quite similar. For this reason, perhaps, archaeology appears frequently as a metaphor in discussions of photography, particularly photography devoted to objects or documentation. For instance, the photographer Berenice Abbott wrote about Eugène Atget, the dedicated photographer of old Paris in the late nineteenth and early twentieth centuries, that: 'He saw the old and the new, as an archaeologist excavates strata of past civilizations.'[4] Atget's characteristic photographic stance was that of an archaeologist, fixing traces of a vanishing Parisian past embedded in its modernizing present.

Walter Benjamin well elaborates the nature of Atget's particular brand of absence. 'It has justly been said that he photographed [deserted Paris streets] like scenes of crime. The scene of a crime, too, is deserted; it is photographed for the purpose of establishing evidence. With Atget, photographs become standard evidence for historical occurrences.'[5] Archaeological photography too is largely deserted, and often to be scanned with a forensic gaze, toward finding evidence of what took place previously. Indeed, archaeological sites today can be cordoned off and controlled in a manner not unlike that of crime scenes in their related search for traces of past activity. In both, photography is the premier instrument of distanced presence looking out towards palpable absence, scanning for traces of the past. Looked at as a whole, then, both presence and absence, both photographer and photographic subject, are available in a single frame to the viewer of a photograph, in a way that comports with the interaction of present and past which is both archaeology's subject and governing metaphor, in the process spanning positions of art and science, subjectivity and objectivity.

Consider a photograph made by Joseph Lawton, a single print mounted among the pages of four magisterial albums largely devoted to Sri Lankan antiquities (illus. 2). Lawton was a professional photographer active in Ceylon (Sri Lanka) during the 1860s and '70s, hired to document ancient ruins, which the Ceylon branch of the Royal Asiatic Society was just beginning to investigate.[6] A striking photograph of a facade near the bathing pool, on the sacred Buddhist mountain of Mihintale, confronts us with the remains of an ancient structure. The building is well along in the process of being reclaimed by nature, as the vines of a nearby tree and weight of soil movement at its top and side have powerfully pushed it out of the rectilineal registers in which it was built. We can almost feel it as the columns move toward horizontal, the threshold is twisted upward and the lintel becomes detached and unstable. This photograph lets us gauge the effect of time on the structure and even consider its future, while also recuperating something of the

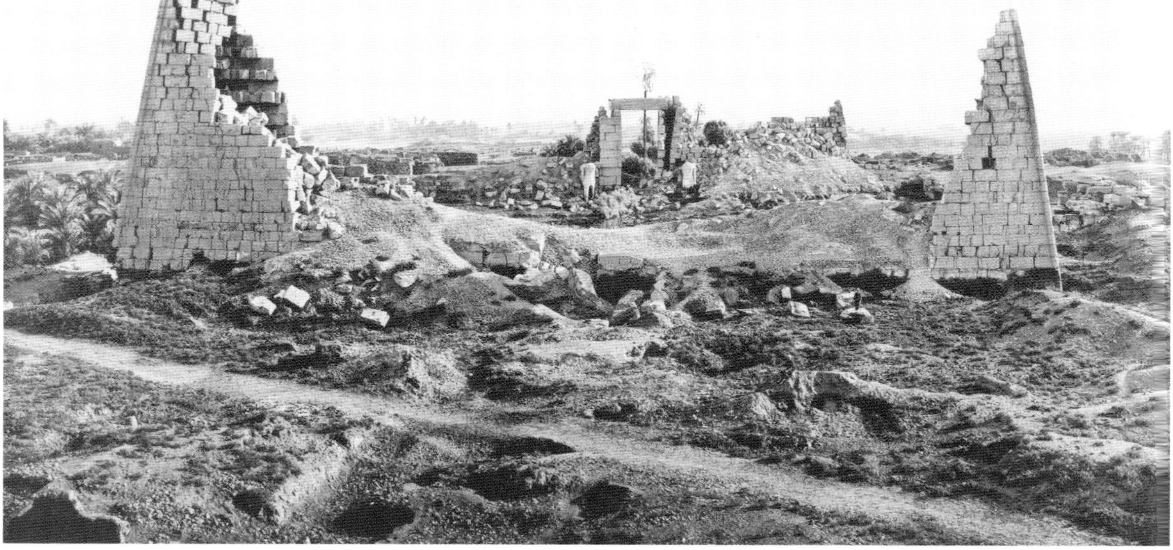

3 Émile Béchard, 'Pylon of Horus, Karnak, Egypt', 1887, photomechanical print.

ancient monument. It is not just a dramatic view of natural forces but also a sort of naturally occurring diagram of ancient building technique, as it is dismantled and disorganized.

A different kind of example is a photograph made a bit later, in 1887, by Émile Béchard in the ancient Egyptian temple complex at Karnak (illus. 3). Whereas Lawton was pressed into archaeological service, Béchard's photo was made toward the end of two decades devoted to a massive photographic documentation of sites and artefacts of ancient Egypt, in association with some of the leading archaeologists of his time. It is a document of the formalization of archaeological vision in Egypt. Béchard's photograph confronts us most of all with what is left of an ancient pylon. Through his choice of viewpoint we can gauge the width and, through the fragment at left, the height and overall shape of the original structure. Béchard places both edges of the photograph at a uniform distance from the edges of the presumed structure, in effect delineating a space that the viewer is invited to scan. Most of this structure, of course, is absent. Most of the space represented is empty, ruined. This emptiness, however, is occupied by the viewer's imagination of what can be reconstructed within its bounds, positioning this present absence in a way that invites our consideration of its past. The photograph is something like a stage set in which archaeological vision can be acted out.

These are two images, then, of archaeological ways of seeing, of fixing the ancient monument and presenting absence for the modern viewer. These are indeed like crime scenes, photographed to understand the dynamics of destruction and allow a reconstruction of the object. But much as photography serves the understanding of antiquity, antiquity itself has been fundamental to photography throughout its history. Writing on the range of interaction between archaeology and photography, the archaeologist Michael Shanks observes that 'even when photographs are acknowledged as artefacts, they may also take on something of the status of found objects, harnessing the magic of the real'.[7] What begins as a copy of the real, then, acquires its own reality. In this sense, one might say that even as archaeology uses photography, indeed relies on it as an essential scientific tool, photography can also enact a certain operation on the things it records which resembles nothing so much as archaeology, resurrecting unique, and past, moments in the life of a structure. Atget is one example, but the effect is only more exacerbated when one thinks of daguerreotypes, unique, negativeless images, technologically obsolete less than a generation after their invention, and notably artefactual in their own right.

A monument from near the beginning of photography is a daguerreotype by the French photographer Joseph-Philibert Girault de Prangey, whose remarkable work we'll consider in more detail later (illus. 1). An image from 1842–3, just a few years after photography's official invention, depicts the facade of a small temple at Djèbel Selsêleh, near Philae in Upper Egypt. The temple sits among boulders and rubble, while behind it a low ridge climbs diagonally in a way that echoes the temple's broken, slanted architrave. The squarish grouping sits safely within a rectangular photographic frame, hugged by the iris outline of the image area. Girault de Prangey's photos are quite varied in size and format, often tailored to their antique subject. What is most striking and dramatic here is surely the architrave itself, which seems almost to be held up by force of will. Even more, the uniqueness and irreparability of this moment is figured in the uniqueness and irreparability of this object. It is a daguerreotype, a sort of photographic format which itself became quickly extinct, a trace of the past. Like most daguerreotypes, this one clearly exhibits marks of its own particular past, in the scratches and unresolved areas of the image, a sort of correlate to the traces of wear to the temple itself.

For its level of popular interest and support, archaeology is among the most fortunate of sciences. Its results bear the imprimatur of scientific validity, and yet often stir a thrill that goes beyond fact-finding, connecting somehow to the poignant drama of human history. But archaeology's unique appeal among the sciences may not be so much inherent as constructed, as much a question of medium as message. Indeed, from its very foundation archaeology has cultivated public interest, and perhaps its greatest instrument has been photography. The anthropologists Curtis Hinsley and Melissa Banta state directly that 'few scientific fields have used photography as variously and experimentally as archaeology, and few have enjoyed such public enthusiasm mediated by this technology'.[8]

A case in point is that of the most famous archaeological excavation of the twentieth century: Howard Carter's finds at the tomb of Tutankhamun in the Valley of the Kings in Upper Egypt. From Carter's entry into the sealed doorway of the burial chamber in February 1923, it was the focus of intense public interest, and has remained so to the present day. This is a mark not only of the value of the finds, but the then-unprecedented publicity devoted to their promulgation, and the remarkable photographic evidence of it available. In fact coverage was carefully controlled and meted out, with few journalists present at any stage of excavation, as if hoarding a rare commodity. The excavation itself, however, was one of the first to be systematically documented by photography. The photographer was Harry Burton, on loan to Carter's excavation from an Egyptological team from New York's Metropolitan Museum. Burton made well over 1,000 photographs. From the start, his photography was more than artefactual documentation. Burton first took up photography as a tool for representing works of art among the art scholars and connoisseurs with whom he had grown up in Florence. An Egyptologist states: 'one sees in his Egyptian photographs the influence of the concerns of the European art historians with whom he had worked'.[9] With delicate, even lighting, respect for composition, as well as concern for texture and balance of tonalities, Burton made his photographs of Egyptian artefacts responsive to the criteria of art. And as such they were passed on to the world.

Burton's photos were published and republished for years, as magazines and newspapers worked to satisfy and encourage public interest. The formats in which they were presented enabled the public virtually to experience the finds. In February 1928, nearly five years after the discovery, *The Illustrated London News* still presented them in its place of honour. On the first page directly below its masthead was a photograph of a canopic chest, hidden beneath the linen pall that had covered it for over 3,000 years (illus. 4). The reader is informed that 'What it is exactly will be found fully explained and illustrated on the succeeding pages of this number.' With one turn of the page, the viewer sees the object no longer hidden by the cloth, but an elaborately inscribed, semi-transparent alabaster vessel, rising from a dado of gold on a sled-like wooden base (illus. 5). Further pages reveal other aspects of the object: the gilded gesso outer canopy with four guardian goddess figures, followed by close-ups of the statuettes themselves.

Through Burton's photography, and *The Illustrated London News*'s treatment of it, a viewer could not merely learn of but even somehow participate in the archaeological process of uncovering and analysis. It is an effect we can still experience here, in the pages of this book. Whether or not the Tutankhamun discoveries stand out qualitatively above all previous Egyptian finds their photography certainly does. Public engagement with the remains of Tutankhamun is as much the product of how they were represented as of what there was to be seen. Here, as we shall see throughout, the history of archaeological photography connects with

THE ILLUSTRATED LONDON NEWS,

REGISTERED AS A NEWSPAPER FOR TRANSMISSION IN THE UNITED KINGDOM AND TO CANADA AND NEWFOUNDLAND BY MAGAZINE POST.

SATURDAY, FEBRUARY 4, 1928.



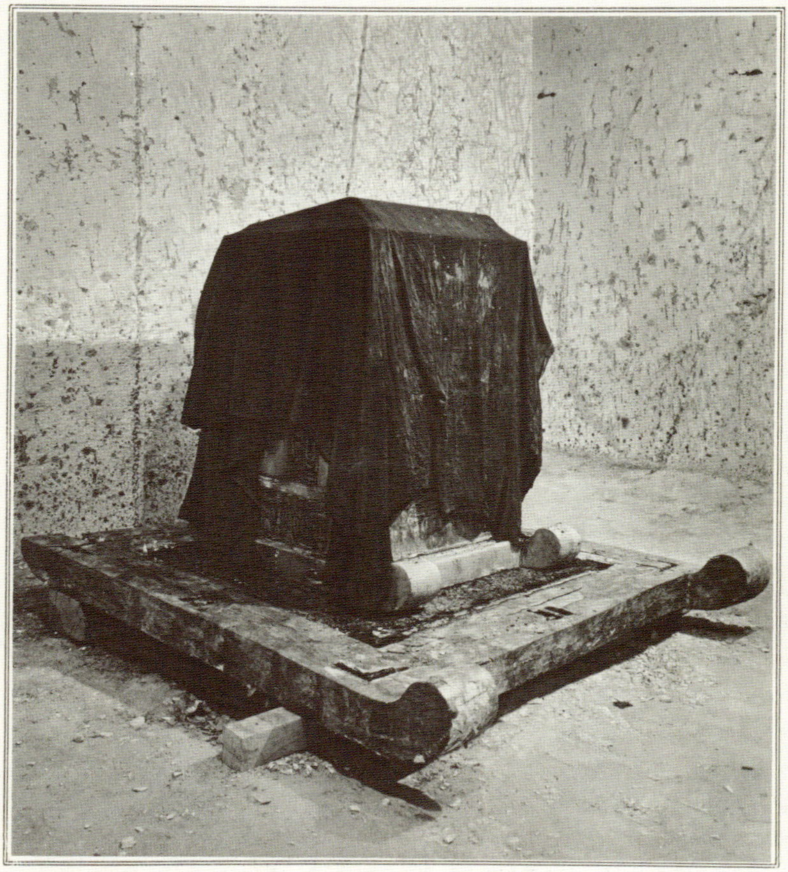

**AFTER REMOVAL OF THE CANOPY: THE VEILED SECRET OF THE INMOST RECESS IN TUTANKHAMEN'S TOMB— THE MOST IMPORTANT OBJECT (AFTER THE MUMMY) COVERED IN ITS LINEN PALL OVER 3000 YEARS OLD.**

Of all the wonderful things found in the Tomb of Tutankhamen, the mysterious veiled object shown above comes next in importance to the actual mummy of the king with its coffins and sarcophagus. What it is exactly will be found fully explained and illustrated on the succeeding pages of this number. Here it stands as it was revealed to the eyes of its discoverer, Mr. Howard Carter, when the canopy that enclosed it had been removed. It is seen still covered with the linen pall draped over it when the king was buried, about 1350 B.C., 3278 years ago. The sight of it causes a thrill of curiosity as to its nature and contents.

PHOTOGRAPH BY MR. HARRY BURTON, OF THE METROPOLITAN MUSEUM OF ART, NEW YORK. (WORLD COPYRIGHT STRICTLY RESERVED.)

a variety of audiences: scholarly, scientific and popular. Indeed, it points to connections among them, just as *The Illustrated London News* format bears notable similarities to those of the large-scale albums that have dominated archaeological documentation virtually from its start.

As we shall see in more detail in the next chapter, modern archaeology and photography emerged at a common moment in European history, within the culture of positivism of the mid-nineteenth century. Archaeological practice differed from that of the solitary discoverers who had dominated sciences like chemistry and biology. Archaeological excavation was, and remains, a collaborative, often vast, enterprise. It was also public in a new way, generally sponsored by governmental bodies, and thus beholden to a dispersed constituency. The need for communication of finds was made even greater by the, often immense, distances between excavation and sponsor, inherent to the age of European expansionism in which archaeology first thrived.

Images, perhaps even more than artefacts, held (and perhaps still hold) the archaeological enterprise together, knitting together not only its practitioners themselves but also its sponsors and audience. Julian Thomas has argued at length that archaeology, as distinguished from older antiquarianism, is a pure product of modernity.[10] Photography, the paradigmatic image technology of modern times, could not have found a better host.

Yet now photography has become so common to our world that we hardly see it. While the widespread availability of Photoshop and other digital software appears to have spawned the first generation that takes for granted the later manipulation of photographic imagery, photography remains our dominant medium for conveying what we agree upon as objective reality. Yet this very generation, and perhaps digital technology more generally, signals a certain crisis for the future trust of photography as a realistic medium. Whatever it means for the future, this presents a good moment to look back at the rise of photography, the forces behind its initial adoption, and to what extent it fulfils the functions assigned it.

4 Harry Burton, 'Canopic Chest, Enshrouded', from *The Illustrated London News* (4 February 1928).

Archaeology too faces a crossroads. Though the days of artefactual treasure-hunting are long gone, its very status as an object-based science is much in question. First there are the particular circumstances that

# THE SECRET REVEALED: TUTANKHAMEN'S MAGNIFICENT CANOPIC CHEST.

PHOTOGRAPH BY MR. HARRY BURTON, OF THE METROPOLITAN MUSEUM OF ART, NEW YORK. 

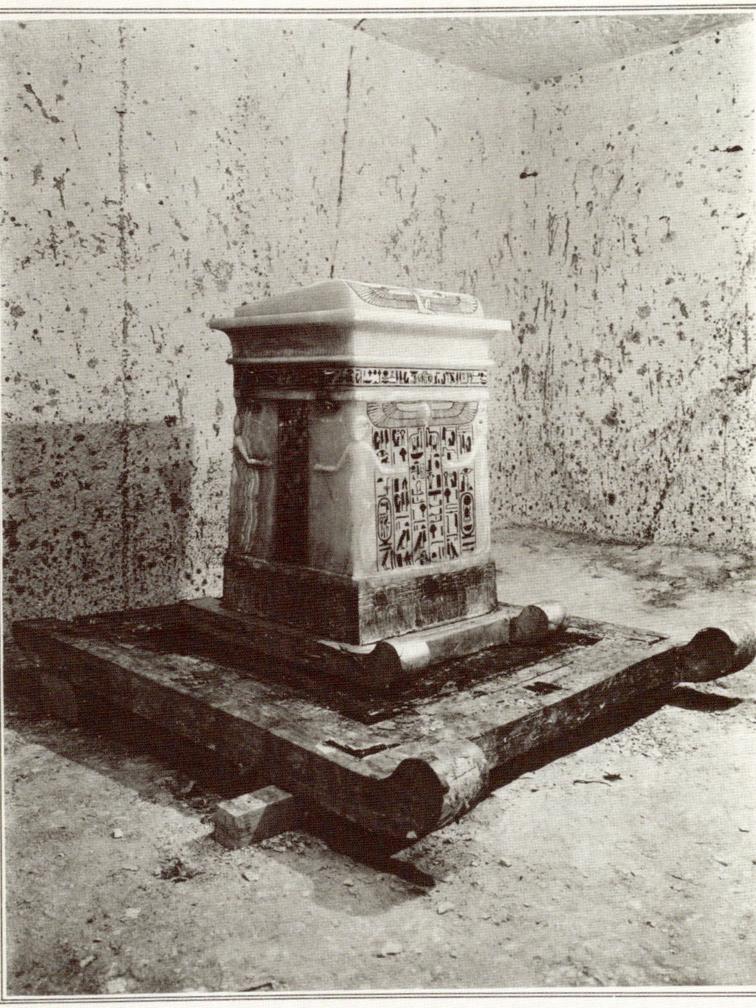

WITH CORNER FIGURES OF GUARDIAN GODDESSES, AND INSCRIPTIONS: THE BEAUTIFUL CANOPIC CHEST OF ALABASTER, ON A SILVER-HANDLED SLEDGE, RESTING ON THE LARGER SLEDGE-LIKE BASE OF THE REMOVED CANOPY.

The secret of the Innermost Recess in Tutankhamen's Tomb here stands revealed in all the beauty of its outward aspect. This magnificent Canopic chest is the mysterious object disclosed to view by removal of the linen pall, which had covered it for over 3000 years, as shown in the photograph on our front page. It was originally enclosed within the great gesso-gilt canopy known as the Canopic shrine, of which an illustration appears on the opposite page, and in the above photograph it is seen still resting on the sledge-like base of the shrine. At the corners of this platform, and in the centre of the front, are visible the sockets into which the posts of the shrine were fitted. The base of the Canopic chest itself is similarly shaped like a sledge, with handles at the side. The chest itself is an exquisite structure of semi-translucent alabaster, and at its lower edge runs a dado of gold. Like the sarcophagus in the sepulchre, the Canopic chest has the figures of the guardian goddesses, Isis, Nephthys, Neith, and Selket, carved in relief at the four corners, and on the sides their respective formulas are cut in bold hieroglyphs filled in with black pigment. The massive lid was fastened by four seals attached to gold staples. The contents appear on succeeding pages.

constrain artefacts in modern times, such as recent agreements throughout the world that forbid transport of finds from the nation of discovery, if not findspot. The devastations of war, from Sarajevo to Rwanda to Iraq, are a further burden, masking or even destroying archaeological contexts as well as objects themselves. Newer, 'non-invasive' archaeological techniques, which have grown strongly in recent years, are in part a response to international covenants but also represent a new kind of environmentally sensitive approach. In both cases, the results involved are less and less palpable objects and more and more two-dimensional representations: graphs, plans, digital images, descriptions, drawings, inventories and, hardly least, photographs. Yet as circumstances conspire to arrest access to the object itself, the current 'crisis' of photographic representation is all the more pressing for archaeology.

Archaeology has many forms of visual recording, a measure of its different objectives, and the ingenuity of its practitioners. Consider the work of Ernst Herzfeld, a leading archaeologist of his time and pioneer in four decades of exploration of the Ancient Near East. Herzfeld's copious documentation records his experience of sites in every way imaginable, including beautifully drawn sketches, squeezes (direct paper impressions of inscriptions), plans, travel journals and even descriptions of dreams. Yet the largest component, in number of items, are his photographs.

Perhaps the most common scheme for ordering a series of archaeological photography is to begin with a large, or even panoramic, image of a locale (sort of a proto-cinematic 'establishing' shot) and then move to closer-in views of portions of a site, followed by even more detailed views of individual features or artefacts. Thus Herzfeld's panoramic photograph of the Taq-i Kisra, the only visible remnant of the ancient city of Ctesiphon, southeast of Baghdad in modern-day Iraq, views the scene from a distance (illus. 6). Significantly, while the photographer's shadow here fords the stream separating the view, the shadow itself was suppressed from a later, published version of this image. The remaining structure (a vault over 30 m/100 ft high) rises from its site, bounded at left by the distant mounds of Harim-i Kisra, which Herzfeld rightly inferred as interring remains of the palace complex. This is just the sort

5 Harry Burton, 'Canopic Chest, Uncovered', from *The Illustrated London News* (4 February 1928).

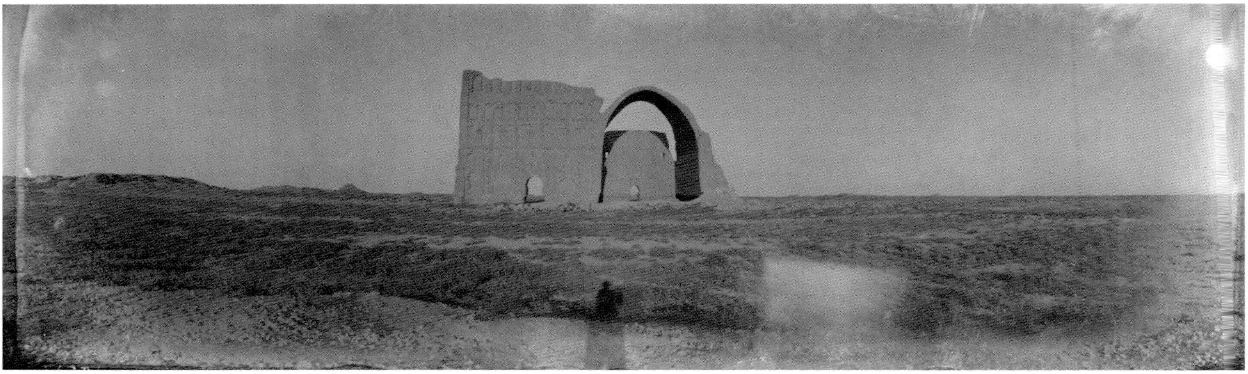

6 Ernst Herzfeld, 'Ctesiphon, Taq-I Kisra at Sunrise', Iraq, 1923–33, gelatin silver print

of image that might be used to begin an inquiry into the palace's structure, function and design, anchoring subsequent photographs of details in a larger whole. The photo works to restore the context of the monument, the spaces where the rest of the grand palace once stood. As Hauser notes, every archaeological photograph is an image of absence, and of something beyond the frame. 'What is seen in the photograph of a ruin is understood to be the remains of something which is not pictured, and which can no longer *be* photographed.'[11] The archaeological photograph is always somehow elegiac, inhabited by a consciousness of loss. The considerable empty space around the ruin certainly offers room to the viewer, as well as an almost still, funereal quality corresponding to absence, but also to possibility. At the same time, this kind of framing affects the monument itself. The overwhelming horizontality of the photograph, and lack of human scale common to the resolutely positivist viewpoint of the mid-twentieth century, distinctly diminishes the vertical grandeur of the high arch. This photograph, that is, is not precisely some unmediated reality, but the result of a choice of interest, if not placement and focal length. Herzfeld, a paradigm of the scientific, object-minded inquirer, makes a photograph that is a portrait, in a sense, of a point of view.

Such a conception is especially germane here, as another panoramic photo by Herzfeld portrays that viewpoint literally (illus. 7). The photographer is set at left, with a view camera and chemical case, pointed at a mound which clearly bears the shape of an ancient fortification in an otherwise unrelieved landscape. The camera precisely intersects the

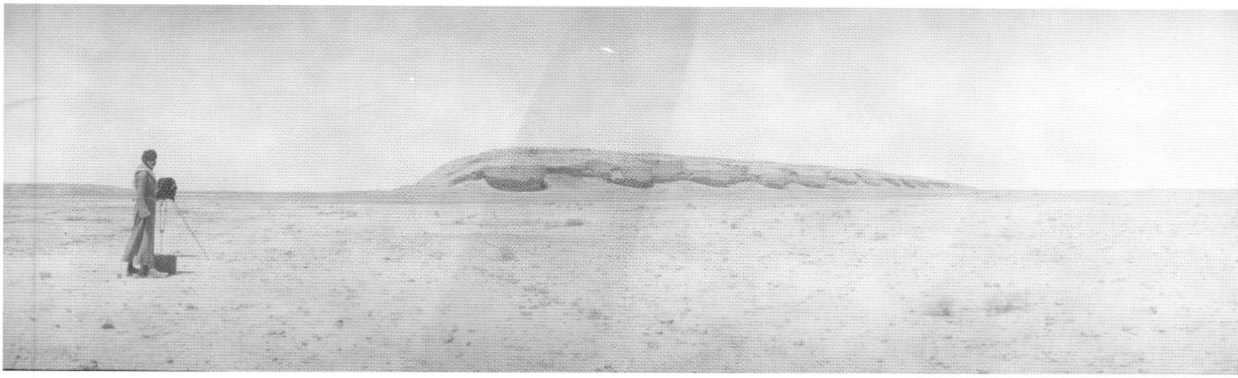

7 Ernst Herzfeld, 'Dastagerd, from East', 1905–11, gelatin silver print.

landscape's horizon line. Of course, this image is not made by the camera pictured, but by another hidden to us, which orchestrates the relation between camera and object. It is a tenuous relation, identifying a sort of centre and periphery of archaeological inquiry, with the vast looming ancient mound at its heart, but the small modern invention and its operator standing as nearly its equal. The image goes to some length to effect this equivalence, as the photographer is far closer to the camera, increasing his relative size in the camera's frame and diminishing that of the mound. It is an image that works to make plausible the almost impossible job of making the past visually present.

Yet, powerful as it is, archaeological photography does not exist alone, but in relation to other visual modes of archaeological recording. When it first arose, such photography made a point of setting itself in context. A good example can be found in Félix Teynard's photographic atlas of Egypt and Nubia. The product of a tour begun in 1851, Teynard's album is one of a number of the first generation of photographic summations of Egypt and its antiquities, by photographers of many nations, such as Maxime Du Camp, Francis Frith, Wilhelm Hammerschmidt and John Beasley Greene.

On the title page Teynard described his album as a 'photographic atlas . . . serving to complement the large Description of Egypt'. From the very start, Teynard presented his photographs not only for their impact as context-less images, but also as ways to supplement the vast systematic study of an earlier age by means of the new medium of photography.

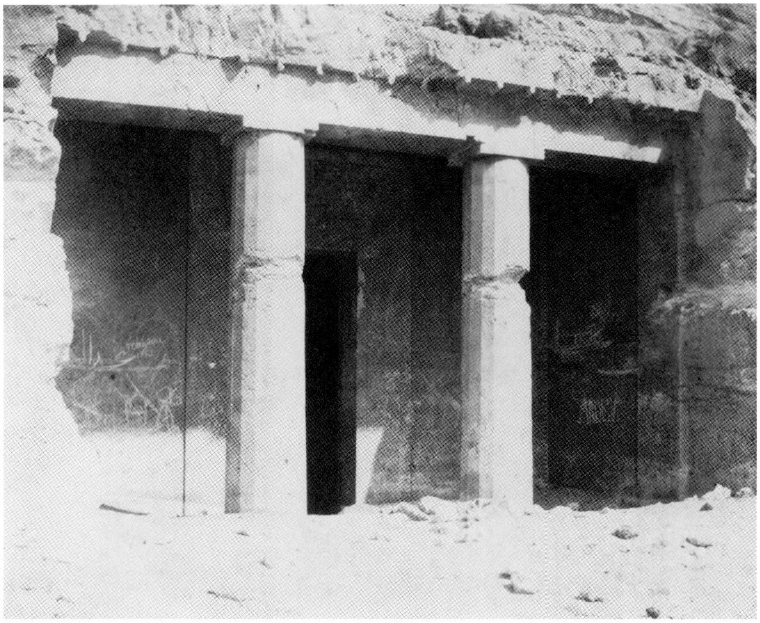

8 Félix Teynard, 'Beni-Hasan, Rock-Cut Architecture – Tomb of Khnumhotep III', from *Égypte et Nubie* (1858), calotype.

The *Description de l'Égypte* is among the most famous works of French Orientalism. Published in 23 vast volumes starting in 1809, it served as a definitive reference for Egypt (both ancient and modern) in nineteenth-century France, as well as a model for the archaeological representation of many other areas of the world then coming to the attention of the incipient French empire.

Teynard's itinerary was the same as that of the earlier volume as well as most other photographic voyagers in Egypt in the nineteenth century: up the Nile, starting at its delta above Alexandria, through lower and then upper Egypt and on into Nubia. But if his album partook of a common sequence of monuments it also presented them in a unique way, partly through the effect of photography, and partly by hewing to the particular interests of a civil engineer. In a typical image by Teynard, of one of the rock cut tombs at Beni Hasn, he places the camera to closely match the cut-out shape of the tomb opening with the edges of the photographic frame (illus. 8). This image of the tomb of Khnumhotep III details the stone lintel and two worn facet-cut columns that hold it up. One also finds, almost offhandedly, traces of its later life. A palimpsest of modern graffiti, in a variety of languages, shines out from the dark recesses of the tomb porch.

The tombs and the kind of information presented about them here differ notably from that of the page of plates devoted to them in the *Description de l'Égypte* (illus. 9). First, the older folio, which makes clear its examples are taken from 'diverse' tombs, restores its subjects to a pristine ideal state. We may recognize the tomb opening (in the centre), but clearly note differences, notably in state of preservation. Second, on the basis of its researches the description recreates whole tombs, with plans and elevations. Finally, the *Description de l'Égypte* includes details of decorative patterns, which are almost wholly absent from Teynard's resolutely structural focus. Teynard's photography effortlessly corrects the perfected, and sometimes imagined, imagery of the place given in the *Description de l'Égypte*. His dramatic and austere images are a remarkable contrast to the varied aspects of the same site described in Denon's book. To be sure, one would barely know that these two images represent the same subject, for they represent it quite differently, in a way that offers a distinction fundamental to understanding photography's role

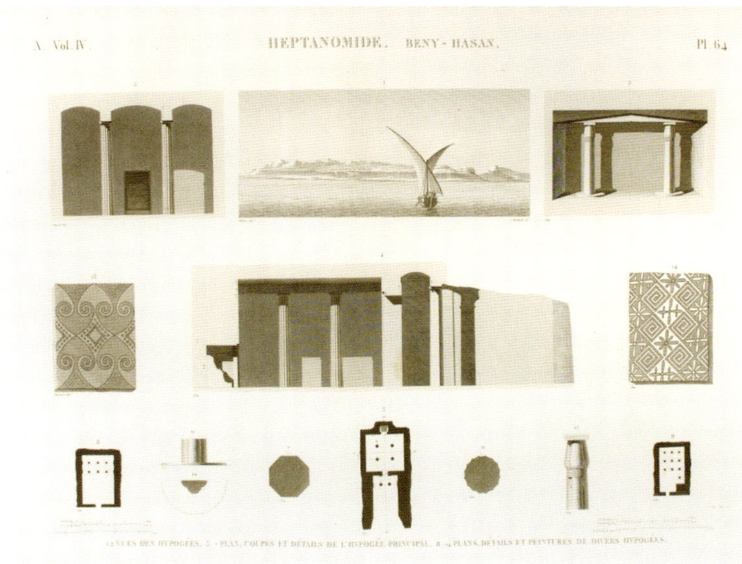


9 'Heptanomide, Beni-Hasan', from *Description de l'Égypte* (1809–28), vol. IV, plate 64, engraving.

in archaeological research. Teynard's album, one might say, presents a particularized *physiognomy* of the ancient Egyptian monument, in contrast to the more generalized *anatomy* of it given in the earlier work. This is a key distinction for understanding the work of archaeological photography.

At the heart of Teynard's physiognomic approach is photography's essential incarnation of the monument: its material, structural – indeed, sculptural – solidity. Considered more broadly, this representational effect of photography is not merely supplemental (as Teynard's title suggests), but also transformative of the *Description*'s engraved imagery. It might not be too much to associate the difference between these two reproductive modes – the earlier engravings versus Teynard's photographs – with the distinction between the antiquarian interest in the past of the eighteenth century and the new archaeological investigations of the nineteenth century. In this sense, what Alain Schnapp calls the 'invention of archaeology' in the nineteenth century is fundamentally linked to the invention – or perhaps the intervention – of photography at the same time.[12]

Natural and self-sufficient as photography may seem, it comes to archaeology as part of a larger array of tools for visual representation. As we shall see at several points in this book, photography has been the source of considerable anxiety within archaeology. The invention of photography brought an effortlessly perfect physiognomic vision to archaeological inquiry. It could fix the appearance of objects and sites, allowing them to be transported, for any reason, to a distant gaze. But recreating the unseeable past requires anatomical imagination as much as physiognomic objectivity. Throughout this book we will see the two working both together and against each other. Because of its dual nature, archaeological literature to this day is replete with drawings, plans, diagrams and related visual representations, as much as with photographs.

But if photography is hardly able by itself to transform knowledge of the past into a science, it nonetheless bears a good portion of the burden of objectivity for the discipline. The rarest sight in archaeological photography from formal excavation practice is the trace of the camera, that index of the subjectivity behind the lens. It is an axiom, for instance, of George Andrew Reisner, one of the founders of twentieth-century

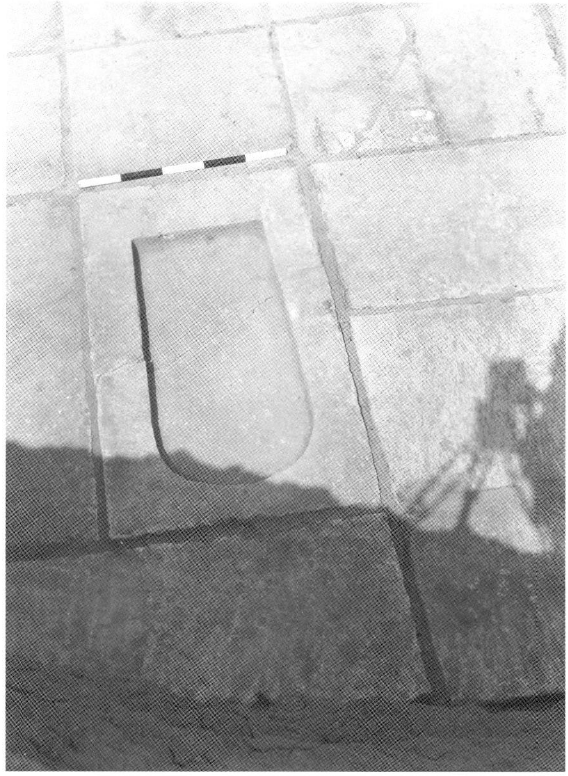

10 Unknown photographer, 'Pavement Detail, Khorsabad Field Image', 1929, gelatin silver print.

archaeology (see p. 50), that 'the less there is of the recording apparatus shown in the picture, the better the record'.[13] An image from the University of Chicago's Oriental Institute of its excavation at the site of Khorsabad, seat of ancient Assyrian kings, in modern-day Iraq, is a portion of the daily documentary tasks of an archaeological photographer, his identity unrecorded in the photographic record (illus. 10). It details paving stones around a niched indentation, set to scale with a standard measure. But another scale is also present, through the shadow of the photographer and tripod-mounted camera that took the picture. This trace of presence (no doubt unavoidable given the necessary viewpoint and availability of lighting) wrenches the image from its attempted stance in objectivity, uniquely adding a casual self-portrait to the essential documentary project. (For a more routine image from the same excavation, see illus. 29.)

The shadow that seems out of place in Khorsabad stands for much more in a photograph from just a little earlier, remnant of a different

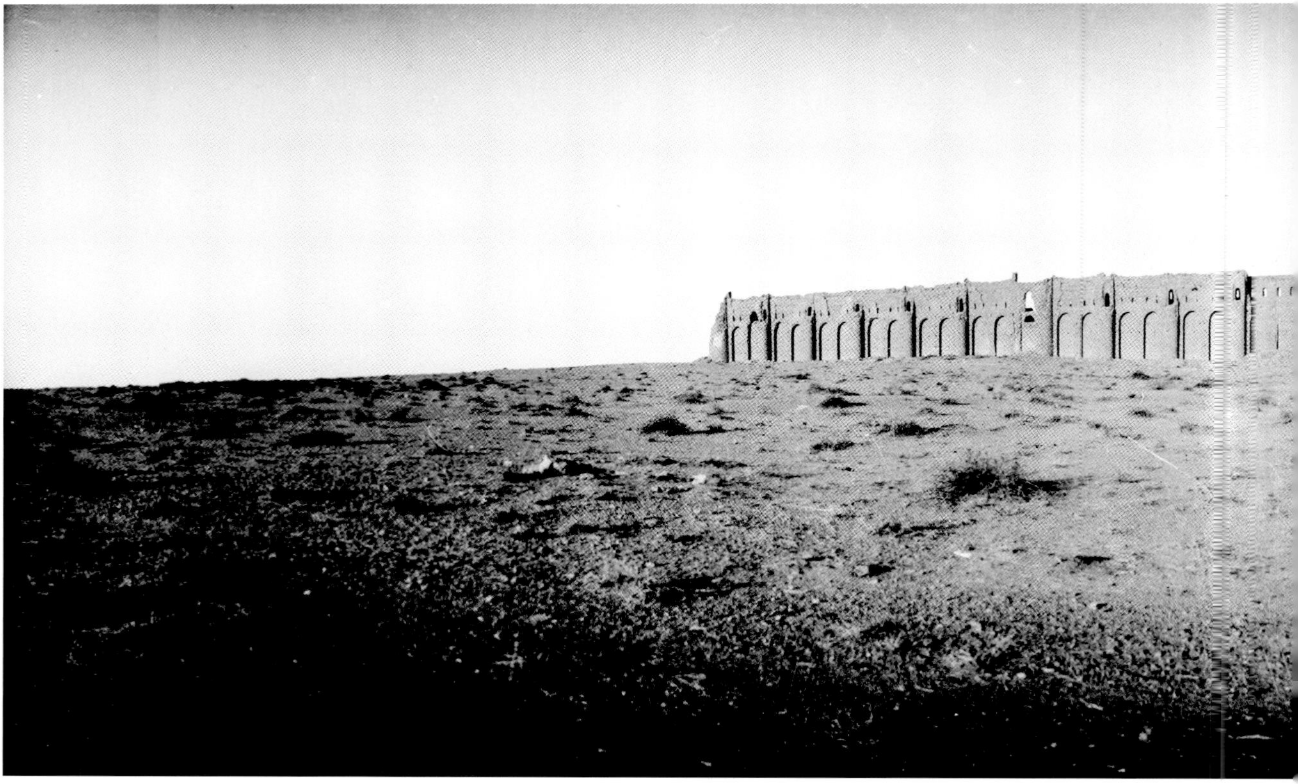

11 Gertrude Bell, 'Khedar from NE, Ukhaydir, Iraq', 1909, gelatin silver print.

archaeological vision, as well as an earlier moment in the history of Iraq. Gertrude Bell is among the pioneers of Mesopotamian exploration, a figure who remarkably brought together archaeological and ethnographic knowledge with real political engagement. Bell is among the founders of modern Iraq in the aftermath of the First World War. In early 1909, among one of her extensive tours of the country, she spent several months at Ukhaydir, in central Iraq. It is the site of a remarkable Abbasid palace and fortress, called 'the father of castles', erected in the eighth century AD, and then largely unknown in the West. Bell's delight in it was palpable. As she wrote soon afterwards: 'A subject so enchanting and so suggestive as the Palace of Ukhaidir is not likely to present itself more than once in a lifetime, and as I bring this page to a close I call to mind the amazement with which I first gazed upon its formidable walls.'[14]

Like any committed explorer or archaeologist of the time, Bell photographed extensively. Her photograph of the palace uses the panoramic

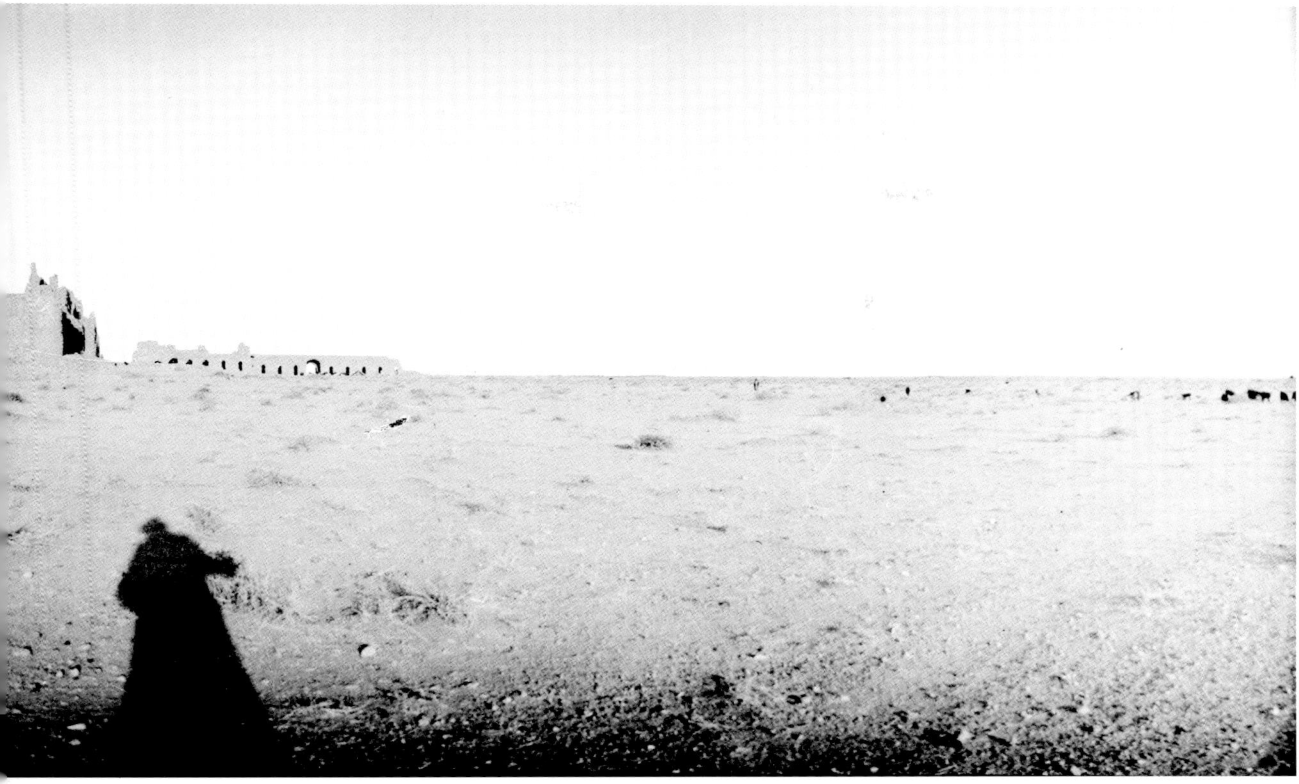

format to place the full experience of the monument in its desert setting (illus. 11). But the photograph is even more animated by the large shadow of the photographer herself, moving toward the building, carrying the enchantment and amazement she describes. This is a photograph that does not at all eschew an engagement between photographer and subject.

In the twenty years between Bell's photograph and that of the Chicago team, Iraq has changed, as has its photography. Hatched from a British mandate after the First World War, it was taken from a loose tribal confederation, with a distant connection to the Ottoman Empire, into a putative modern state with clear dependencies on Western powers. Bell's individual vision of its ancient monument is subsumed into the collective realm of archaeological endeavour, in which the photographer is a hired member of a team. The distinction between these two photographs is that between these two moments, as the rise to objective standardization and de-personalization of archaeological vision coincides with the modernization of both the locale and the discipline. As we shall see elsewhere in this book, this moment of transition is a major break, and crisis, within the history of archaeological photography.

At its most scientific, archaeology seeks to approach the photographic image as document, not to look *at* the photograph so much as to look *through* it to the object pictured. The trace of the photographer makes this more difficult, distracting the viewer with a sense of the temporality and contingency involved in making archaeological photographs. This book, by contrast, will be devoted to the range and history of the larger process involved, looking both *at* and *through* photographs, examining the subjects of archaeology through both archaeological photographers and their photography, from conception through production through circulation.

At the same time, this small book about what are (literally) often very big books is in no way meant as a comprehensive treatment of its subject. It will suffice if it can help to frame some of the questions involved. Barthes calls photography a 'certain but fugitive testimony'.[15] The aim of this book is to follow the traces of that fugitive – photography itself – from its first appearance at the site of the archaeological monument as it leads us through the times and spaces of the modern apprehension of the past.

one

# Science, or Truth

Photography has come to be about almost everything in the world, but in the eyes of many of its founders and early supporters it was particularly about archaeology. The astonishingly rapid rise of photography began largely with developments in the year 1839, which brought to public attention the varying processes for picture making of William Henry Fox Talbot in England and Jacques-Louis-Mandé Daguerre in France. This is merely two years after the first usage of the term 'archaeology' in a modern sense, as 'scientific study of the remains and monuments of the prehistoric past'.[1] Archaeology emerged from a centuries-long tradition of antiquarianism at almost precisely the same moment that photography emerged from the even longer desire to fix permanent images of the external world. As even the wording of the definition of archaeology suggests, this development took place under the aegis of science, a term itself only coined in the modern sense earlier in the same decade.

From the start the two almost seem made for each other. Archaeology and photography are surely among the first proud pairings of a scientific goal and the technological machinery for accomplishing it. Although photography was adopted as a tool throughout the sciences, from its very start archaeology in particular was at the centre of the justification of photography's worth.

This is strikingly evident in the first major testimony on behalf of the invention, François Arago's report submitted to the French Chamber of Deputies on behalf of Daguerre (and his forerunner Nicéphore Niépce). While this lengthy document speaks generally on the significance of photography to science and the fine arts, toward the start Arago takes pains to single out its import for archaeology in particular:

> Had we photography in 1798 we would possess today faithful pictorial records of that which the learned world is forever deprived of by the greed of the Arabs and the vandalism of certain travelers.
>
> To copy the millions of hieroglyphics which cover even the exterior of the great monuments of Thebes, Memphis, Karnak, and others would require decades of time and legions of draughtsmen. By daguerrotype one person would suffice to accomplish this immense work successfully. Equip the Egyptian Institute with two or three of Daguerre's apparatus, and before long . . . innumerable hieroglyphics as they are in reality will replace those which now are invented or drawn by approximation.[2]

This brief passage suffices to convey the enthusiasm for photography contained throughout the report, as well as the particular hopes attributed to it for archaeological research. Photography is, first, an agent of preservation and restitution, a means to salvage and to forever hold objects that are in danger of being lost. Second, it is a technology of efficient surveillance, using the machine's capability for speed and consistency to dramatically decrease time required for labour. Third, and perhaps most crucial of all, its product is systematically, effortlessly, objectively 'true', presenting images of unfiltered reality free of the embellishment and invention prone to the work of even the most practised artist.[3] As we shall see in detail throughout this book, while none of these claims are unconditionally true, all remain nonetheless fundamental to the archaeological employment of photography.

The theorist Pierre Bourdieu observes that 'photography is considered to be a perfectly realistic and objective recording of the visible world because (from its origin) it has been assigned *social uses* that are held to be "realistic" and "objective"'.[4] Seen this way, Arago's words are not descriptive so much as prescriptive. They work less to inform us about the essential nature of the new discovery itself than to guide us in our evaluation of its products. Writ large, the history of archaeological photography is a history of the response to the fundamental paradox of photographic truth, a lengthy and ever less innocent unravelling and then shoring up of the basis for acting on the core beliefs stated by Arago. Indeed, the entire history of archaeological photography might be divided into two parts: an early phase of elation at this new vehicle for objective representation followed by a later one of resignation, using it despite its faults.

Arago's report is prophetic in other ways as well. Notably, archaeology for him brings to mind Egypt more than anywhere else. Little has changed from this moment to the era of Indiana Jones and Lara Croft. Though this book is designed to sample a broad range of world archaeology, it can rarely stray too far from Egypt and the greater Mediterranean, both sites of the field's earliest investments and innovations. Another sort of investment is evident here too: of political power. Arago refers at the start to the Napoleonic expedition cum invasion of Egypt, a move seen as politically disastrous in Arago's time, despite the magnificent attempt to repackage it that is the grand folio *Description de l'Égypte* (1809–28). The restitution offered by photography could be not only placed at the service of the disinterested realm of science, but might also work toward political recuperation, justifying a nation's investment however conditions changed 'on the ground'.

The origin of photography in France plunged it into the public, governmental discourse of large-scale archaeology in a formative and deeply influential way. In entrepreneurial Britain, by contrast, it has a more private history, quickly becoming involved with smaller projects of representing antiquities and abetting research. Yet here again we find photographic representation being pulled in opposing directions. Talbot is best known today as an inventor of photography, but he was at least as renowned in his own time as a scholar of ancient languages. He was involved in controversies over biblical and other ancient Near Eastern Languages, and was one of four scholars involved in the demonstration in 1855 of definitive mastery of Assyrian Akkadian cuneiform writing. Talbot's interest in photography is a very paradigm of its employment by a philologically oriented archaeological scholar and connoisseur.

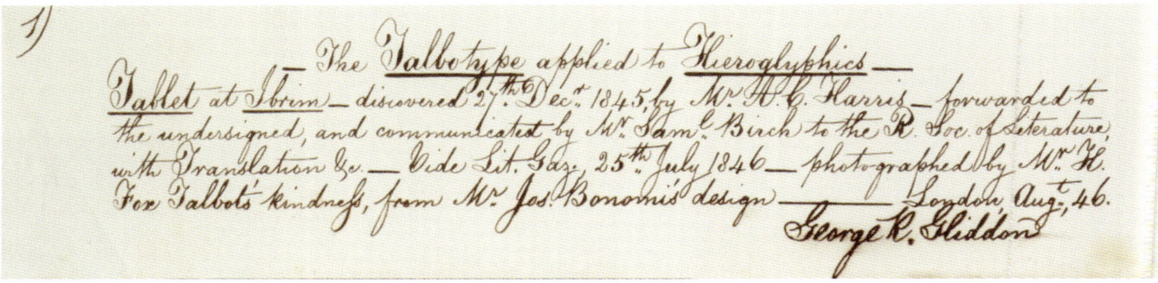

1) — The Talbotype applied to Hieroglyphics —
Tablet at Ibrim — discovered 27th Decr. 1845, by Mr. A. C. Harris — forwarded to
the undersigned, and communicated by Mr. Saml. Birch to the R. Soc. of Literature,
with Translation &c. — Vide Lit. Gaz. 25th July 1846 — photographed by Mr. H.
Fox Talbot's kindness, from Mr. Jos. Bonomi's design ——— London Augt. 46.
George R. Gliddon

12 (*above and right*) William Henry Fox Talbot, 'The Talbotype applied to Hieroglyphics' (1846), p. 1, two-part salt print from a paper negative.

Some of Talbot's work on antiquity embodies Arago's conception, notably employing the collaborative mode proper to the scientific model then emergent. Talbot was behind the publication, in 1846, of a four-page pamphlet consisting solely of calotype prints, entitled 'The Talbotype applied to Hieroglyphics' (illus. 12).[5] It reproduced Joseph Bonomi's transcription of a hieroglyphic inscription of an ancient Egyptian rock stele in Ibrim, Nubia, together with a translation of the inscription prepared by Joseph Birch, Keeper of Antiquities at the British Museum, and an account of its discovery by Anthony Charles Harris, a British antiquities dealer and antiquarian. Talbot, never precisely a leading scholar, made a contribution that was not substantive but instrumental: a new medium allowing scholars to exchange visual information more easily. This pamphlet, the first use of photography in Egyptology, is a fully scientific, and reductive, treatment of an ancient artefact. Indeed, any photo of the artefact itself is absent from the pamphlet, which in effect equates the signs of the inscription with the discovered object. Photography here is not a means of artfully revealing an object's complexity but rather of foreclosing on the ambiguities of the object in the process of communicating determinate visual information to a scattered learned community.

Yet one also finds in Talbot's work an opposite tendency, dealing with a different portion of antiquity, the more highly valued works of classical sculpture. In 1844 Talbot published *The Pencil of Nature,* renowned as the first photographically illustrated book. Its 24 plates illustrated a range of subjects that might be depicted by photography. The only object pictured twice was its single antiquity, a cast of an antique bust identified

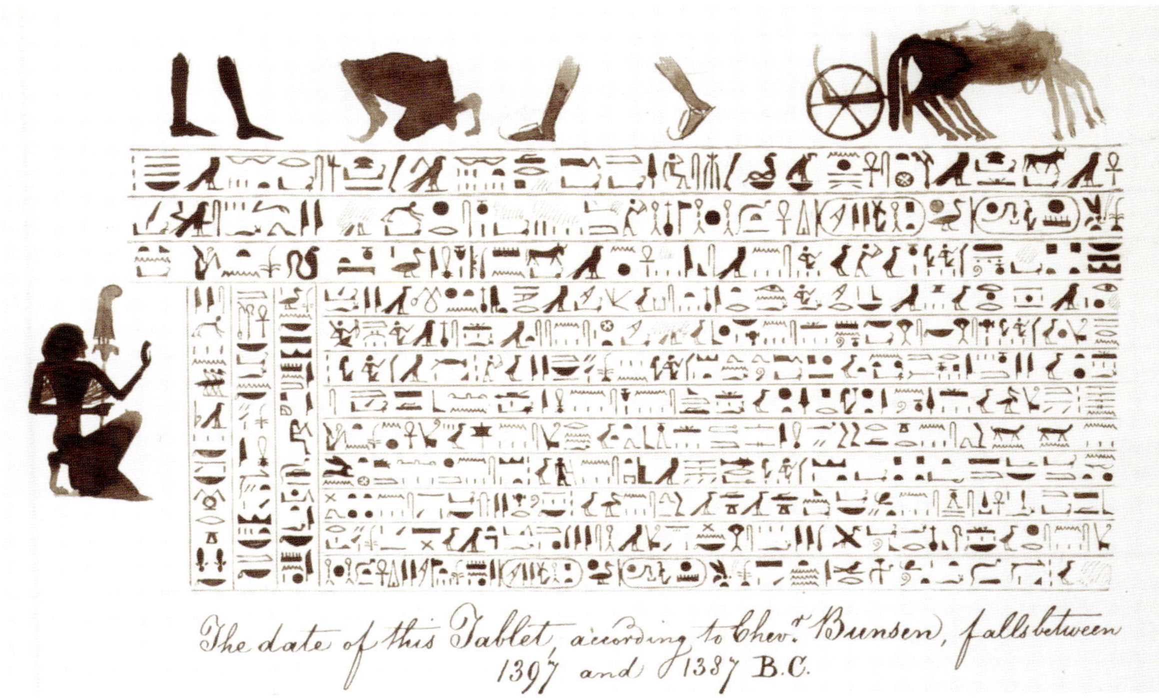


as Patroclus, made after an original in the British Museum (illus. 13, 14). Talbot's text notes that 'Statues, busts, and other specimens of sculpture are generally well represented by the Photographic Art' and stresses the 'almost unlimited variety' of images that can be made from a single such object, especially given the way lighting can also be infinitely varied.[6] He made over 30 different images of the cast altogether, in a quest, according to Susan Taylor, 'motivated more by a desire to express emotion than a wish to document'.[7]

The two images both isolate the object against a black background, while approaching it from different angles with different kinds of lighting. The setting against a blank backdrop is now a common technique of artefact photography, repeated to the present day and described in innumerable photographic manuals. Talbot's use intimates also the openness toward aestheticization that is abetted when the camera removes the object from its original physical context and remakes it in a new one.

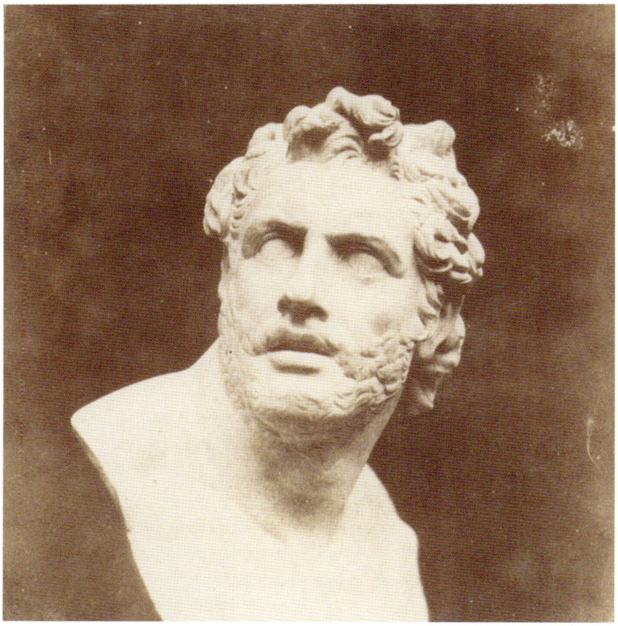

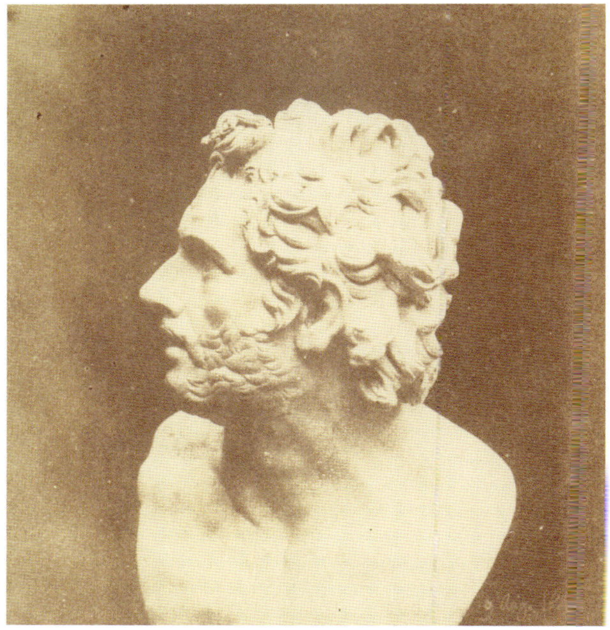

13 William Henry Fox Talbot, 'Bust of Patroclus', from *The Pencil of Nature* (1844–6), plate 5, salt print from a paper negative.

14 William Henry Fox Talbot, 'Bust of Patroclus', from *The Pencil of Nature*, plate 17, salt print from a paper negative.

In the process of displaying 'Art', Talbot's conception could not be more different from that of philological science. The two images together chip away at a conception of a single photograph capturing the reality of an unvarnished past, literally displaying the same thing with different appearances. It draws attention away from the object before the lens and toward the photographer himself, presenting the particular images chosen of the object as mark of a singular vision and aesthetic choice.

The tension between what I've called looking at and looking through photographs of ancient artefacts, seeing the objects in contexts of art versus science, was thus present from the very start in archaeological photography, and very much dependent on preconceived notions toward the worth (the social use, in Pierre Bourdieu's terms) of the object pictured, Greco-Roman work being at the opposite end of the spectrum of aesthetic value from Egyptian. On which topic, a third image in connection with Talbot must be considered. Among the greatest challenges to the conventional understanding of early human history during the decades following the invention of photography was the discovery of vast caches of ancient

Assyrian artefacts, excavated from sites in the Middle East during the 1840s.[8] Many were inscribed with cuneifom writing then in the process of being deciphered. Talbot had met the British Museum directors and broached the possibility of using photography to aid in the process.[9] In 1854, in a makeshift studio on the Museum's roof, Roger Fenton photographed several hundred inscribed tablets.[10] These photographic replicas could be consulted, transported and juxtaposed far more easily than the objects themselves, thus facilitating scholarly attention. It is a hallmark not just of discovery but also of a method of scientific analysis, the first concerted project of a sort envisioned by the Photographic Society of London. In 1853, the very year of its founding, a writer suggested that through photography the study of the past could learn from procedures of natural science, so that 'when once adopted exchange of photographs will become as indispensable to antiquaries as the exchange of plants is to botanists'.[11] It is a concept now as common to us as the Internet.

Talbot's own work as decipherer is evident in his, sometimes copious, annotations to Fenton's prints (illus. 15). A print of one tablet is annotated at places corresponding to the text. Numbers one to four are drawn directly on the print and also organize much of the notation, which speculates on the meaning of particular signs at the right, and word conjugations, at top left. Much of the sign decipherment is correct by modern standards, but this particular tablet is a special challenge, as it is an ancient table of linguistic correspondences, between Sumerian, to the left, and Akkadian, to the right.

The textual overlay works to reduce the image to text, while the numerical marker puts the text in processual order. 'K. 248' refers to the mound of Kouyunjik, in which the tablet was found, and the order in which objects were retrieved. Yet this image differs considerably from that of the hieroglyphic inscription. This photograph confronts us with the materiality of the object, its fracture, incompleteness and tentative arrangement against a storeroom wall. It is an image not just of the text, but also of the painstaking, collaborative job of documentation and decipherment. Strikingly, just as the worth of Assyrian artefacts was located somewhere between the aesthetic value ascribed to classical objects and the lesser 'prescriptive' worth of the Egyptian, so too the very format of

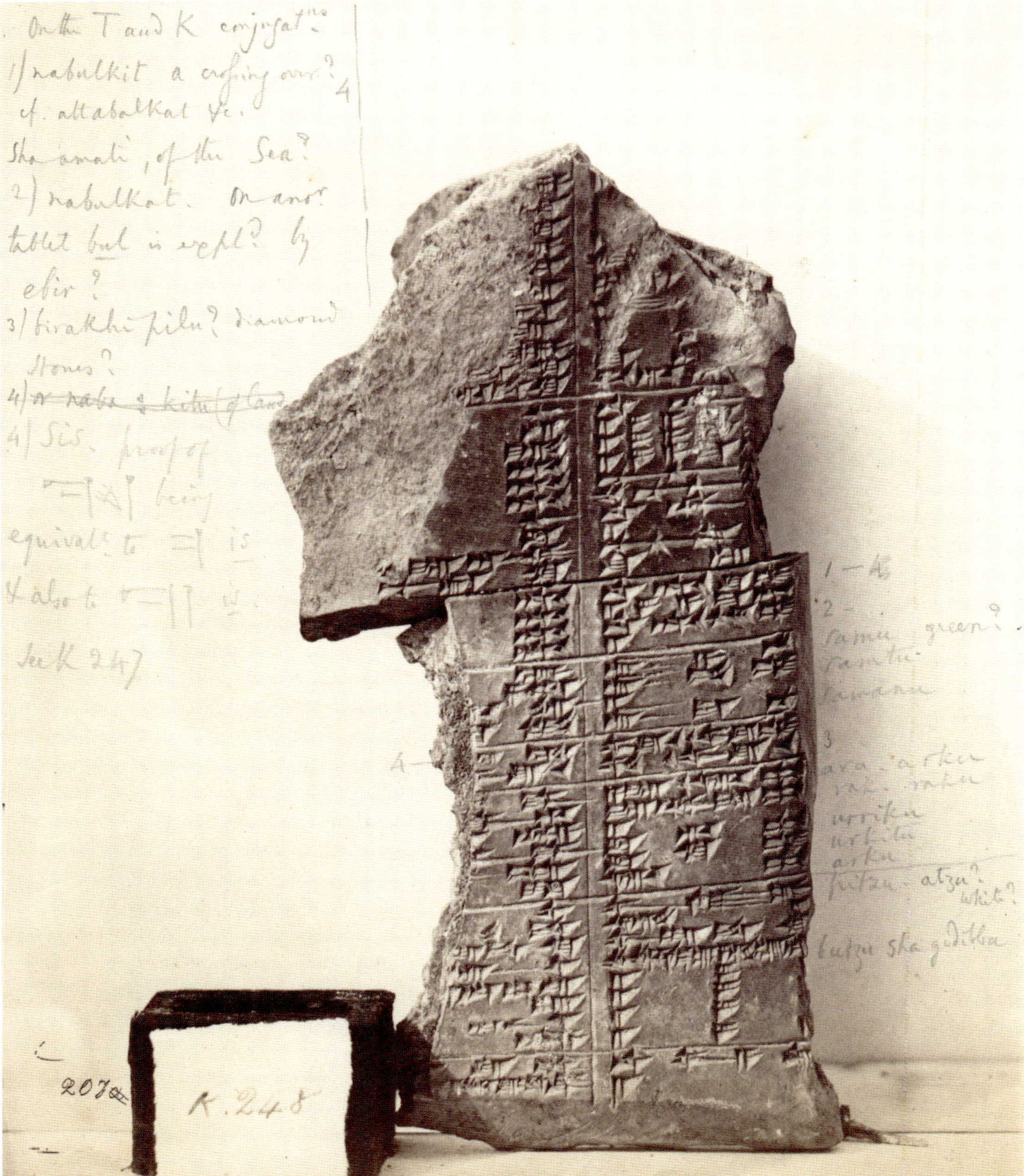

On the T and K conjugat.
1) nabalkit a crossing over?
cf. attabalkat &c.
sha amati, of the Sea?
2) nabalkat. On anor. tablet but is expl. by
ebir?
3) birakhi pilu? diamond stones?
4) Sis. proof of
see K 247
K.248

the photograph is attuned to recording different kinds of information, now material as much as linguistic. Whatever scientific objectivity is ascribed to capturing what is in front of the lens seems supplemented by the work of the sensibility present behind it, virtually photographing a sculpture, with attention to framing, background and lighting.

This variety of photographic forms and motivations is particularly striking since all involve a single person during a relatively short time span. It is also formative, if not prophetic, for as photographic capability became more widely available in antiquarian, artefactual and archaeological representation, the array of photography that evolved, while more varied and complex, still bears the traces of Talbot's initial activities.

Photography's first formal engagement with archaeological excavation took it to Egypt. Within three years of Arago's announcement, the Egyptian expedition led by Karl Richard Lepsius in 1842–3, sponsored by the Prussian royal house, included photographic equipment among its tools. In conscious emulation of the Napoleonic *Description de l'Égypte*, the campaign produced a series of twelve massive folio volumes, the first of which appeared in 1849. Lepsius, a leading hieroglyphic scholar, paid most attention to inscriptions, from sites throughout Egypt and Nubia. But his work provides engravings recorded in traditional form. Indeed, the very title of the book is *Denkmäler aus Aegypten und Aethiopien nach der zeichnngen* ('Drawings of Monuments . . .').

Lepsius may have been in touch with the latest technology but was not alone in rejecting it, as we shall see. There is an evident conflict between the pace of technological change and the ability of an audience to absorb it, a reason for scepticism about photography even in the moment of its triumphant introduction. The camera's promise of effortless, precise rendering, when further pressed, was distinctly mediated, even compromised, by the context in which it appeared.

Just one year after Lepsius set out, Paul-Émile Botta, the first excavator of Mesopotamia (ancient Iraq) described excitedly his thoughts in 1843 on discovering an Assyrian palace complex in a mound in Khorsabad. He wrote: 'I had the first revelation of a new world of antiquities.'[12] Botta was more interested in sculptures than the inscribed tablets we have seen with Talbot. His arguments for the age and, notably, the aesthetic quality

15 Roger Fenton, 'Kouyunjik Tablet', with pencil annotations by William Henry Fox Talbot, 1854, salt print.

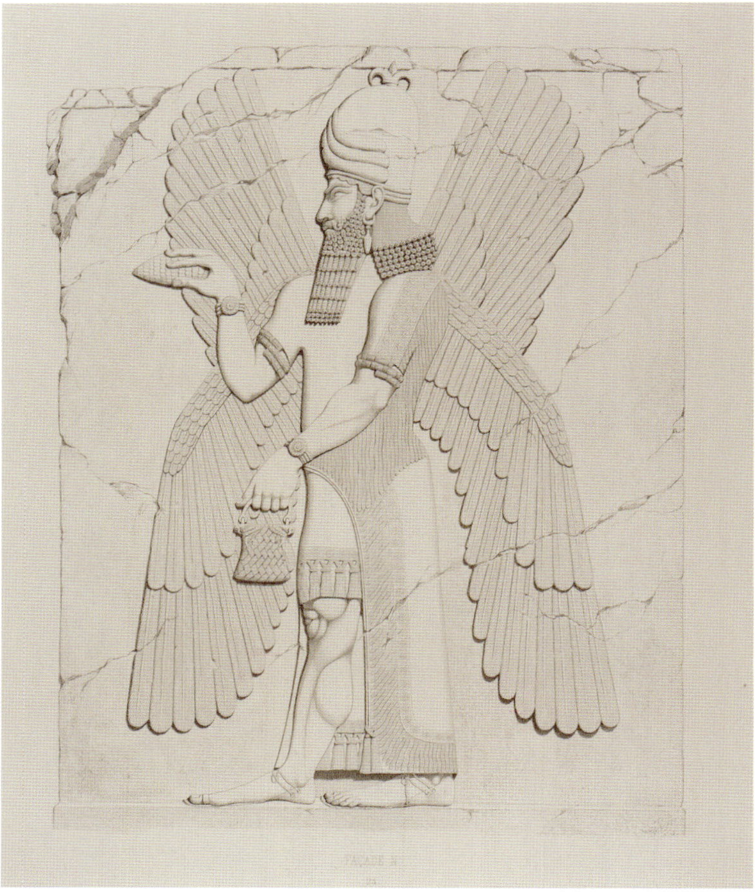

16 Eugène Flandin, 'Assyrian Winged Genie', in Paul-Émile Botta, *Monument de Ninive* (1849–50), vol. I, plate 28.

of Assyrian art, were attested first by his own less than perfectly revelatory drawings (made with the aid of a *camera lucida*, an optical device used as a drawing aid) published together with his initial report. They were then pictured with considerably more force in elaborate engravings after drawings by Eugène Flandin published in the multi-volume *Monument de Ninive*. This large folio, produced by the French government soon after the discoveries, sought to treat Mesopotamian art, and France's own discoverers, with the same honorific quality as that of the earlier *Description de l'Égypte*. Flandin, an accomplished artist specializing in archaeological rendering, produced, for instance, a recondite image of an ancient Assyrian relief figure, one of the winged genies that entranced and puzzled Western viewers (illus. 16). His image painstakingly details every visual aspect of the object, not just the subject and the extraordinary finish and detailing of costume and bodily features, but also the state of the object, its evident cracks and abrasions. Flandin clearly registers and passes on to the viewer the sort of attention demanded by a compelling object that aspires to being a work of art.

The aesthetic worthiness of Assyrian art was eminently debatable in mid-nineteenth-century France. What is striking in the present context is that when French excavation in the area continued, after Botta's work, it strove to do nothing so much as increase availability to the individual gaze that Botta celebrated, and attempted to use photography to accomplish the task. The excavation of Victor Place in Mesopotamia, starting in the 1850s, revisited many of the sites exhumed by Botta, now employing the calotypist Gabriel Tranchand to record them. This indeed was its primary innovation, hailed by photographic advocates such as Ernest Lacan, editor of the photographic journal *La Lumiére* and tireless advocate of photography.

Lacan's breathless encomium is worth quoting at some length. Little more than a decade after Arago's report, it marks a high point in public adulation for photography, as well as the romance of archaeology.

> While descending the Tigris and Euphrates, these old rivers proud with their ancient glory, which flow, diminished by time, through the ruins of destroyed palaces, temples remade [and] broken idols, how many times will the traveller have at his recourse this simple [photographic] apparatus, which demands only a few minutes to record on paper or plate sites where a bygone people have left their trace, and with the help of the sun which having lit these empires now still lights their ruins! One can say that M. Place will bring back Assyria itself in his boxes, in order to deliver them here to scholars, artists and all those who research and study it.[13]

The picturing ability of photography is here joined to the picturesqueness of archaeology. Yet the product of these pictures made by the sun itself is unquestionable, as 'Assyria itself' will be boxed and delivered back to France.

In Place's official excavation report, *Nineve et l'Assyrie* (1867–70), photography's role in representing Assyria proved to be both larger and more problematic. At the start of the volume, Place assures the reader that: 'Every important piece of art or architecture has been consecrated by photography.' Place goes on to praise Tranchand's role in a way that shows it to be one of policing as well as consecrating. He states:

> It is not only the precision apparatus that he [Tranchand] employed, which has permitted me to attach to my discoveries a degree of mathematical exactitude, but also his constant presence at the worksite contributed significantly to maintaining proper order.[14]

Place praises especially Tranchand's vision in finding Assyrian artefacts in the dark mud caverns and his ability to productively command the (mostly Kurdish) workers. The camera, together with its operator, is described as a figure of singular vision, and power. Yet a look at Place's excavation report reveals that he uses photography, the unique trace of Tranchand's presence and the basis for Place's claim to 'mathematical exactitude', as hardly something purely objective or beyond questioning.

18 E. Petit and Antoine-René Digeon, 'Chains and Crampons', in Victor Place, *Ninive et l'Assyrie* (1867–70), vol. III, plate 70.

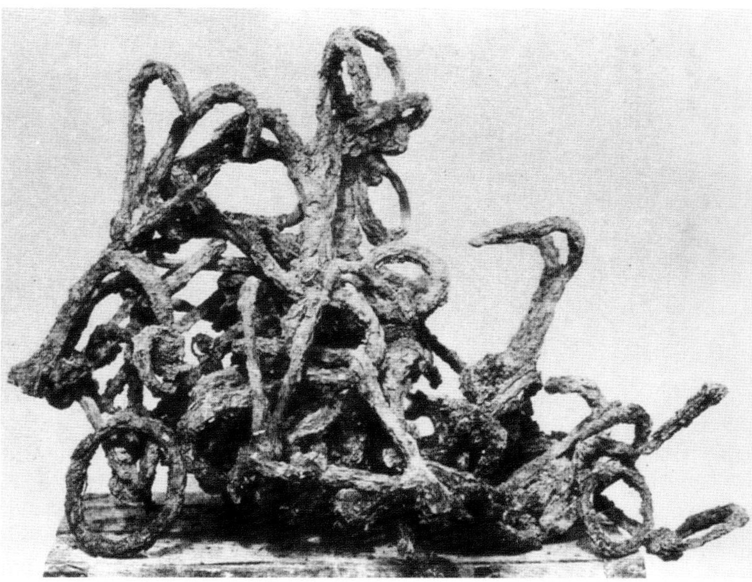

17 Gabriel Tranchand, 'Chains and Crampons', 1852–3, modern silver print from a lost paper negative.

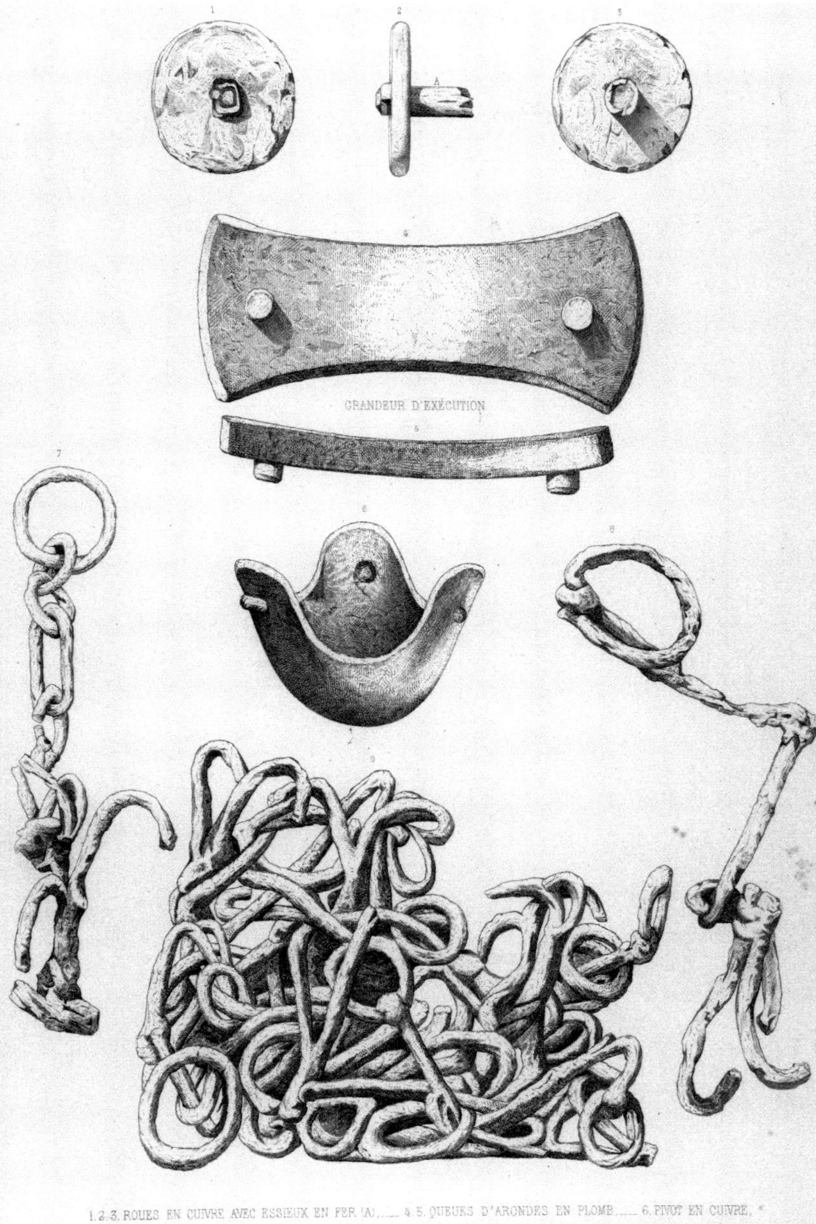


1.2.3. ROUES EN CUIVRE AVEC ESSIEUX EN FER (A). ___ 4.5. QUEUES D'ARONDES EN PLOMB. ___ 6. PIVOT EN CUIVRE,

7. 8. ET 9. CHAINES ET CRAMPONS (MAGASINS et DES DÉPENDANCES)

(Réduction au tiers)

Place's *Nineve et l'Assyrie* was indeed extensively illustrated, but not precisely by photographs. Rather, like many of the archaeological albums of the mid-century, it consisted of engravings made after photographs, a sort of compromise between media. While the majority did represent their photographic sources with fidelity, there are also notable divergences, as in this striking example. A portion of an etched plate shows a variety of implements excavated: a twisted, bundled metal chain, surrounded by two hooks, with a portion of a tripod at the top (illus. 18). For all its studied exactitude, this image is not a direct transcription of any of Tranchand's photographs. First, it brings together two different photographs. The tripod derives from one photograph, and the other images from a second (illus. 17).[15] But that second photograph does not present three discrete artefacts at all, but rather the mass from which the three in the engraving have been isolated.

Place refers in his text to the large engraved image at the centre as 'a photographic view' and says he reproduces it 'in order to present an exact image of the state in which this ironwork was found'. What Place says of the engraved image is even truer of the photograph on which it is based: that 'on first viewing one has under one's gaze only a chaos made of rings, chains and hooks'.[16] But the photographically derived precision of the find is hardly an ending point for Place, who instead uses it as a basis for visual speculation about Assyrian metalwork, as in the two portions of chain represented at either side. These two side images, however, are purely imaginary. They were constructed according to Place, by isolating, re-working and imagining portions of the whole. Only as engravings can both levels of antiquities, the precisely found and the more properly imagined, the find and the conception of the find, coexist on a single page.

Here, then, is a prime example of the different interpretive operations of different representational media as used by archaeologists, uncoupled from a drive to mimetic fidelity or unmediated transcription. The etching works to interpret the mass while the photograph is most adept at describing it. At play here is a perfect distinction between the print's interpretive anatomy and photography's descriptive physiognomy, mixing both interpretive levels on a single printed page.

Further, in its own way, the photograph of a strange, compelling object sitting on a base (unlike the floating object in the print), marks what might also be deemed as a drive toward aesthetic objectification. Indeed, a scholar of the ancient Near East once told me that such objects only began to be studied in detail after the metal constructions of artists such as Picasso or Julio González became known (through photographs, of course). As we shall consider in more detail in a later chapter, photography thus ushers the object into a new realm of circulation and comparison.

In the most rigorous scientific and scholarly practice, then, photography revealed antiquity only within distinct limits. Yet the fascination for the photographic image of antiquity as expressed in Lacan's encomium to Place did nonetheless find an outlet. After the public announcement of the process, photographers were almost immediately on the move, taking the photographic apparatus throughout the world and concentrating especially on the areas of greatest interest to Western audiences. By November 1839, just months after Arago's announcement, the Frenchmen Hector Horeau, Frédéric Goupil-Fesquet and Pierre-Gustave Joly de Lotbinière were said to be in Egypt 'daguerrotyping away like lions'.[17] The work of the last two was utilized in the *Excursions Daguerriennes*, which appeared the following year (see p. 106).

Their activity is the vanguard of a wholesale drive toward documenting, and often salvaging, built structures of every portion of the past. This is evident, for instance, in the French Mission Héliographique of 1851, a governmental project that sent five photographers to various regions of the country to photograph historic structures of all ages, preserving what was seen as a material patrimony threatened by circumstances both physical and ideological (see p. 116). Surprisingly, perhaps, the same activity was endorsed in England by John Ruskin, who was otherwise often critical of modern developments. In his second preface to *The Seven Lamps of Architecture* (1855) Ruskin implored photographers 'to bear in mind that while a photograph of landscape is merely an amusing toy, one of early architecture is a precious historical document . . . this architecture should be taken not merely when it presents itself under picturesque general forms, but stone by stone, and sculpture by sculpture'.[18]

Such an attitude was behind the work of subsequent decades and practised throughout the world. Hardly least was India, given its immense stock of monuments, and eager British, as well as colonial, readership. James Fergusson, primary scholar and purveyor of works on the history of Indian architecture, prefaced the first edition of his *History of Indian and Eastern Architecture* (1876) with a paean to photography.

> For the purpose of such a work as this, however, photography has probably done more than anything that has been written. There are now very few buildings in India – of any importance at least – which have not been photographed with more or less completeness . . . For detecting similarities, or distinguishing differences between specimens situated at distances from one another, photographs are almost equal to actual personal inspection.[19]

Fergusson reports the accomplishment in India of the same sort of photographic project recommended earlier by Ruskin for Europe, a mark of the worldwide inundation of a photographically motivated vision of the material past. Fergusson tellingly states that photographs are 'almost' equal in value to a visit to the actual monument, attributing to the photograph itself a second-order, documentary nature. As we shall see, it could not always be confined to this status.

But as important as the actual making of photographs was the matter of reproducing and circulating them, which vexed popular and amateur audiences as much as scientific ones. Books from the *Excursions Daguerriennes* to Fergusson's work more than 30 years later suffered from the same handicap as Place's volume, consisting of engravings after photographs, not photographic images themselves. The technical difficulties in mass-producing photographic books at reasonable prices were first solved by the French entrepreneur Louis Désiré Blanquart-Evrard of Lille, who started the first large-scale printing house in France. In 1852, just a year after its foundation, Blanquart-Evrard published Maxime Du Camp's *Egypt, Nubia, Palestine and Syria*. The bulk of Du Camp's work consisted of a portfolio of salt prints made from the paper negatives he produced during a two-year tour of the region.

19 Maxime Du Camp, 'Propylon of Temple of Khons, Karnak,' in *Egypt, Nubia, Palestine and Syria* (1852), plate 27.

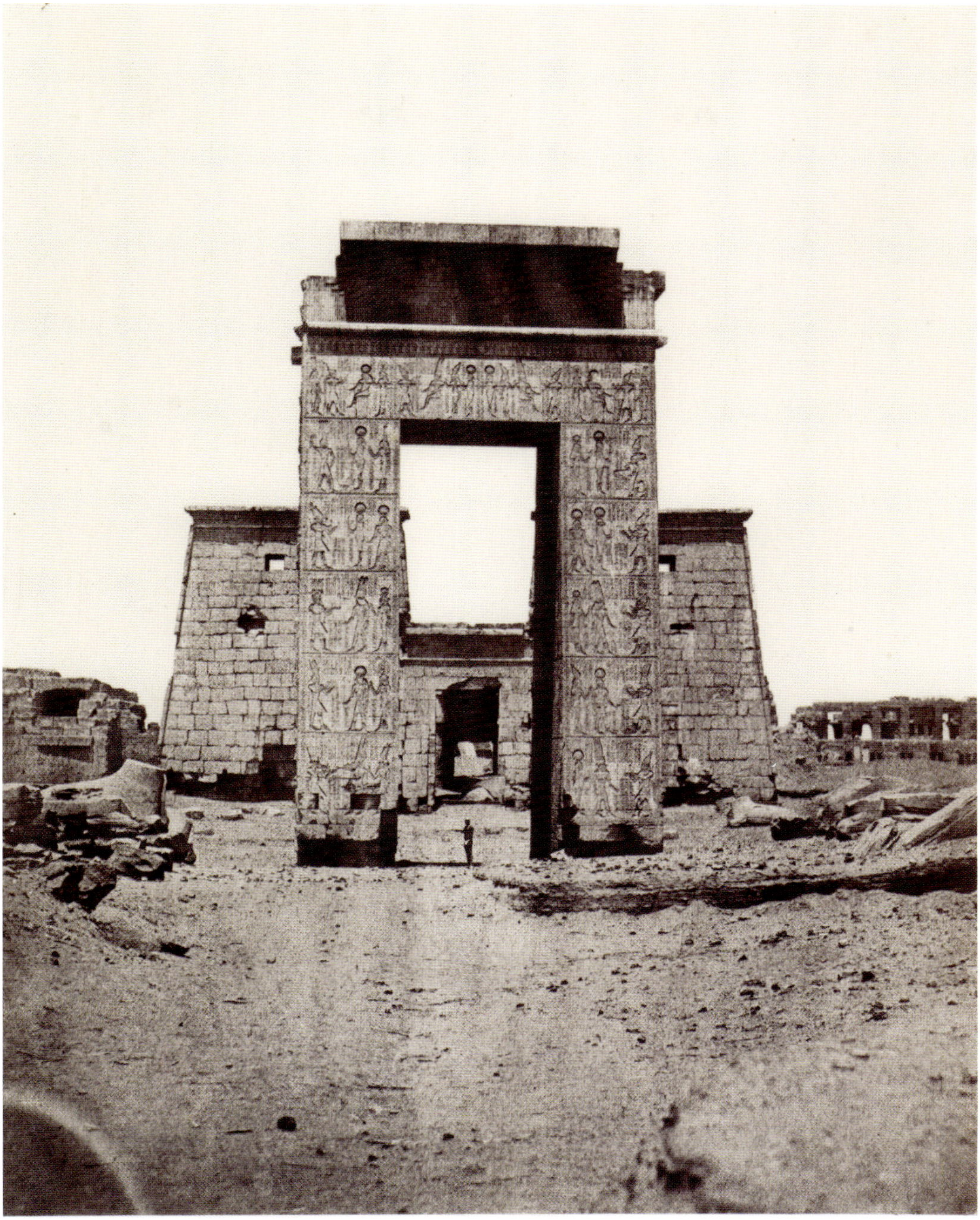

Via photography, Du Camp brought Egypt's presence to the French viewer, and he was named to the French Legion of Honour for the accomplishment. Though Du Camp's work is the product of what is largely a touristic experience, it is presented to the reader as a pseudo-scientific topographical account, with an accompanying text that marshals ancient scholarship and physical details in a manner reminiscent of traditional antiquarian texts and other contemporary travelogues. But this textual component of the book is considerably smaller than its array of 125 images, displacing the burden of narrative from textual to visual evidence.

In all, it was a work as novel in representational medium as it was unchallenging and traditional in content.[20] Du Camp's image of a temple approach at Karnak, for instance, while dazzling with its size (established by the tiny staffage figure at its centre) is stolid and rigidly symmetrical (illus. 19). Nothing in the photograph detracts from the viewer's sense of entering the temple precinct. Du Camp's image presents the principle of 'straight' documentation that presages the style of much twentieth-century archaeological recording.

Du Camp never returned to photography after his Middle Eastern trip. He had seized on a contemporary innovation, rode it to fame, and then abandoned the often frustrating process for other pursuits. A different background and trajectory is that of Joseph-Philibert Girault de Prangey. Born in Langres in 1804 to a noble family, Girault de Prangey was a lifelong artist particularly dedicated to architectural drawing and recording. After a tour in Spain in the early 1830s, where he spent time studying and drawing Islamic architecture and monuments (later lithographed and published in a formal volume as *Monuments Arabes et Moresques de Cordue, Séville et Grenade*), he had both the means and the experience to utilize the photographic apparatus to similar effect.

In 1842 Girault de Prangey began a three-year tour through the Mediterranean and Middle East which produced as many as 1,000 daguerreotypes. Formally trained as a draughtsman and painter, Girault de Prangey's images are anything but purely straightforward in the manner of Du Camp. They are an object lesson in the challenges of representing the archaeological subject: in what can be recorded within the visual frame as well as conjured in the viewer's mind. Girault de Prangey was among the very first to photograph the Acropolis. An image of the Parthenon is hardly frontal, instead placing the building's corner precisely at the centre of the image, its steps jutting directly into the viewer's space, while at the top an extant portion of the pediment moves similarly to engage the upper edge (illus. 20). The image seems to be constructed in accordance with the capability of both camera and viewer. Lindsey Stewart observes that 'the temple ruins tower above the rubble' in a way that almost enacts visually the adulation felt among educated Europeans for the cultural heritage of Greco-Roman antiquity.[21] The photograph of the Parthenon creates a meaningful, engaging structure out of the inert raw material that surrounds it, product of more recent shocks. It is an enduring trace of the past, worn but vital. Just to the left of the stylobate's corner sits a small camera on a tripod, aimed at a detail of the site. This may be the first archaeological photograph to depict the process of archaeological photography.

Human subjects are rarely captured in Girault de Prangey's images, in part due to the lengthy exposure times required. Yet the exclusion is not only technical. It serves the basic vision of archaeology, not just by

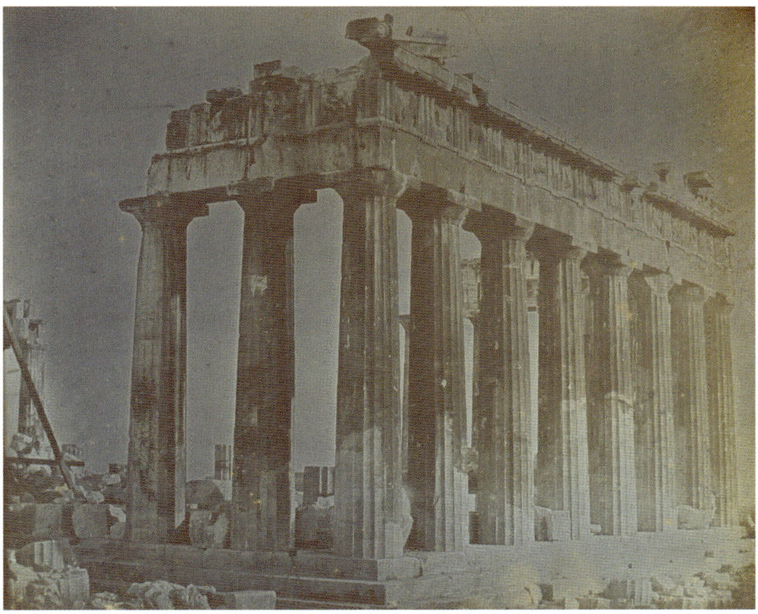

20 Joseph-Philibert Girault de Prangey, 'Facade and North Colonnade of the Parthenon, Acropolis, Athens', 1842, daguerreotype.

diminishing the present for the palpable suggestion of the past, but also by systematically excluding what, for travellers from Western Europe, was the troubling, less-settled presence of the contemporary inhabitants of what were better known as ancient lands. Greece at the time was a welter of peoples and religions, only recently having won its independence from the Ottoman Empire.

A photograph from Jerusalem, from two years later into Girault de Prangey's tour, adopts a related mode of seeing, and looking away from the cotemporary, to a different sort of site. A half-plate daguerrotype of 'The Probatic Pool, Jerusalem' is devoted to the curative pool in which those suffering from illnesses were said to be cured by the periodic visit of an angel, and near where Jesus was reputed to have healed a man too ill to even reach the waters (illus. 21). Girault de Prangey's subject here is not so much palpable as imagined. It is thus not exactly detailed in a bright light, but found within a dark, mysterious empty space. Both images, in different ways, play on the viewer's imaginative investment, and correspond to different kinds of archaeological subjects (not least the differences between above- and below-ground archaeology). The first connects with the past via present experience, providing the viewer an explicit, detailed vision, almost reaching beyond the frame, and drawing the viewer's eye upwards. The second, perhaps more common in archaeological photography, thrives on absence, looking down an empty space into the projected past. Girault de Prangey's image takes the viewer into the darkness of the pool after traversing the barrier wall that confines it. With the new, detail-rich rendering that was the daguerreotype's métier, the viewer can descend the wall almost brick by brick through vegetation and signs of human habitation, its stones becoming larger and rougher, the enclosure itself becoming smaller, and the entire act of looking itself a kind of archaeology: scanning progressively more distant times.

Girault de Prangey's work spans a considerable array of types of archaeological photography, not least including what may well be the first panoramic photographs in the field. Key among them is a type located between grand or establishing views and specific artefactual photography, namely that of site details. A photograph of a cistern

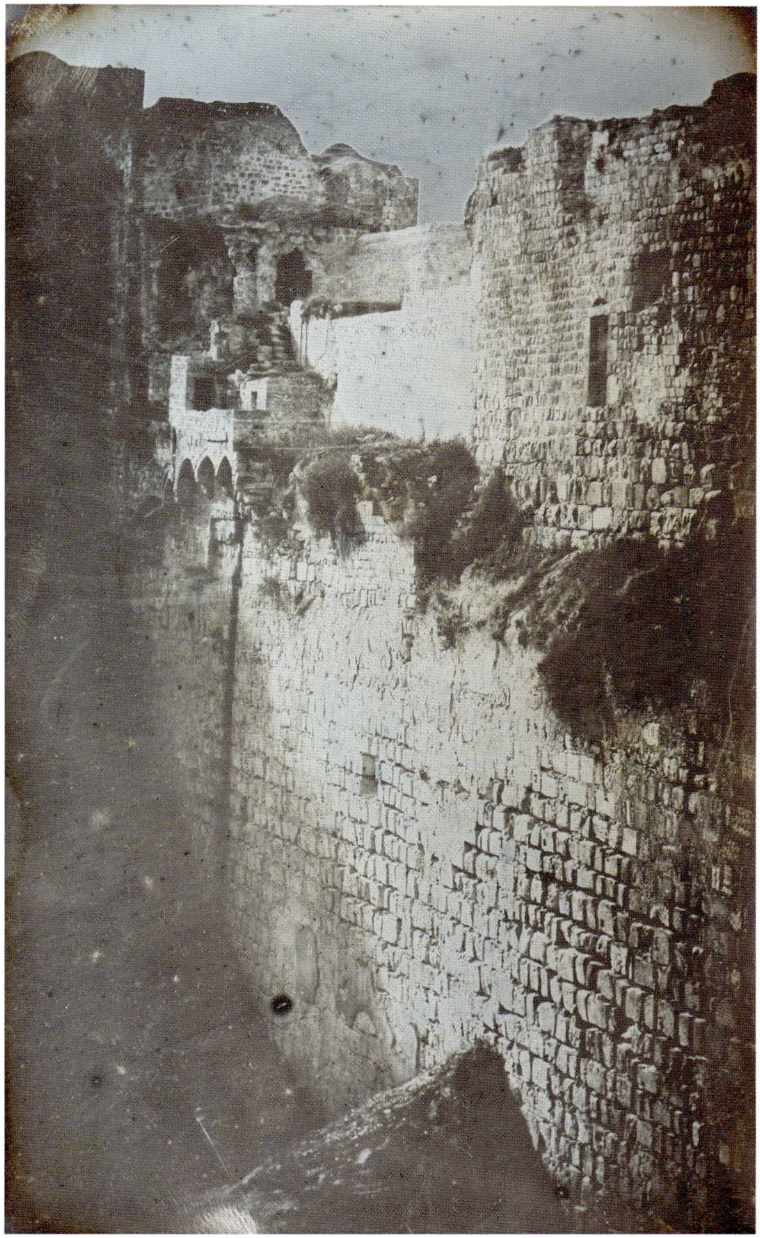

21 Joseph-Philibert Girault de Prangey, 'The Probatic Pool, Jersualem', 1844, daguerreotype.

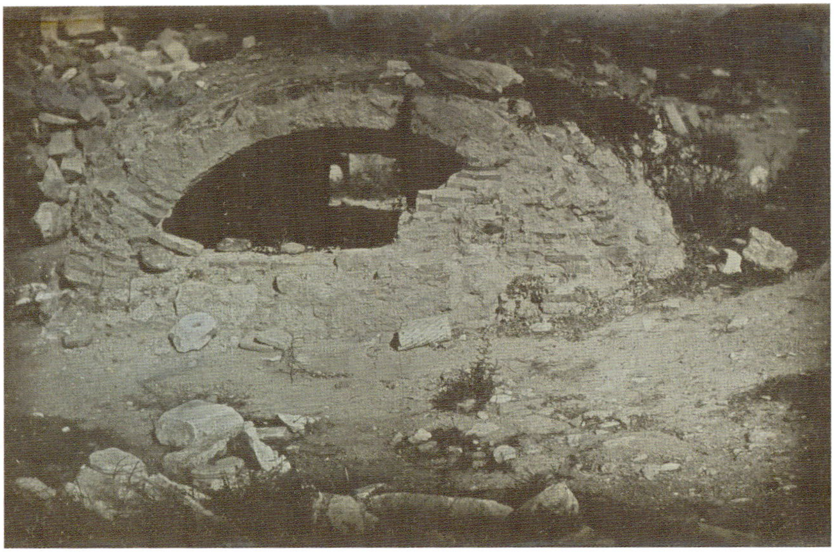

22 Joseph-Philibert Girault de Prangey, 'Cistern Opening at the Foot of the Erechtheion, Acropolis, Athens', 1842, daguerreotype.

opening at the foot of the Erechtheion, also on the Acropolis, focuses on the opening itself and surrounding structure (illus. 22). Details of bricks and stone, soil and rubble strewn throughout the visual field tax the camera's ability to focus on them all, while once again a space of watery darkness anchors the eye. But here the image is centred rather than framed, directed by intellectual rather than experiential criteria. For all that it says about ancient building practices, it says far less about the experience of viewing them. This sort of image, which minimizes viewing subject for viewed object, has come to embody most of all the photographic work of the dispassionate eye of science. Its echo can be traced nearly 40 years later, in 1880, when Alexander Conze published one of the first archaeological treatises extensively illustrated with direct photographic reproductions, his *Neue Archaeologische Untersuchungen auf Samothrake*. Though best known for several images that isolate and detail striking fragments from his Samothrace excavation, the vast majority of Conze's illustrations are devoted to the less striking but essential details of understanding the site as a whole, such as this drain, similarly centred and pictured from several directions, in the systematic manner still practised in scientific excavation photography (illus. 23).

We know little of Girault de Prangey's underlying motives. But his photography itself elaborates a fundamental choice that obtains in archaeological photography. There are images of wholes, intact organic segments, and of portions, noteworthy features that bear recording. These are images that seem deliberately striking, to affect the viewer's sensibility and offer him/her an immediate, almost visceral, purchase on the subject. However, there are those which seem just as deliberately unstriking, highlighting the objective testimony of the recording photographer and deliberately eschewing artifices of lighting, viewpoint, composition and so on. Each of these modes has found a place in archaeological photography. In the play between them is a flux between art and science.

23 Wilhelm Burger, 'Sacrificial Pit "A" seen from North', in Alexander Conze, *Neue Archaeologische Untersuchungen auf Samothrake* (1880).

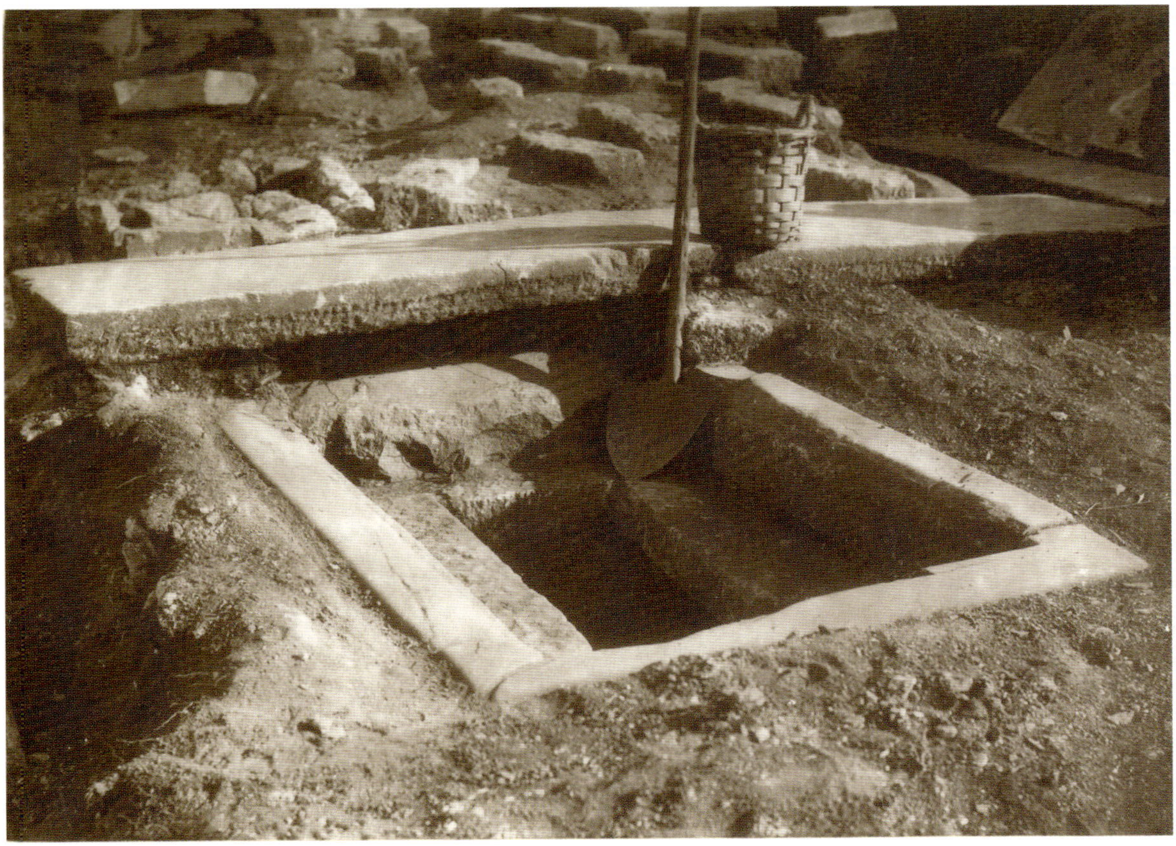

Almost no corpus of archaeological photography employs the 'objective' mode exclusively, but it is a measure of the scientific claim of modern archaeology that its photography largely eschews aesthetic or experiential effect for systematic, exhaustive documentation. Compared to Du Camp's views to enable the armchair tourist, or Girault de Prangey's aesthetic vision of the Parthenon, consider the words of George Andrew Reisner. Reisner was a pioneer of scientific archaeology in the early twentieth century, a Harvard professor who directed many of the most important excavations in Egypt, Nubia and Palestine, perhaps most famously that of the Giza necropolis. Also an expert photographer, Reisner took many excavation photographs himself. His 1924 treatise on the use of photography in excavation begins with a single general principle: 'This fact must always be borne in mind: *the excavator can only photograph what he has observed* . . . Photographs . . . serve as reminders to the eye of the excavator but are not much better than blank paper to one who has not seen the object photographed.'[22] At its heart, Reisner's conception of archaeological imagery, still a core of the modern scientific conception, is not visually so much as functionally distinct. It is less concerned with what is represented than with who can properly do the looking. The photograph is an instrument for a privileged memory, a second-level image and souvenir to be looked *through* to its moment of origin and not *at* as an object in its own right.

As archaeological photography floats among different conceptions tied to different audiences, one can even see tensions play out between these modes at moments of crisis. John Henry Haynes served as photographer to the University of Pennsylvania excavation to Nippur (Iraq) in the last decade of the nineteenth century. It is an excavation today known to Mesopotamian archaeologists largely as a cautionary tale. This also applies to its photographic documentation. Haynes had studied photography with William J. Stillman in Athens (see pp. 95–7), and his work reflects Stillman's structural, even lyrical, approach. After some touring and experience of photographing classical monuments, Haynes was named field photographer to the Nippur excavation, as well as American consul to Baghdad, in 1889. Before photography's spread created useful local photographers, the staff photographer was quite often the lowest of imported Western excavation workers, and often had administrative functions as well. But Haynes's greatest misfortune was that the Iraqi desert, and Nippur's mudbrick structures, did not respond well to the classical aesthetic in which he had trained, nor did his resultant photographs fit the functional criteria of his director.

John Peters, the excavation leader, states about Haynes's first two years of photographic work that 'I had failed to have the camera used as I wished during my work', deeming the whole enterprise 'to so large an extent a failure, that it was at first proposed to dispose with all photographic outfit this time and so reduce expenses'. It is striking to hear that as late as the 1890s some considered photography expendable. Yet Peters continues: 'It seemed to me that photography was essential, if it were our intention to excavate scientifically and report our results intelligently to the world.'[23] Peters wished for 'photographing the work in the trenches frequently and systematically, and photographing objects found *in situ* and again in camp', which is still a good summary of the fundamental documentary use of photography in object-based archaeology.

A photograph by Haynes of a deep trench made early in the Nippur excavation provides a good example of the situation (illus. 24). The view glances across the trenches rather than down into them. It does not detail their holdings or features so much as it presents, even revels in, a sort of complex calligraphy of earth, a surface all the more compelling as it seems obscurely connected to the topography of hills beyond the excavation site. Haynes's view is visually striking, but that is just its failure. It does not document so much as it discovers visual material. It sees for itself, rather than through the eyes of the archaeologist. A glance at Maurice Cookson's *Photography for Archaeologists* (1954), for instance, discusses and illustrates 'the Need for a high viewpoint' to allow seeing into individual trenches (illus. 25). In just this visual comparison, Cookson's work eloquently lays out a fundamental principle of one of the leading archaeological photographers of his time, who worked for nearly three decades with Sir Mortimer Wheeler.

Wheeler was not only among the most influential and successful archaeologists of the twentieth century, but also one particularly devoted to the use of the photographic image. In his didactic *Archaeology from the*

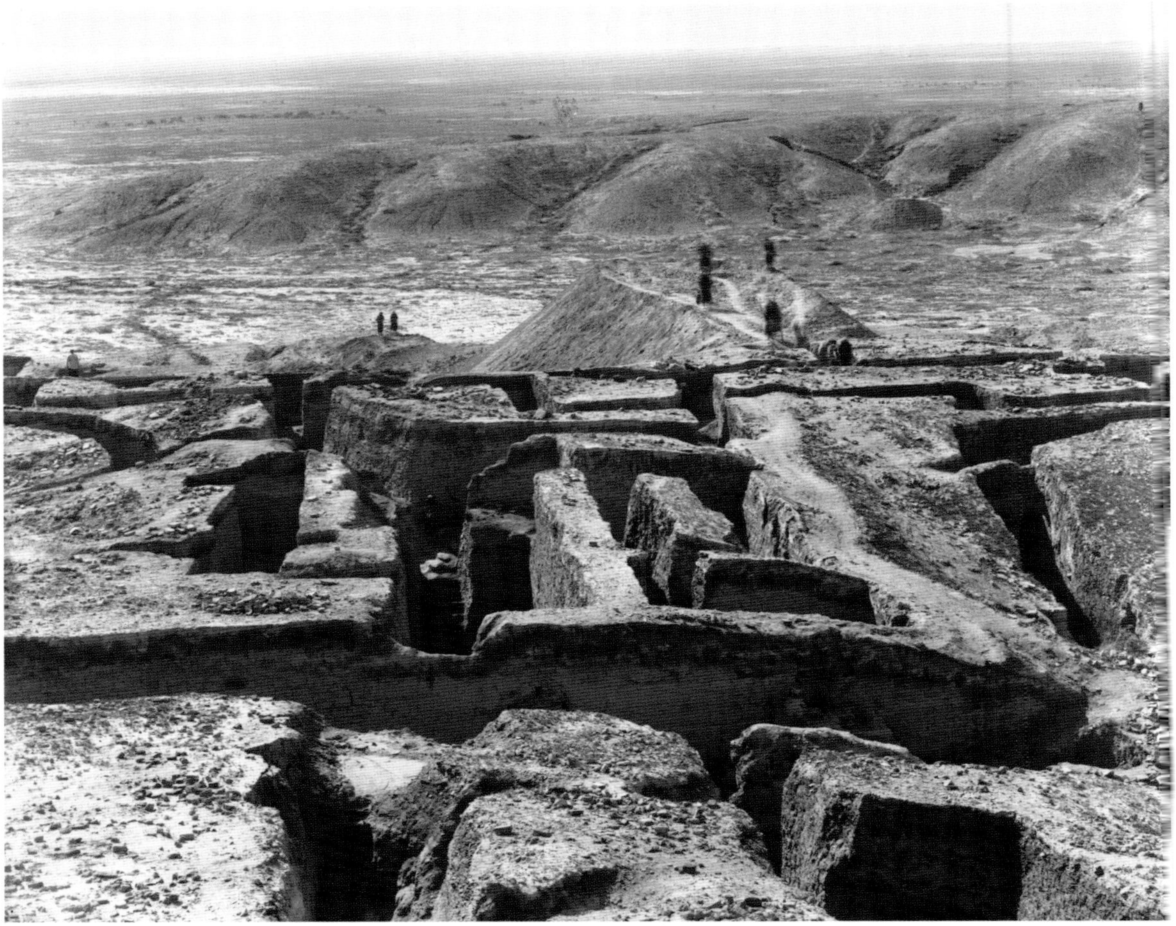

24 John Henry Haynes, 'Trenches in Mounds West of Shat-en-Nil, Nippur, Iraq', 1889–90, albumen print.

*Earth*, Wheeler even provides photographs that allow us to look from the standpoint of the archaeological director, one deeply concerned with the performance of the excavation enterprise with quasi-military precision. Thus, in a similar binary comparison, a plate distinguishes a chaotic excavation from one of proper 'discipline' (illus. 26). From Peters to Reisner to Wheeler, then, the history of archaeological photography is intermingled with the history of codification or even the enforcement of a certain brand of archaeological practice. The specification of how to dig includes the specification of how to represent and evaluate.

25 Michael Cookson, 'The Necessity for a High Viewpoint', in *Photography for Archaeologists* (1954), plate 5.

26 '(a) Chaos: Excavation in the East, 1935' and '(b) Discipline: Excavation at Arikamedu, South India, 1945', in Mortimer Wheeler, *Archaeology from the Earth* (1954), p. 64

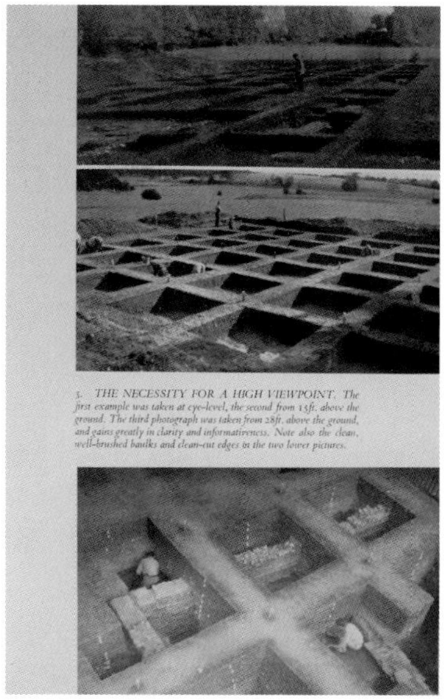


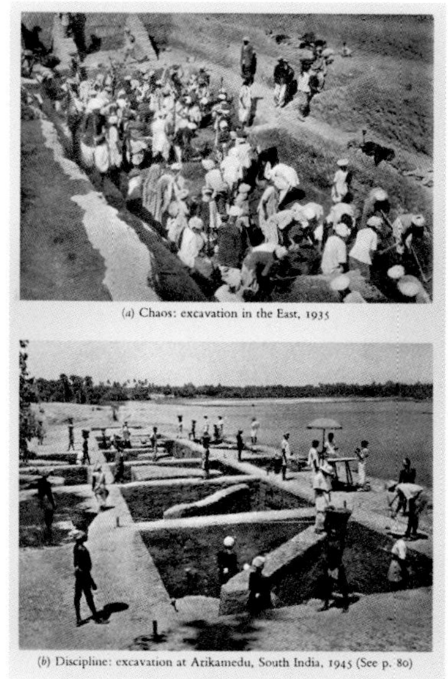


Indeed, it was Wheeler's axiom that just a look at an excavation would indicate its fundamental nature. The scene of chaos at the excavation of 'an archaeologist of considerable repute' is contrasted by one, as Wheeler states, which 'unblushingly represents an excavation of my own'.[24] In Wheeler's description it is 'a site neatly parceled out in readily controllable areas; small groups of workmen are directed by supervisors (distinguishable in the photograph by their sun helmets); the basket carriers are working in orderly procession along clear pathways; and in the middle distance on the right, the survey-party is conveniently at work at a table shaded by an essential umbrella'. Beyond the documentary value of this image for Wheeler's text, one cannot help but be struck by the visual sensitivity involved, presenting an image glossed by thick description, in a manner reminiscent of the strict principles for design of traditional history and narrative painting. What was even more to be disciplined for Wheeler, as we shall see in more detail later, was the photographic medium itself.

The one photograph by Haynes that Peters deemed the best after two years of the campaign was an object photo, an image of a selection

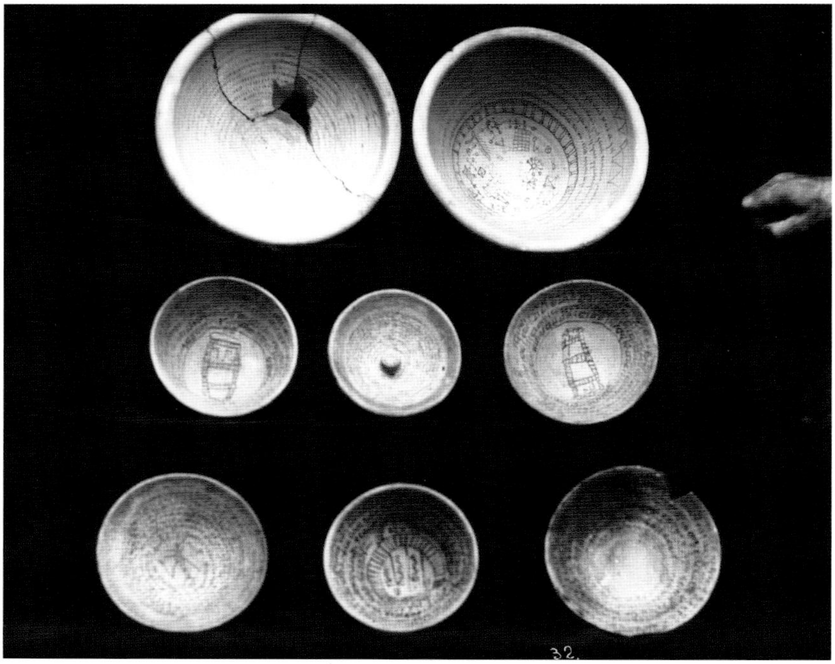

27 John Henry Haynes, 'Nippur, Eight Aramaic Incantation Bowls', 1889–90, albumen print.

of discovered artefacts set against a black background. Haynes worked repeatedly at object photography, sometimes under improvised conditions, as in this example where a hand holds up a backdrop for a group of inscribed bowls (illus. 27). As Peters stated, for him the primary function of archaeological photography was to allow archaeologists to document and communicate their finds to each other. Object photography and site photography make up the bulk of standard archaeological photography because they are the primary things about which archaeologists wish to communicate. Within a particular archaeological project, the balance between these types reflects the different interests of the directors of the project as well as the nature of the site itself.

'Standard' archaeological photography, made under the dominance of the scientific method, is designed to be looked at by a forensic investigator. Visually, it shares much with the ethnographic photography that also began in the nineteenth century, applying to an ancient monument the physical rulers and grid system commonly used for measurement of

28 John Burke, 'Ruins of a Temple at Norwah, Kashmir,' in H. H. Cole, *Ancient Bulidings in Kashmir* (1869), plate 34.

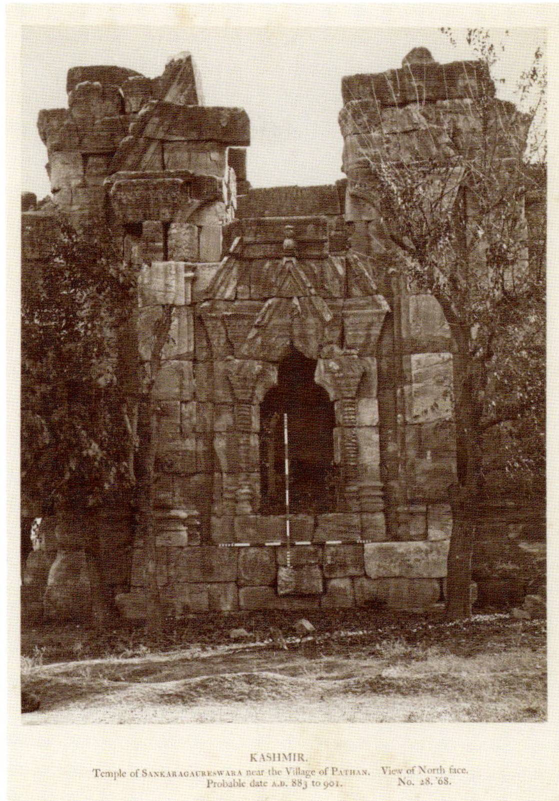


facial and bodily features of specimens of indigenous peoples. A particularly explicit example can be found in a photograph by a British colonial survey team of the remaining facade of a temple in Norwah, Kashmir, which uses two perpendicular rules to allow the mapping of a full grid (illus. 28). This embodies the historical segment of a larger drive, in the words of Maria Antonella Pelizzari, 'to know, archive, and classify Indian diversity'.[25] In line with demands of archaeologists like Reisner, the ruler itself soon took a place that was less central, so as to allow the photograph's subject to be approached more directly.

This later visual modality can be elaborated by two American images from the mid-1930s, the very decade in which professional archaeology was fully institutionalized.[26] A stratigraphic view made in Khorsabad

(Iraq), by the University of Chicago excavation there, is a vertiginous drop as it glances across layering of soil above a smoother, excavated floor at the lower left (illus. 29). The view is disorienting for its seeming lack of central focus, arbitrary placement of edges and perhaps most of all by the diagonal axis of the space, accentuated by the rule. What is on view is an idea about how to find the past, within a process of painstaking documentation, as much as any physical evidence. It is not a photograph taken for publication so much as for possible consultation at some later time, a fact waiting for a theory and jog to memory.

Archaeological teams under the Works Progress Administration extensively examined and documented sites of Native American habitation prior to the flooding of the area by the Tennessee Valley Authority during the 1930s. These images soon became first-order pieces of evidence, as the sites themselves were largely submerged beneath the TVA dams project. The photographic image here stands for, indeed virtually becomes, the object of study in its own right. An archive of tens of thousands of extant photographs traces the excavation process.

But again the viewpoint behind the camera intervenes. These photographs also document the expectations of archaeologists, including a panoptic, even transgressive, drive to examine what is culturally fraught,

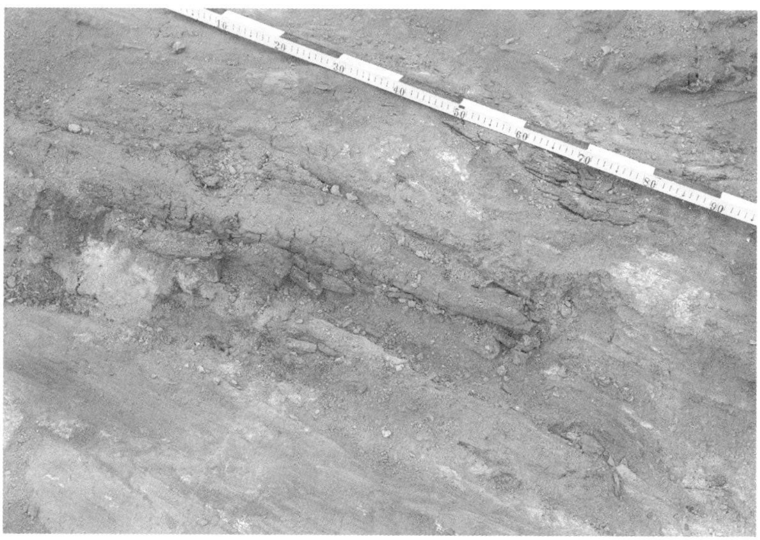

29 Unknown photographer, 'Detail of Stratigraphy, Khorsabad Field Negative', 1934.

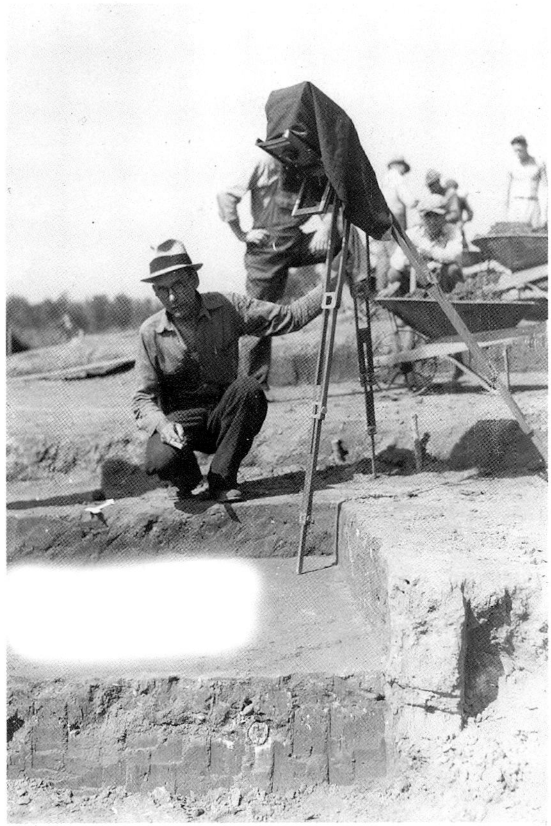

30 Wendell C. Walker, 'Photographing a Burial at Hixon Site, Chickamauga Reservoir, Hamilton County, Tennessee', 1936, gelatin silver print. A portion of the image is intentionally obscured.

indeed today forbidden. The WPA teams examined Native American burial sites, though among all reputable New World archaeologists today such examination is forbidden without explicit permission from and collaboration with relevant indigenous peoples. Even the process cannot properly be depicted without obscuring and keeping the human remains themselves out of view to non-indigenous eyes (illus. 30).

A photograph of a portion of a different burial mound is numerically tagged. According to its field record it includes 'six triangular projectile points and miscellaneous worked stones including a crude celt'.[27] With admirable candour, we learn that the artefacts 'have been slightly rearranged' but the report assures us that the 'position is essentially accurate', thus minimizing the investigator's tampering. This is especially striking because the image's main testimony is to what is not before the lens. Besides the artefacts, the record tells us of 'bones of burial completely disintegrated and nothing left'. It is just this 'nothing' that, here, is made into 'something'; it is absence itself that is documented. We see here, not for the last time, the paradox of photographic testimony in archaeology, in the way the photographic image requires human intervention while also seeming to be independent of it. If 'the stones speak' they do not do it alone, but are placed within a set of expectations, sometimes, as here, in a way that violently intrudes upon the cultural norms of the realm being investigated.

Indeed, the evidentiary power of photography under an excavator's control leads to the even more delicate question of the possibility of falsification. For instance, recent examination of the publications (from just the same time as the WPA images) of Sir Arthur Evans, renowned discoverer of the Bronze Age site of Knossos on Crete, has found photographs to have been altered, and even occasionally falsified, to support his sometimes controversial historical interpretations of the site's findings.[28]

Like any other image, the archaeological photograph requires decipherment. To be useful in archaeology is not the same as being obvious, unmediated or natural, despite claims from publicists and archaeologists alike, as we have seen, of the photographic image's pure accuracy and identity with the real. Rather, the truth of the photographic image in archaeology is intimately linked to new scientific modes of evaluating evidence. Its truth is decreed at least as much by scientific usefulness as by visual accuracy. Indeed, usefulness versus accuracy mark two distinct kinds of evaluation, related to different visual habits. Turning back to the origins of photography, one can see these two paths contrast with particular force in the early study of antiquities of Central America.

At just the moment of photography's invention, the American travel writer John Lloyd Stephens had embarked on a project exploring Mesoamerican antiquities. The first volume of his two-volume expedition report, *Incidents of Travel in Central America, Chiapas and Yucatán*, appeared in 1841. For illustrations Stephens employed the British artist Frederick Catherwood, a meticulous draughtsman previously experienced in recording archaeological imagery in the Middle East. Catherwood was astonished and awed by the size and complexity of the monuments, almost to the point of despairing of ever capturing them. He eventually was able to produce the impressive, often detailed images that were key to the book's success by drawing with the aid of a *camera lucida*. However, by the time of the tour that led to the second volume, *Incidents of Travel in Yucatán* (1843), the claim for authority of the photographic camera had decisively intervened. Thus the volume's preface assures the reader that 'the descriptions are accompanied by full illustrations from Daguerreotype views and drawings taken on the spot by Mr Catherwood'.[29] While such a statement may have been required to guarantee veracity to the public, the text itself makes clear that Catherwood did not find the camera adequate at all for the grandeur and vastness of the monuments. On site at the Governor's Palace in Uxmal, for instance, with a camera proudly described as 'the best that could be procured in New-York', Catherwood deemed the results 'not sufficiently perfect to suit his ideas'. Among Catherwood's complaints about photographs was that: 'At times the projecting cornices and ornaments threw parts of the subject in shade, while others were in broad sunshine; so that, while parts were brought out well, other parts required pencil drawings to supply their defects.'

Stephens continues: 'He [Catherwood] therefore completed everything with his pencil and *camera lucida* while Dr Cabot and myself took up the Daguerrotype.'[30] The camera's presence may have been necessary to public acceptance of the project, but it was virtually antithetical to the figure responsible for representations and was operated instead by the two non-artists. It played little role in any of the ultimate illustrations of the book. The greatest role played by the camera in Stephens's narrative is when it is used for portraiture of women in Yucatán towns. Photographic images may have been *true* to precisely how the monuments appeared in the dappled light of deep forests, or dramatically shadowed at some times of the day, but were not *useful* to the artist's/archaeologists's project of representation. The artist used to full delineation of grand monuments, and blocking out the rest, was distinctly disappointed by photography's surface-oriented, undiscerning visual results.

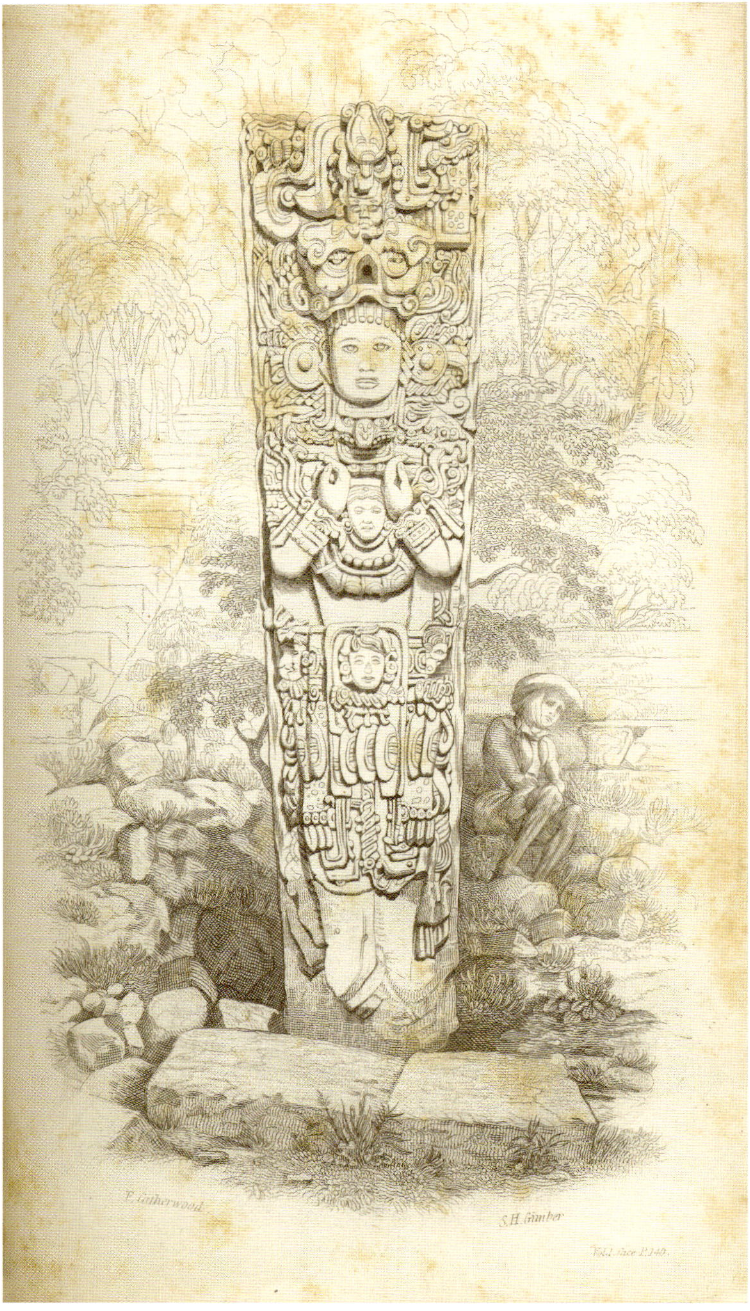


31 Frederick Catherwood, 'Discovery of a Sculptured Monument', in John Lloyd Stephens, *Incidents of Travel in Central America, Chiapas and Yucatán* (1841), vol. I opp. p. 140, engraving.

Catherwood's illustration, such as one of a 'stone idol' at Copan, from the earlier volume, operates on a different logic from the camera (illus. 31). The monument is elaborated in detail, including its iconography, surface, shading and even the rocks that surround it. On the other hand, the seated figure, like the natural setting and stone structure, are only lightly sketched, as if behind a scrim, thus singling out the monument from the whole almost as if with a spotlight. Catherwood plays the role not of photographic recorder but discerning viewer, knowing what to minimize.

A further step in the history of photographic delineation of the region works to bring the two roles – trustworthy photographer and informed draftsman – closer together. Desiré Charnay was a French school teacher who had been settled in America for years when he embarked on the tour that led to his publication *Cités et ruines américaines* (1862), a survey of ancient Mexican monuments. Charnay's work spans two formats. It consists of a quarto volume of texts and engravings, much the same as Stephens's works, but is accompanied by a very large folio of 50 photographic illustrations. In consulting the work, its images seem to subordinate textual knowledge to visual experience. This is accomplished in part by the sheer size of the images as well as their detail and complexity. Charnay's painstaking prints from wet-collodion negatives contain vastly more to catch the eye than the smaller daguerreotype format. Yet at the same time they hark back to the tradition of the vast 'sublime' prints used to portray the same antiquities in pre-photographic times, such as those of Jean-Frédéric de Waldeck and José Luciano Castañeda, which had served as models for Catherwood as well.[31] A photograph such as the view of the principal facade of the so-called nunnery (actually a governmental palace) at Chichén Itzá details its structure, ornamentation and imagery together with the clotted jungle foliage picturesquely retaking the site (illus. 32). It combines the appeal of photographic veracity with the visual fullness associated with the graphic print.

Yet such an image still would be unlikely to satisfy Catherwood, or the assumptions of the print tradition. The photograph still has areas of darkness that occlude the structure, and the difficult terrain does not

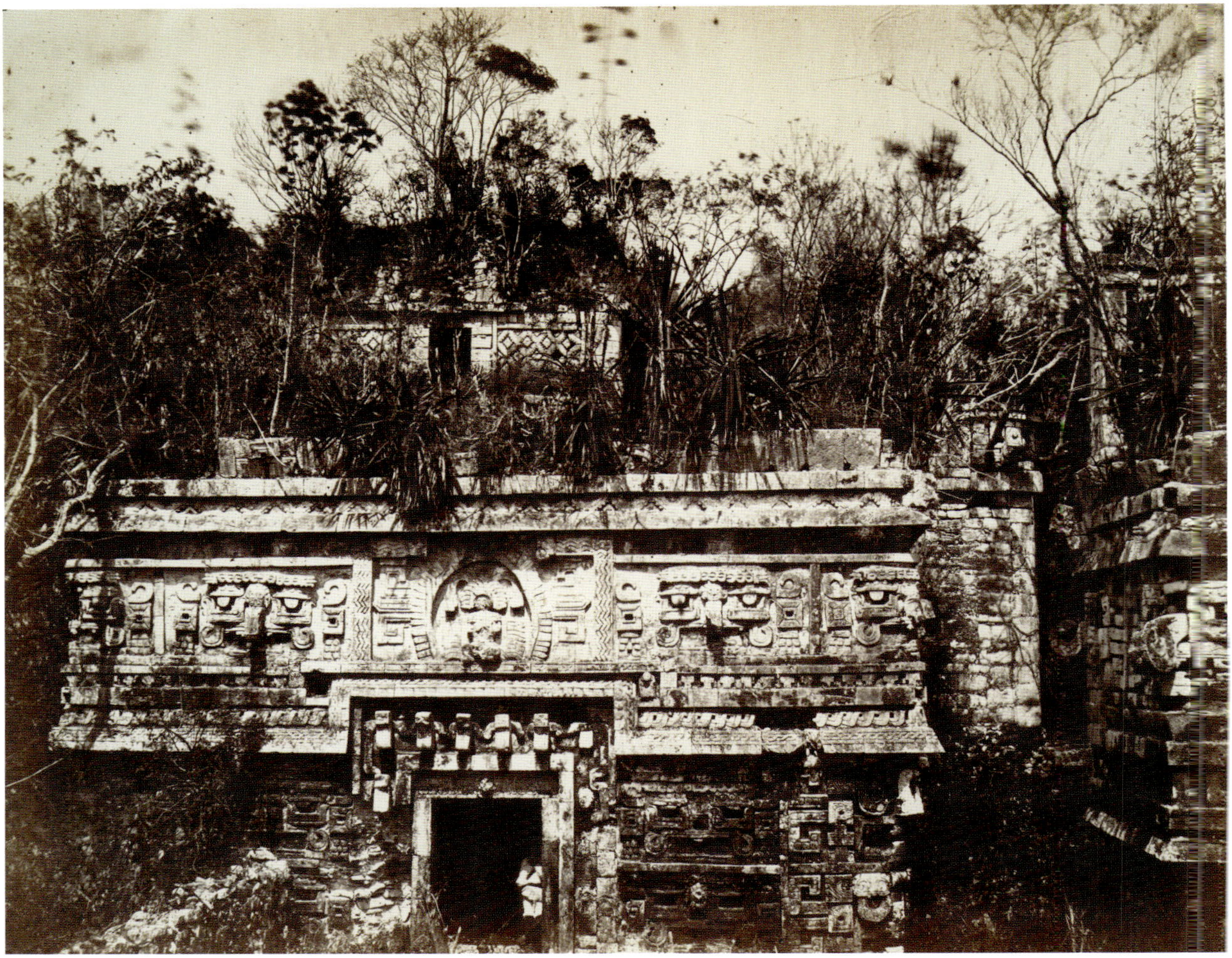

32 Desiré Charnay, '"Palace of Nuns", Principal Facade, Chichén Itzá', in *Cités et ruines américaines* (1863), plate 30, albumen silver print.

provide the ideal viewpoint and framing for concentrating solely on the subject. What distinguishes Charnay from Stephens is not just visual, but epistemological: the overlay of science. Charnay's text had much in common with Stephens, with travel stories, descriptions of places and people, struggles with photography, historical speculation and many other matters strewn throughout. But it was preceded by another text, more than 100 pages long, by one of the foremost theorists of cultural formation of the time: Eugène Viollet-le-Duc. Viollet-le-Duc's treatise is devoted to applying Charnay's work to a central question of the time: that of racial identity. Were the temple builders Aryan or Semite? Viollet-le-Duc used Charnay's evidence to deem the builders a *mélange* of the two. Stephens had used Catherwood's engravings to make observations on the same question, but Viollet-le-Duc stands as an expert imported into Charnay's travel enterprise. Moreover, Viollet-le-Duc employs the very fact of Charnay's images to buttress his arguments. He states that 'constructions as significant as those of which M. Charnay has delivered the photographs, which require the concentration of so many arms, of immense effort, are constructed by inferior races under submission to a theocratic or aristocratic regime'.[32] Viollet-le-Duc, indeed, was among the most enthusiastic supporters of photography, as we shall see. It is his intellectual framework, as much as any visual feature involved with Charnay's particular process, which harnesses together accuracy and usefulness. Viollet-le-Duc's hypothesis used Charnay's photographs for support, testimony to the inviolable truth attributed to the actual monuments in a way inaccessible to hand-drawn imagery. But as much as photography was fundamental within Viollet-le-Duc's conception, it also took on a lesser, evidentiary role (just as Peters later wished for Haynes's photos), not creating its own narrative, but serving that of a historical argument found in an accompanying text. Viollet-le-Duc is thus a pioneer not just in the use of photography but in its harnessing to a greater project.

Throughout its history, photography in archaeology has proven both indispensable and always in need of discipline. It remains a live issue in archaeology today. The revelation of photography's imprecise identity with its object has several implications within the field. First, the same belief in technology that led to photography's rise has moved on to more recent devices for correcting its errors. One cannot go to a conference on archaeological imaging without hearing an array of enthusiasts of various, sometimes proprietary, techniques. For instance, a team of specialists from many fields working on the site of Sagalassos in Turkey has produced a number of three-dimensional renderings by sophisticated computational techniques that stitch together and adjust photographic (or video) imagery of sites, structures and artefacts (illus. 33). Such 'virtual archaeology' has considerable advantages over using the cumbersome real objects, allowing the researcher to take points of view that are difficult to access, as well as to try to fit together fragments, no matter the size, weight or location, and to compare visual and structural details of distant objects. Yet the paradox of this drive to replicate three-dimensional archaeological reality is that it presents an opening towards an ideal in which 'the ultimate goal is to make it impossible to differentiate between real and virtual objects', in effect challenging the premise of photography as documentation of an external reality: no longer images to look *through* at all, but rather a past contained, its absence evacuated by virtual presence.[33]

The visual invocation of the archaeological object, as embodied not only by photography but other physical methods – like squeezes (direct soft paper impressions) or drawing – is just one edge of the virtual. The 'image-based' work of the Sagalassos group might be contrasted with a non-visual method, such as that of a Spanish team at work in the palaeolithic site of the Gran Dolina cave in northern Spain. In these dark depths archaeologists use not sight but sound. Large wand-like objects are placed within the cave and emit acoustic signals that are received, compared and registered by computer to allow a very high level of accuracy in elaborating details of a pre-mapped spatial structure. They allow measurement not just of location, but outline, shape and orientation of objects such as fossils.[34] As they resemble nothing so much as giant pencils, photography's status as 'pencil of nature' is somehow usurped by these devices, which make a claim to objectivity by a different route.

More important, as a new vehicle for a longstanding project, they mark that photography, in the age of Photoshop, no longer enjoys its

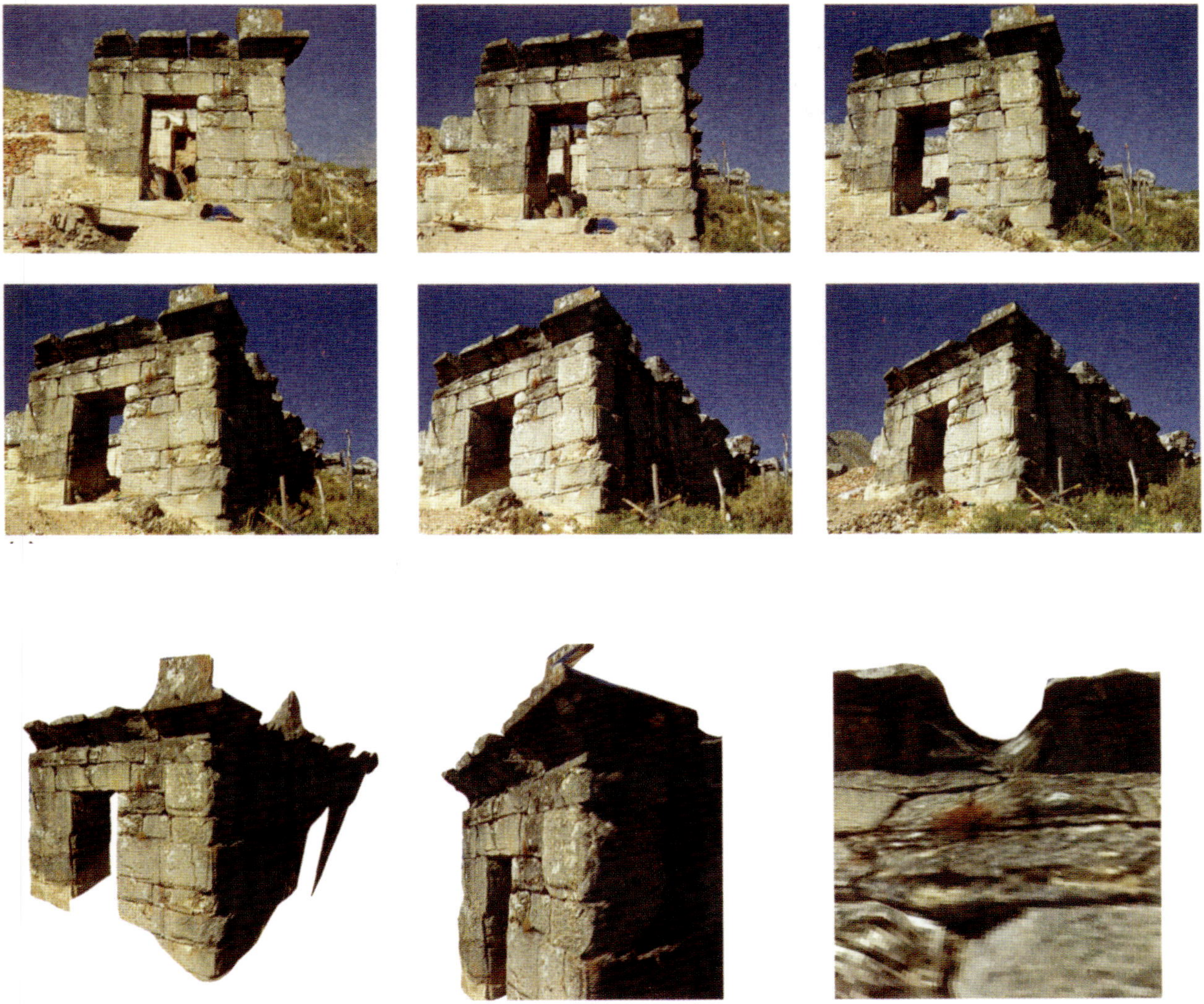

33 Marc Pollefeys, Luc Van Gool, Maarten Vergauwen, Kurt Cornelis, Frank Verbiest and Jan Tops, *Digital Reconstruction of a Corner of the Roman Baths*, Sagalassos, Turkey, three digital images (bottom) based on six contemporary photographs from 2003 (top).

customary authority. Archaeologist Jonathan Bateman observes: 'The technological nature of photography has endeared it to archaeology's scientific aims – offering a perceived bedrock of objectivity to a discipline that has become consciously worried by the subjectivity of its endeavour.'[35] These sorts of projects are a continuity of the same drive, now looking to anchor its claim in newer, less assailable, means.

Yet archaeology itself has also changed. While it will always be dedicated to exploring the material past, how rightly to accomplish this, and what precisely is to be studied, is a matter of considerable debate. The past few decades have seen the rise of a 'post-processual' archaeology, influenced by the social sciences and humanities, which is as concerned with exploring how archaeology works in the present as with what it discovers about the past. Photography here takes up a new role, somewhere between official and vernacular, which not only focuses on traces of the past that may be left in the present, but also conveys to the viewer what is really in front of the archaeologist: the complexity of that very present and what it takes to construct, or conjure, its history. This photography is not solely handmaiden to studying objects or sites, but can also become an object in its own right. It is not designed solely to buttress or disprove a given hypothesis, but rather to explore the contradictions of lived experience.

A perfect example is that associated with the team at work at Kalaureia, excavating the ancient sanctuary of Poseidon on the Greek island of Poros.[36] Most of its work goes into excavation, but, as has always been true, such activity is only possible through relations with townspeople, governmental authorities and indigenous site workers. Any archaeologist would recognize that this is as central to archaeology as digging and recording. But with the new anthropological consciousness of post-processual archaeology, it is seriously worth studying in its own right, not just for its inherent interest but as a window on the social, political and cultural factors that affect archaeological work and that condition its findings.

In the Kalaureia project, photography is a basic way to examine this theme. Photography, today an immensely democratic medium that can be made by anyone on apparatuses from digital cameras to mobile phones, buttresses the experience of everyone on an archaeological site. The project

34 Aris Agnostopoulos, Yannis Hamilakis and Fotis Ifantidis, still from *Kalaureia in the Present*, 2009, digital collage.

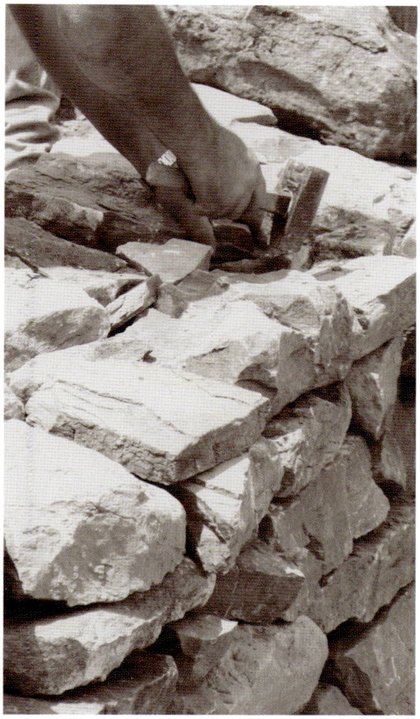

Archaeological workmen/women do not just dig; most enjoy building things, crafting, creating, making things with their hands. The supervising archaeologist was concerned that the new terrace wall built by the workers looked "too ancient"...

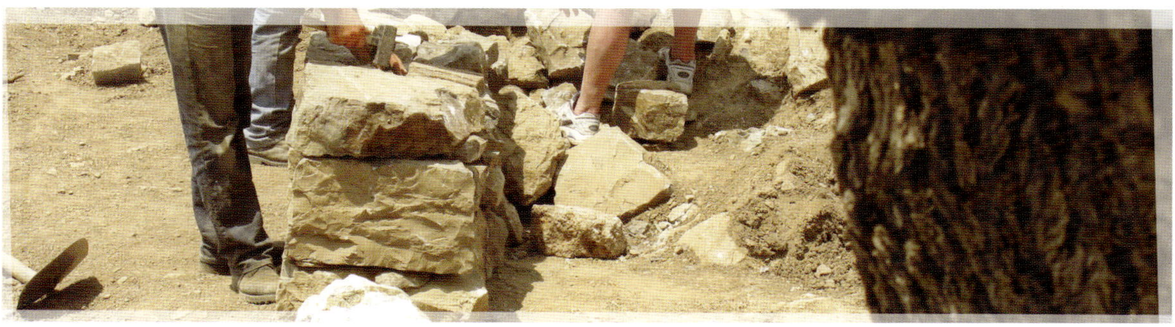

of 'Kalaureia in the present' admits these different, even competing experiences, and welcomes the ironies they can create. In one photo, a panoramic image designed to echo, or perhaps speak back to, the traditional format of the archaeological photograph, a 'humble olive tree' stands at the centre, decentring the nearby ancient stoa that more commonly dominates the archaeological viewpoint. In another, we look directly at the site through its workers, both directors and underlings. 'The supervising archaeologist was concerned that the new terrace built by the workers looked "too ancient"' (illus. 34). The photograph confronts us with the workers and stones themselves, objects both ancient and modern. It even reveals something of the code involved in setting up an archaeological site for the public, and that the distinction between ancient and modern is far less clear than is often made out.

Photography like this introduces questions that have always swirled around archaeological photography but have rarely been directly addressed by it. Photographs of people on site have always been taken, but rarely treated with the same seriousness. Thus from its origins in detailing sites and objects, archaeological photography now stretches to formally include its own cultural present. This might be either deplored or celebrated, seen as a loss of scientific purpose or focus on the past, or a welcome new opening to repressed, but essential, experience for evaluating how archaeology makes its facts. In either case, it is a development stemming from the nature of archaeological photography, which, sometimes inconveniently, pictures as a whole the never-quite-commensurable complexities of archaeological practice itself. This is precisely the topic to be pursued in the following chapter.

two

# Travel, or Presence

> It is easier to photograph than describe an ancient site.
> O.G.S. Crawford[1]

Though claims about the fear of photography among non-Western peoples can be overstated, it is worth recalling that the camera was nonetheless an intruder, an imposed Western invention, much like archaeology itself. The same John Peters we have previously noted for his commitment to photographic recording in excavation also proudly described his ability to disguise his photographic activities from local officials. Walking in Palmyra in 1889, while photographing ancient and modern sites, he was accosted by one such official who demanded an account of his party, checked his identification and 'also inquired curiously as to the meaning and use of my Kodak camera'. Fearing that this might lead to its prohibition, Peters states: 'I thought it well, therefore, not to be accounted a photographer if I could avoid it.' He describes a variety of stratagems for avoidance, including claiming to forget the local language and, when that failed, playing on confusion in it between the words for telegraph and photograph. When still pressed by the official,

> I told him that it was a 'remembering machine': that when I wished to remember anything that I had seen I fixed the machine so and touched the little button in this way, where upon the scene was written down upon a piece of paper, and at my leisure afterwards I could take it out and recall to my memory what had interested me there.

> A remembering machine was quite a new instrument, and excited much interest, and no objection whatever was made to its use.[2]

35 Francis Frith, 'The Statues of Memnon', in *Lower Egypt, Thebes and the Pyramids* (1862), albumen print.

Proud of his cleverness and the dazzling fruits of Western modernity, Peters gets his way. His description of the memory machine to the benighted official is a fair summary of how he wished it to function. It is also a trace of the continuing newness of the camera (led by Kodak through a process of miniaturization starting at the end of the nineteenth century), as technological adjustments made it easier to accompany archaeology to ever more remote places.

Most of all, though, it presents the complex cultural landscape in which archaeological research could take place, as difficult to traverse as any physical terrain. As we shall see in this chapter, the factors that actually mediated between the photograph and the reality it was claimed to effortlessly capture were as much cultural as technological.

Few archaeological narratives are complete without discussion of photographic difficulties. Accounts from the nineteenth century are a catalogue of adventure: Desiré Charnay spending months in the jungle waiting for his equipment to arrive; Francis Frith with chemicals boiling over while photographing in the desert; Félix Teynard lamenting the loss to his camera of dark temple interiors; Maxime Du Camp describing unruly locals perpetually interfering with his attempts at recording.

Almost every writer regrets at some time the limitations of point of view, the largely earthbound camera (and human viewer) small and constricted compared to vast, complex monuments. An image by Frith of the colossi of Memnon, on the Theban plain in Upper Egypt, intimates what might be discovered with a closer look at the inscriptions and sculptured features suspended at different levels above the viewer (illus. 35). Frith's image subordinates these difficult-to-capture details for the striking ruination of the monuments as a whole, but he spoke for many when he stated: 'Oh what pictures we would make, if we could command our points of view.'[3]

The words of these practitioners undercut those we have heard from earlier promoters of the initial expectation that photography would simply and quickly capture distant reality. On the contrary, they provide

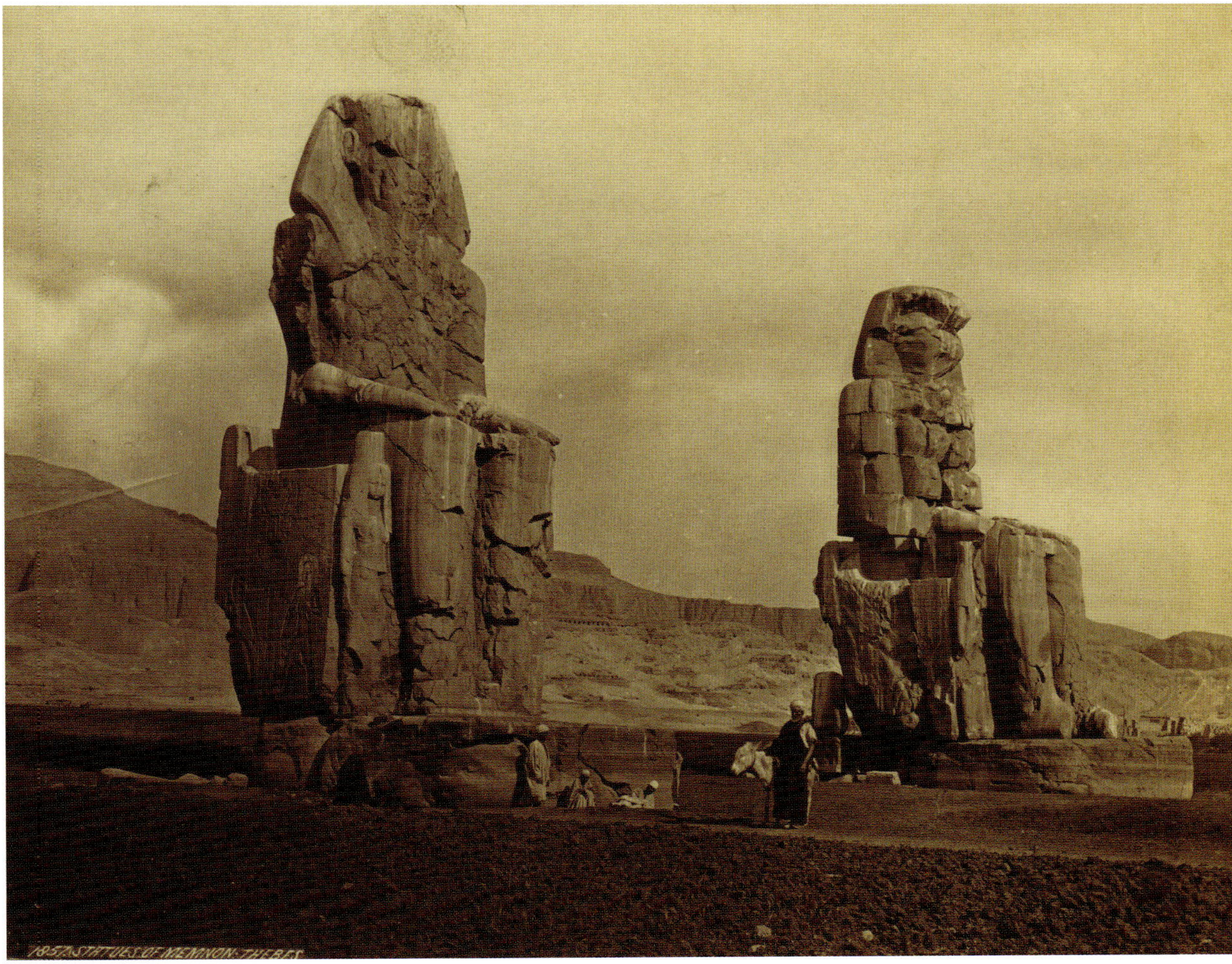


some of the earliest testimony to how difficult the task could be when actually attempted. Yet, far from diminishing photography's perceived value, the actual photographic portfolios subsequently offered were even more precious and valued. While still an unquestioned trace of ancient remains, they were also the product of painstaking modern labour and intense thought about how to represent them.

Many of the earliest pictorial difficulties were met by subsequent technological innovations in photographic process and camera apparatus, as well as the now common construction on archaeological sites of complex tripods and photographic towers for high-angle and detailed views (illus. 36). Developments in transport not only brought baggage faster but also enabled other means of viewing. A Chicago team exploring Abu Simbel in 1906 was able to climb the high mast of a sailing ship to photograph rock-cut stelae hundreds of feet above the river on a near-vertical drop. The rise of the aeroplane, and aerial photography, provided a whole other mode of discovery, as we shall see presently.

But while advances in cameras, film and processing may have ameliorated existing problems, they brought photography no closer

36 James Henry Breasted, 'Photographic Tower, Sudan, Near Island of Tumbos', 1907, gelatin silver print.

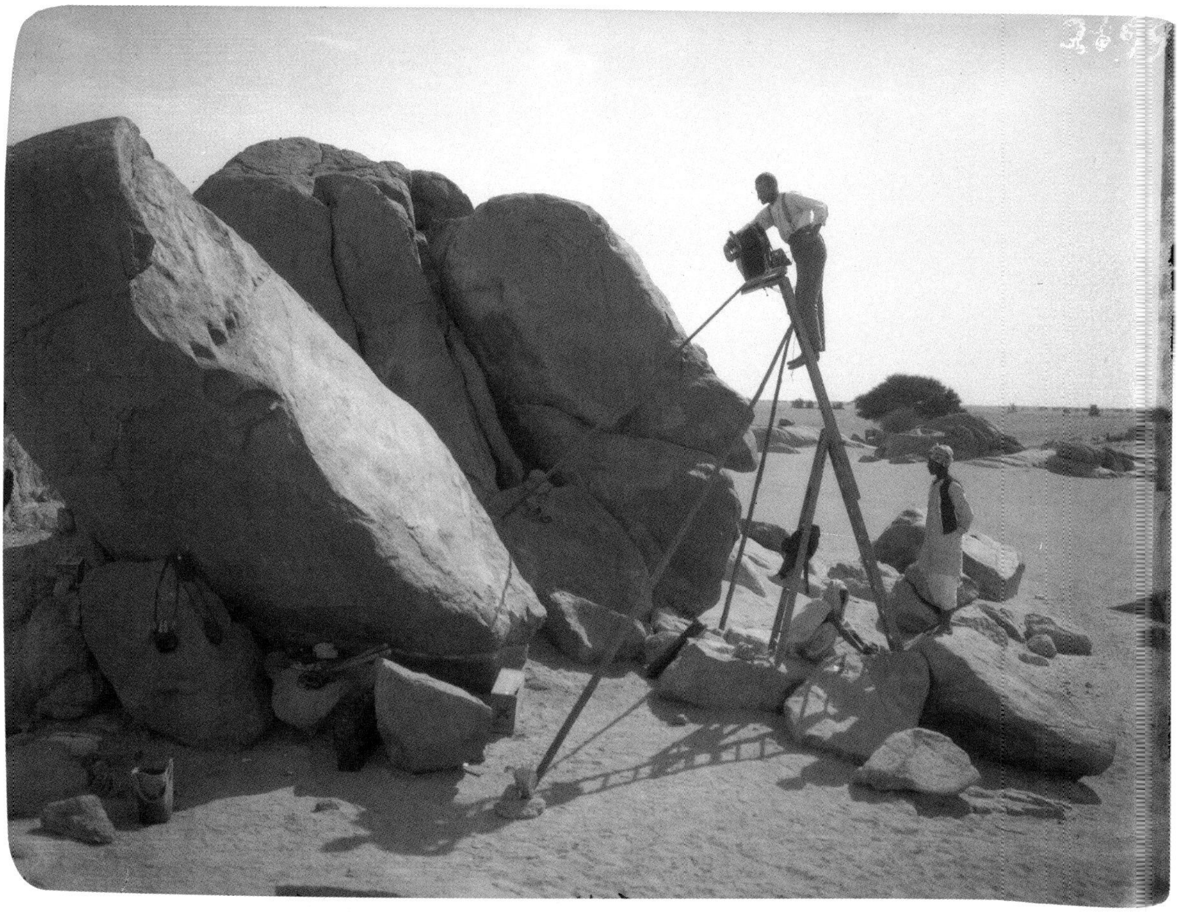

to fulfilling its fundamental promise. In his *Archaeology from the Earth* (1954), Mortimer Wheeler wrote, in a characteristically sardonic tone: 'The overwhelming difficulty of the archaeological photographer is to induce his camera to tell the truth.'[4] Truth, for Wheeler, could only be painstakingly coaxed from the camera. As the public face of British archaeology in the mid-twentieth century, through a stream of books as well as television and radio appearances, the proper imaging of archaeological sites and artefacts was a major concern. Yet Wheeler's entire chapter on photography in *Archaeology from the Earth* sounds resigned to the necessity of photography and seems almost to take delight in criticizing at length (at times even illustrating) the unsatisfactory photographic practices of his contemporaries. In this it is part of a longer tradition among archaeologists of photographic mistrust, which we shall meet again.

Beyond technological questions of representation, archaeological photography is also inflected by social and cultural differences, making distinctions not just about what, but also about who, it is important to record. The photographic record of just about all archaeological digs includes images of staff, both scientific directors and local workers. But they are hardly equally treated. When indigenous workers are portrayed, they are most commonly gathered together in a single group. These can be very large crowds, testifying not only to the scale of organized archaeology, but also the lack of individual identity attributed to workers. A photograph from the French-led excavation at Delphi in 1898, for instance, gathers some hundred workers on a terrace (illus. 37). In pulling back enough to capture all, the camera rather lumps them together as a mass, despite fascinating differences of costume and deportment that are just barely evident.

By contrast, when directing archaeologists are present, they are commonly distinguished from the crowd. Even in Delphi one is struck by the distinct group to the left, closer to the camera than all the others and in distinctly Western garb. Even more revealing in this respect is a photograph made in 1926 in China (illus. 38). The occasion is a visit from the (then) Crown Prince Gustav Adolf of Sweden to Carl Whiting Bishop at the excavation site of His Yin Ts'un in Shanxi province. Three

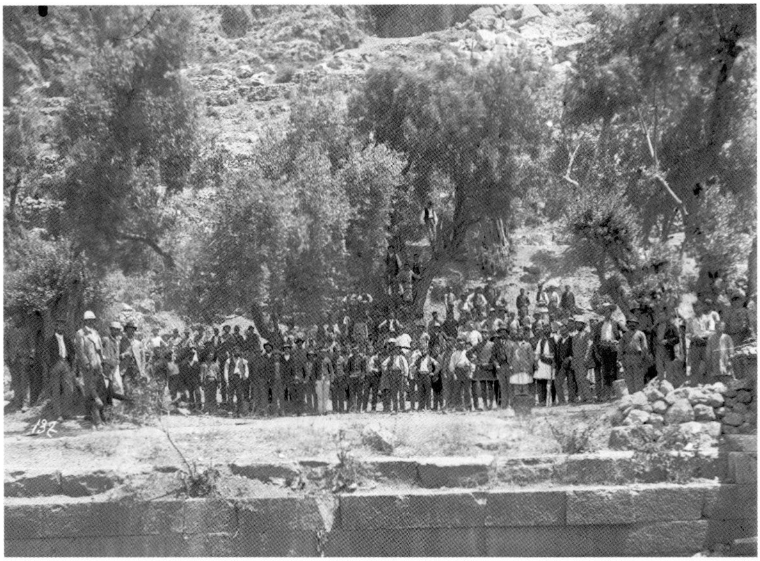

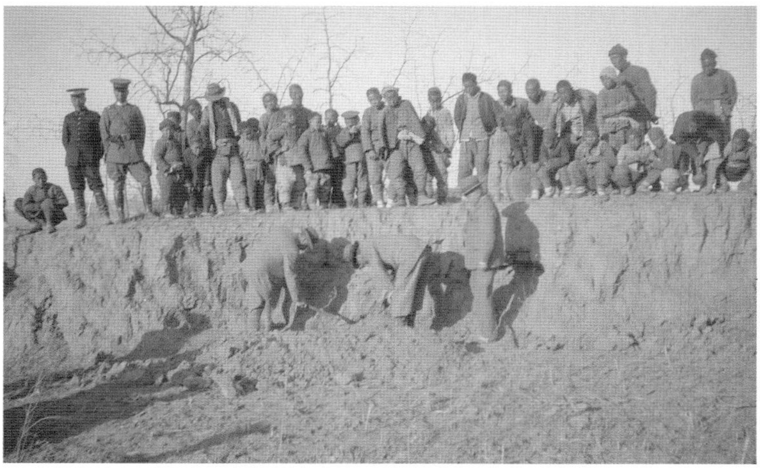

37 Unknown photographer, 'Excavators on Upper Terrace of Gymnasium, Delphi, Greece', 1898–9, print from glass negative.

38 Carl Whiting Bishop, 'Crown Prince Gustav Adolf and Carl Whiting Bishop on Site, Shanxi Province, China', 1926, modern print from film negative.

years before, Bishop had made important finds at Hsin Chêng Hsien in Hunan, notably of bronzes, offering the first material traces of the Chen dynasty. In their formal garb, Bishop and the Crown Prince huddle together to examine a wall, as an attendant stands nearby. While the Westerners bend to their task, a crowd of men and boys, among them the locals drafted to archaeological work, stands away, their different spatial positions neatly marking social differences. Without the help of the locals, the two spent their time digging fruitlessly.

It is clear in this image who is at the centre of the work of archaeology. The camera watches the group watching, in the process converting an archaeological dig into an occasion for ethnographic observation. We note, for instance, the way two members of the militia to the left, forces of the warlord governor sent for protection of foreigners, stand apart from the peasant crowd.

The anonymity of indigenous workers is not, of course, a given but a function of who controls the camera. In 1993, Dave Webb, a long-time field photographer then on an archaeological site in Essendon, England, began to use his camera in another manner, systematically taking more formal, individual images of site workers in settings drawn from actual fieldwork (illus. 39). After taking and accumulating images for nearly a decade, he created an online repertory, the Diggers Alternative Archive,

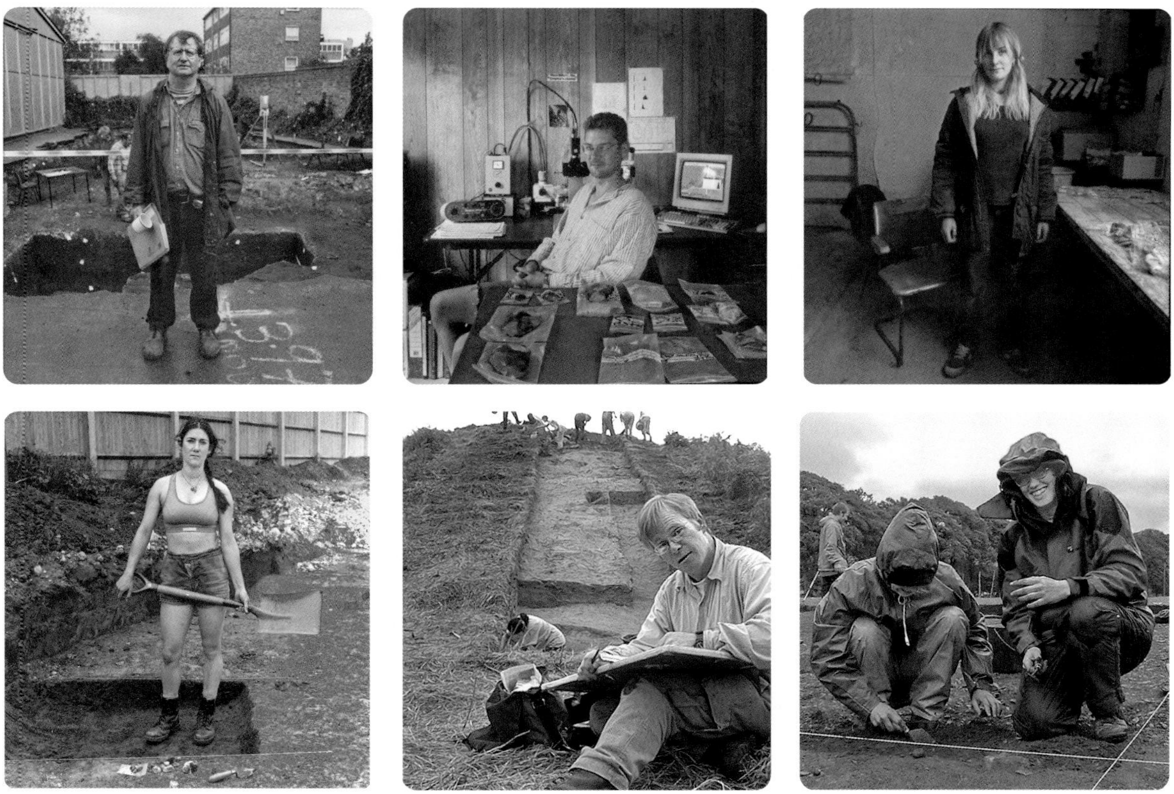

39 Dave Webb, photographs from *The Diggers Alternative Archive* series, 1993–present, bromide prints and direct digital imagery.

to right the fact that he found 'no real documentary work to record the people who do the excavation'.[5] Webb's archive, devoted to sites around the UK, approaches archaeological workers as individuals, posed in every portion of their work environment from trenches to offices to temporary lodging. The website's purpose is 'to provide an alternative view of diggers to the back of the head normally reproduced in most archaeological texts'. Webb's project indeed asserts individuality in what is more commonly shown as a collective, with space not just for name and appearance but also for texts written by the workers themselves. It pictures something that is essential to archaeological endeavour, its very process, but which is almost never deemed worthy of visibility.

But archaeological photography also at times depicts another kind of valuation of its workers, not against others in the present but in connection to its objects in the past. In another, quite unique, photograph from Delphi, a group of workers has been formally posed around one of the excavation's major finds, in 1894, of a largely intact marble figure of Antinoüs, dating from the second century AD (illus. 40). The sculpture was discovered in this upright position, but now is completely cleaned up, set off by (and perhaps even leaning against) a dark background, set in a hollow whose bottom we cannot see.[6] This placement obscures the, much more fragmentary, lower portion of the object. More importantly, it presents a tableau of what is both a sort of archaeological dream, an object virtually emerging from the ground, and a document of the nineteenth-century conception of archaeology as culling of treasure.

This photograph centres precisely on Antinoüs, providing a frame around him and inviting the viewer to play on his features. This effect is created both internally and externally, through operations both in front of and within the camera. The workers stand back from the object, providing a clear sight line to it, staring back at the camera in a mixture of curiosity, anxiety and obedience. These are villagers of the town of Kastri. Their village had for centuries been located directly on the site of ancient Delphi. Despite their protests for more than 50 years, it was eventually relocated by the Greek state to allow the French excavation.[7]

The workers are posed in a way as if realizing the importance of the excavation and unimportance of their own history. Antinoüs is virtually

40 Théophile Homolle(?), 'Discovery of Antinoüs', Delphi, 1894, print from glass negative.

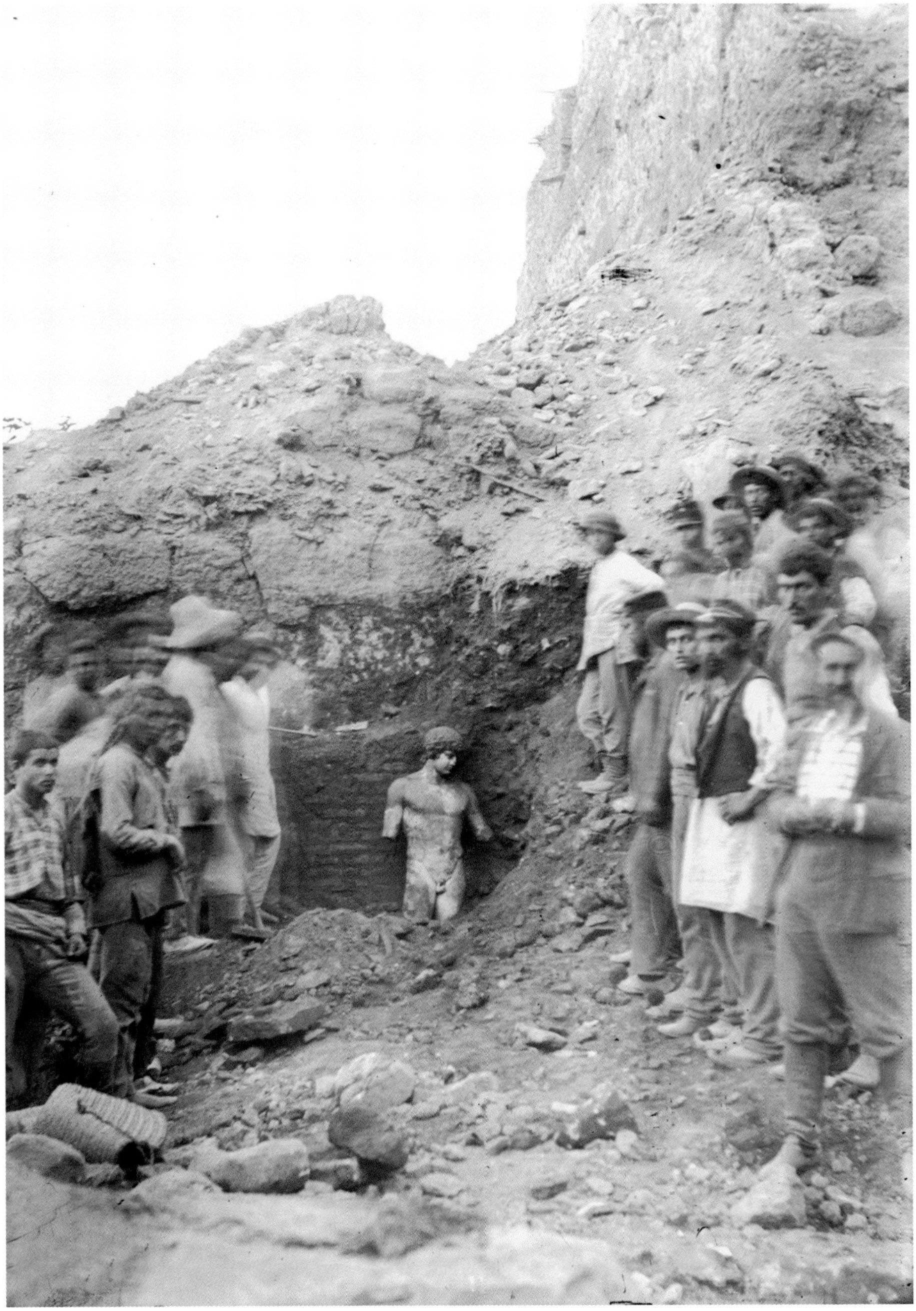

the only figure whose form is not at least partly obscured by another. The statue is, literally and precisely, the focus of the scene. The obscurity of the individual workers for a generalized group identity is a product of both technical and cultural limitation. Technically, it is not so much a question of limited exposure times for a large group, in which individual figures might move (since we've just seen another successful group image from the same dig), but rather of depth of focus. In this scene, the highest definition is placed on the ancient artefact at the back of the grouping. But this placement of focus is also, rather dramatically, a statement about realities, past versus present and imported versus indigenous (especially since it happens to be Antinoüs, a personage who was not Greek but Roman). This photograph, then, exemplifies an archaeological vision that is both questing and controlling, not just looking towards past traces in the present, but also blurring or minimizing what is required in the present to gain access to that past.

The kind of archaeological vision embodied by the image of Antinoüs is far more pervasive than a single image might suggest. Peters's invocation of photography as memory was more prescient than he knew, as modern neuroscience emphasizes that the work of human memory is not total but selective. The project of eternal recall, of artefacts and sites, to which archaeology is dedicated, takes place only at the expense of a simultaneous forgetting of other matters deemed ephemeral.

We can see the process at work in the imagery of the Iranian photographer Antoin Sevruguin. This photograph of the Achemenid tomb of Cyrus at Pasagadae is a perfect example of the illustrative photography Sevruguin provided for his Western patrons (illus. 41). He was a primary photographic source for scholars of the pre-Islamic monuments of Iran, notably the German scholar Friedrich Sarre, whose published works often used Sevruguin's images, and who amassed a much larger collection of photographs for study. Sevruguin was a native purveyor of raw material for scholarly analysis, a nimble subordinate rather as the Alinari brothers were to the art historian Bernard Berenson. Here the tomb sits alone, almost on a pedestal, a pristine antiquity whose natural setting is almost like a museum case. This image format, both its emphases and exclusions, is perhaps the most common mode for

41 Antoin Sevruguin, 'Tomb of Cyrus, Pasagadae', c. 1900, gelatin silver print.

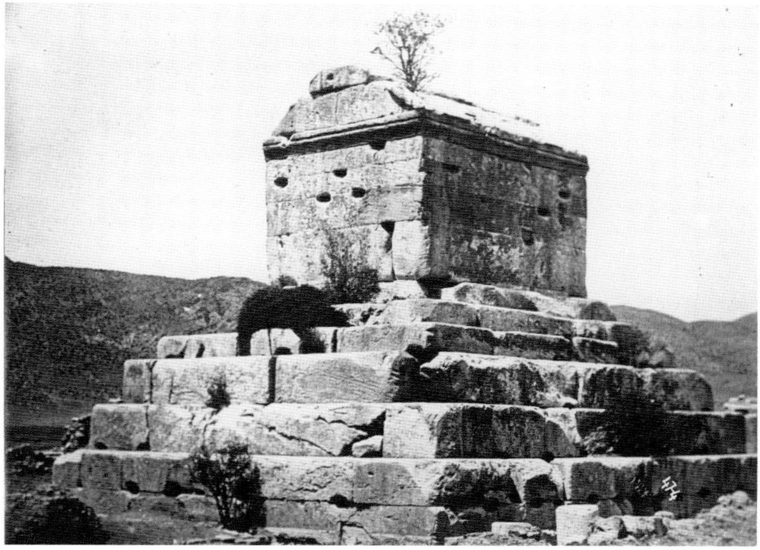

Western photographs of Middle Eastern antiquities. The tomb appears just as clinically detailed in two photos from Ernst Herzfeld's later survey notebook of the site (illus. 42). The only difference is that Herzfeld sets the camera farther back to take more of the emptied site into account, carefully including views from different sides and angles to account for more of the full structure. Both images are purified representations of the ancient structure, with the presence of indigeneous inhabitants evacuated, withholding privileged access to the monument for the Western viewer, most of all the archaeologist and photographer whose shadows mark the view.

What is striking is that Sevruguin's photography is not at all confined to this mode. Rather, his work not only acknowledges contemporary inhabitants, but depicts the very process of creating the standard photograph. Thus another photograph, taken from the opposite side of the monument (note the branch in the roof, clearly evident in both images) and pulled back a bit, clearly displays just how much equipment and human effort was involved in making the other photograph (illus. 43, see also illus. 41). A number of people (both servants and guards), as well as equipment, pack animals, and more are strewn across the image,

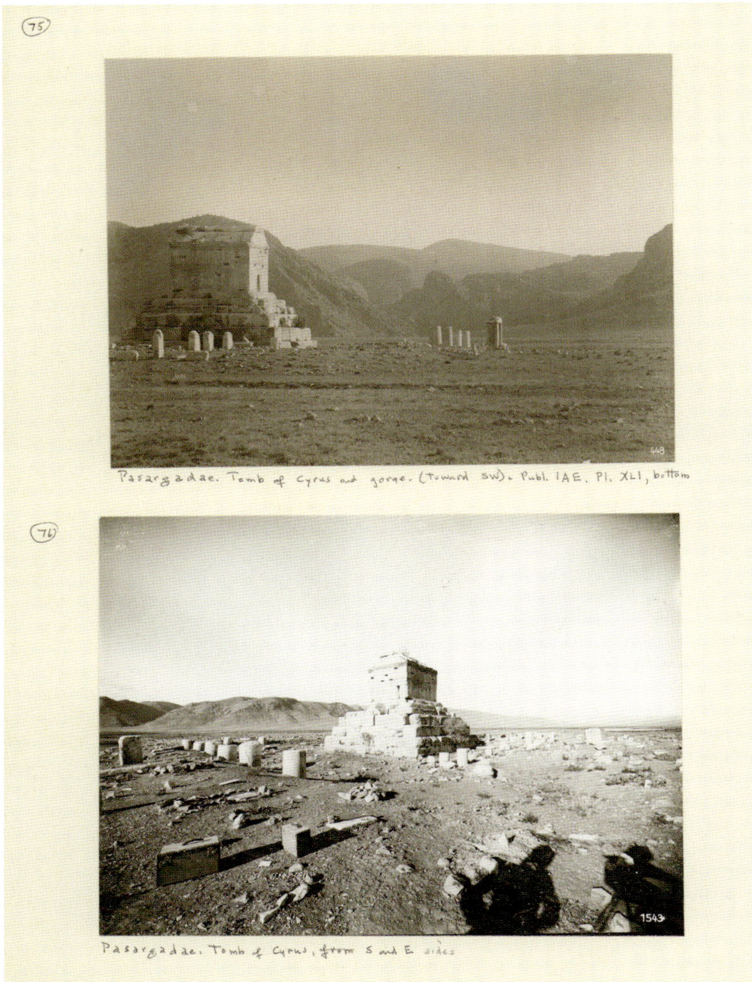


42 Ernst Herzfeld, page from the photo album *Pre-Achaemenian Monuments and Pasargadae*, 1923, toned gelatin silver prints.

testimony to the laborious project of photography in these remote and often dangerous regions of Persia.

Sevruguin's second image of the tomb of Cyrus, then, could be said to temporalize the first. That is, it removes it from the pristine essentialism constructed for the Western scholar, and opens it up to the lived experience of a particular time and place. It is, literally, a representation from another side. It is a subtle sort of reframing of archaeological photography.

The history of archaeological photography as it entered the twentieth century is a history of ever more resolute focus on objects, and equally resolute exclusion of human traces. A look at the first English-language statement of a comprehensive methodology of archaeology makes this clear. W. M. Flinders Petrie is today sometimes deemed the 'real-life Indiana Jones', though depiction of his actual frugality and asceticism would lead to a rather less popular sort of film. Petrie is far more significant as founder of a fundamental tradition of Middle Eastern archaeology, first applying scientific techniques in archaeology throughout Egypt and Palestine. He held the first chair in Egyptology in England, at University College London, wrote 97 books and taught an entire generation of

43 Antoin Sevruguin, 'Tomb of Cyrus, Pasargadae', c. 1900, gelatin silver print.

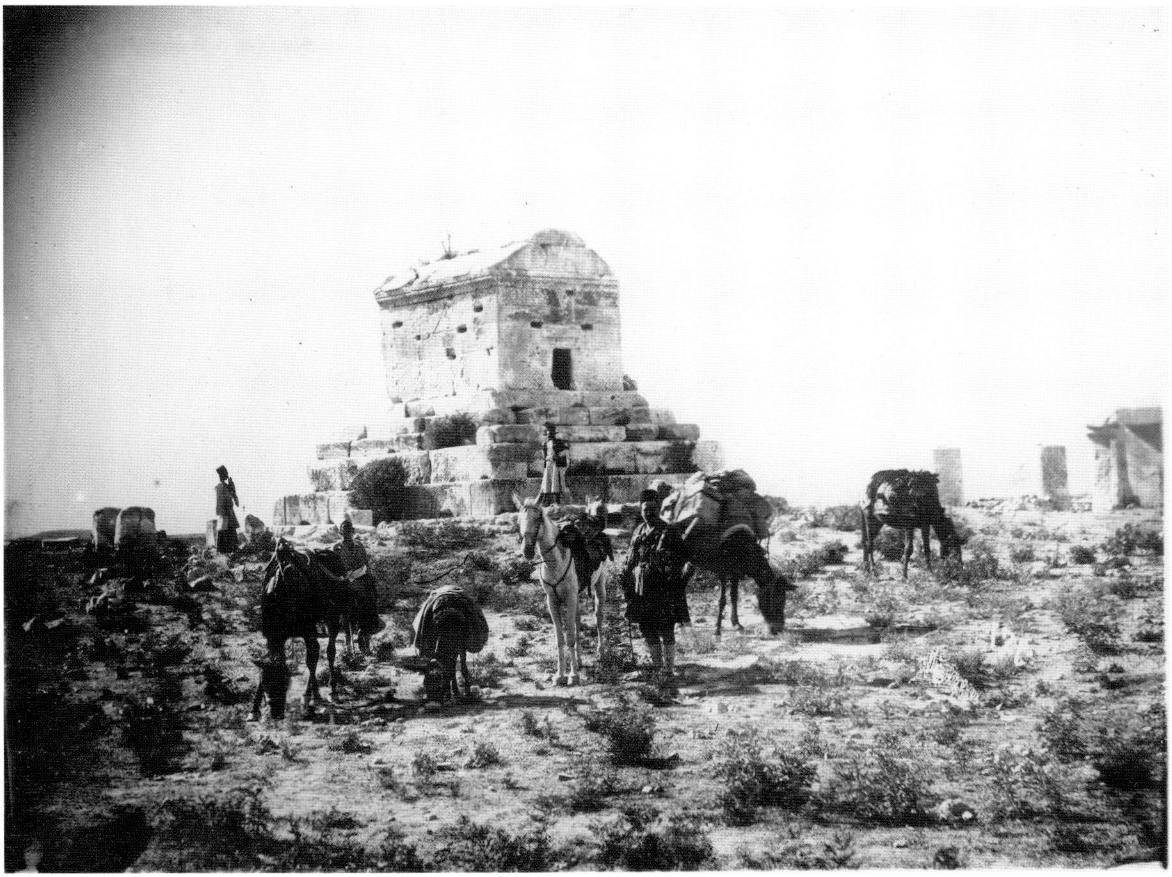

researchers. Petrie's method was resolutely detail-orientated and comparative. He virtually invented the technique of seriation, in which large masses of artefactual evidence are placed in relative chronological order by attention to similarities in shape, material and decoration. To do such, essentially statistical, work requires a 'database' of objects, preferably all known in a uniform manner and conveniently available.

Petrie's *Methods and Aims in Archaeology* was published in 1904, after more than 20 years of fieldwork and more than a decade into his academic career. It is a comprehensive guide to running an excavation site, dealing with labourers, recording finds and communicating them. Two chapters are devoted to recording methods. The first describes 'copying' by means of casts, squeezes, drawings and other measures. The second is dedicated to photographing.

Photography for Petrie, as for most archaeologists since, is not self-sufficient as documentation. His chapter begins by stating:

> Photographs are essential for all objects of artistic interest, and for expressing rounded forms for which elaborate shading would otherwise be needed. Views of the excavations and buildings are also wanted. And it is desirable to publish photographs as well as drawings of very important carvings, in order to guarantee the accuracy of the drawings, which is the more useful edition for most purposes.[8]

There is a tone of resignation to photography as a sort of necessary evil that is generally inferior to drawings both of artefacts and inscriptions. Still, several functions emerge for it. First, when published next to an inscription or other carving, it serves to 'guarantee the accuracy' of the more useful drawn form of visual information. Petrie does not explain why such a guarantee is needed. But it speaks to the anxiety about evidence involved in treating archaeology as science. We shall see in the next chapter just to what extent, in the case of recording ancient Egyptian inscriptions, the photograph can both guide the researcher's hand and be subordinated, hiding its own presence. Second, photography can serve as a more expedient kind of drawing for certain elaborate objects, freeing the quantitative mind to deal with things beside special cases. Third, and perhaps related, 'photography is "essential" in questions of artistic interest'. Though Petrie elsewhere calls museums 'ghastly charnel-houses of murdered evidence' for removing individual objects from context, the photographic elevation of an individual object to aesthetic value is applauded.[9] Even to Petrie, the hardheaded realist, photography has a dual function as guarantor of truth and invitation to beauty.

From Petrie's initial words, one would think photography is of limited value in archaeology. In fact, his chapter takes it quite seriously and indeed establishes in detail the basic principles that still dominate archaeological photography. Arrangement of objects against a black velvety backdrop, the best times of day for outdoor photography, cultivating even lighting from the upper left, the use of reflectors to fill in dark spots and most of the other rules since codified and extended in innumerable manuals of archaeological photography can be found in Petrie's chapter.

What is perhaps more striking are the rules that Petrie establishes for the treatment of archaeological objects before they are photographed. A relief is to be dusted with sand and then wiped off, revealing a different surface than that presented initially (illus. 44). Just as important is what Petrie call the 'dressing' of a tomb, in which every object is brushed clean,

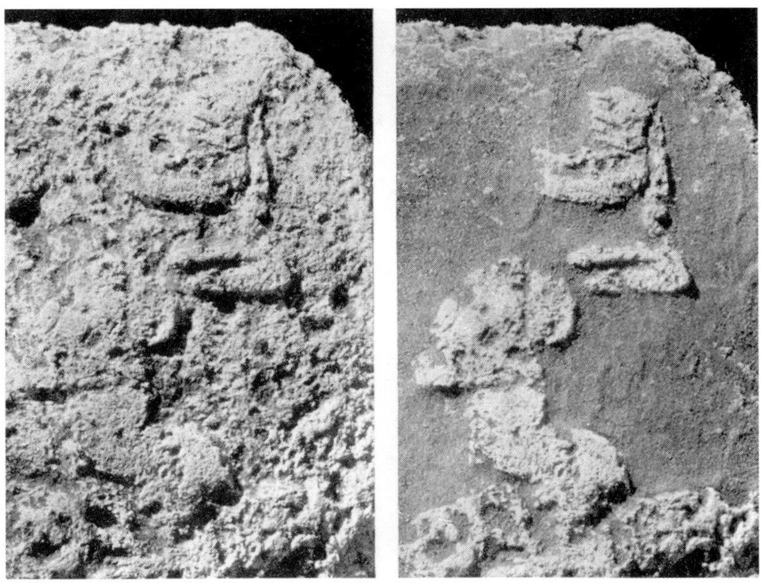

44 W. M. Flinders Petrie, 'Weathered grave-stone, unsanded and sanded', in *Methods and Aims in Archaeology* (1904), fig. 37.

the ground between objects is packed with dark earth for contrast and all objects are entirely cleaned and slightly lifted out of the ground to present a full outline. He acknowledges it can easily be several hours of work to make a site ready.

The procedure stipulated by Petrie is still a norm in archaeology. Perhaps the only fundamental difference is that it is now often performed by a specialist photographer. In an article from 1986, Aaron Levin, a longtime archaeological photographer whose work illustrates many books on Mediterranean and Near Eastern archaeology, describes a day on a dig. Whereas Petrie assumes the archaeologist takes his own photos, Levin states: 'it's much more practical to teach archaeology to an experienced photographer than to expect a marginally interested grad student to pick up the nuances of photographic principles needed to solve the myriad problems of excavation photography'. As in any other scientific endeavour, specialization takes command.

Levin describes an exhausting regimen that starts two hours before dawn, with a crack team of volunteers devoted to quickly clearing, trimming and sweeping a 5 × 5-m (16 × 16-ft) plot, so that it can be systematically photographed within the 25-minute window of proper ambient light. He stands on a ladder and methodically photographs the same plot from each cardinal direction. But the principle of keeping the ground pristine is the same as that enunciated by Petrie: 'Each time I change direction, someone steps in behind me and quickly sweeps out my footprint.'[10]

Just as with portrait photography, this brand of site photography hinges on getting the subject ready for its close-up. It is not a question of photographic documentation, as the camera always documents what is before it, so much as archaeological preparation, if not artifice. Even at its most seemingly straightforward, then, archaeological photography records how a site virtually never looks, but rather how its directors want it to be for the record. It is the product of a field decision that effaces as much as possible the fieldwork, the human presence, itself.

Archaeology's use of the nascent machinery of photography thus often functioned as a kind of protocol, a deliberate way of seeing, and in some cases overlooking, the plenum of archaeological experience. At the same time, starting in the early twentieth century, photography helped to fix a new sort of archaeological vision. Indeed, if there is any form of photography today particularly tied to archeology, it is one that liberates sites from questions of their appearance in human scale, and rather sees them anew on a grander scale: aerial photography. Starting with its great pioneer and popularizer, O.G.S. Crawford, aerial photography was not just archaeological documentation but a basis of crucial discoveries. Born in 1886, Crawford was a Hampshire schoolboy when he first tramped the barrows and tumuli of the English countryside, leading to an early commitment to field archaeology as well as topographical study in the particular British tradition of William Stukeley and Richard Colt Hoare. Trained as a geographer at Oxford, he was a veteran of archaeological excavation before serving in the First World War as an airborne photographer/observer in the then-new field of aerial reconnaissance. While aerial photography made from balloons had occasionally been put to use for archaeological purposes since the later nineteenth century, the concerted aerial reconnaissance studies made during the First World War by English, French and German flyer-photographers constituted a new corpus of systematic, large-scale territorial exploration, providing a new tool for archaeology.

Crawford brought a specific material sensibility to the new vision enabled by aerial photography, a geographer/archaeologist's exquisitely nuanced awareness of surfaces and what can lie beneath, and a tireless energy to deepen awareness of the English past among the general public. Crawford's very first major success was devoted to the most-revered ancient site in England. In late 1923 he used aerial photographs to find a feature of Stonehenge that had long eluded researchers, the location of the avenue through which the site had been reached from the river Avon. With three modest excavation trenches in his proposed path, Crawford found a differentiation of soils that confirmed perfectly his visual deduction.

Named after the war as the first Archaeology Officer of the Ordnance Survey, the British governmental agency responsible for mapping, Crawford also founded the journal *Antiquity* in 1927. Its pages featured short, accessible, well-illustrated articles (most commissioned by Crawford himself) by the giants of the day in both digging and understanding the past, from Leonard Woolley to V. Gordon Childe. Its scope extended throughout terrestrial time and space, from prehistory to the Middle Ages, from Baluchistan to Malta to Fayum, and was particularly committed to evidence derived from the aeroplane's god-like view and the camera's ability to fix it.

Crawford's own greatest and most popular exercise in the fruits of aerial archaeology was his publication *Wessex from the Air* (1928), 'the foundational study of aerial methodology', which made manifest from the sky in extraordinary completeness the palpable traces of the English past.[11] A photograph of the remains of an ancient Roman hilltop camp at Badbury, for instance, details three layers of ramparts as well as roads into the enclosure (illus. 45). The photograph, we learn, was taken at 7.10 p.m. in mid-July, at the point when shadows are longest and just rake the surface. The trees at the top make longer shadows than any of the archaeological features, testifying to the relatively modest size of the topographic differential in the terrain.

Such 'shadow-sites' were among Crawford's most striking images, made in effect by strategic choice of viewpoint, in both space and time. *Wessex from the Air* also presents other kinds of evidence and more visually diffuse archaeological material. A photograph of Barbury Farm, for instance, presents us with a palimpsest of traces of village settlements from prehistoric to medieval, with features far more subtle and less in register with each other, a view of the manifest chaos and contingency of land use, which Crawford often lamented (illus. 46).

Crawford's comments on reading and making aerial photographs amount to a set of rules for looking very closely from above at the English countryside: for the differences to be allowed between looking through plantings of barley and those of beetroot, or what contours that areas of flooding, or drought, or snow-melt might make evident, or to watch for different colourings in swathes of grass. Aerial archaeological photography allows us to know the difference, in Crawford's words, 'between the cat's view of the carpet and ours'.[12]

The homely domestic metaphor endears the process to the reader, and somehow makes it as natural as being human. Crawford's viewpoint

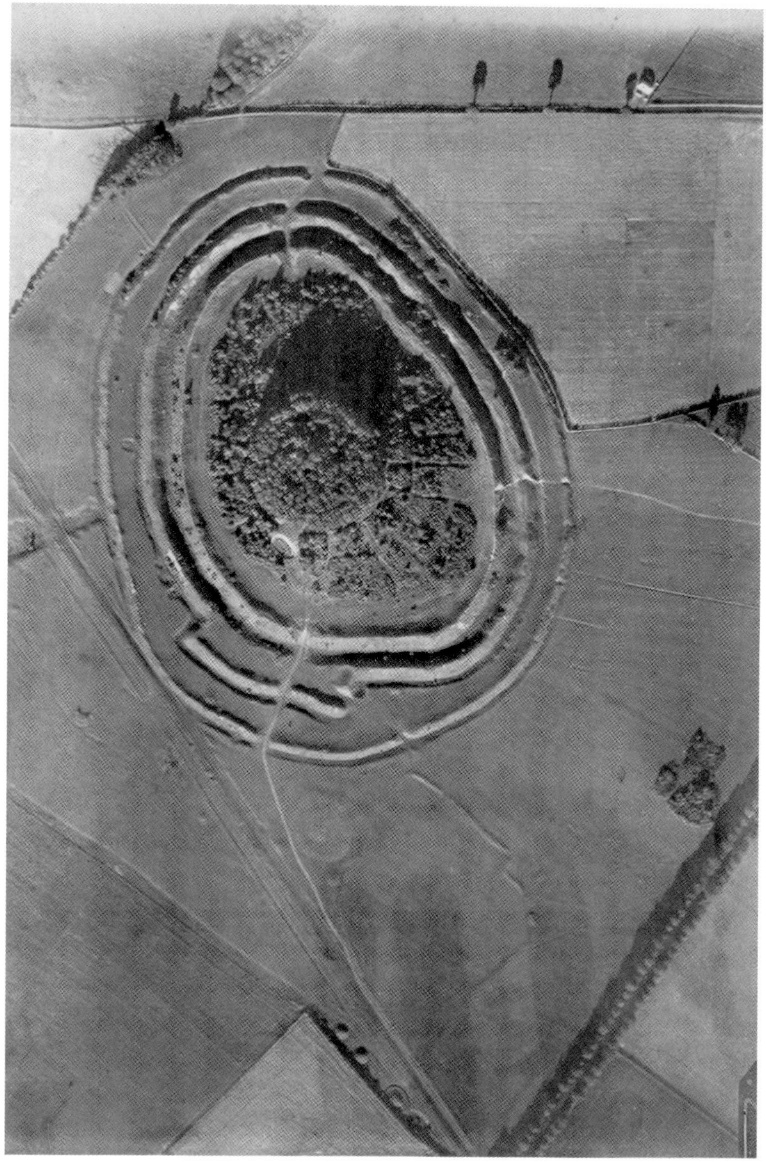

45 O.G.S. Crawford, 'Badbury', in *Wessex from the Air* (1928), p. 58, plate IV, halftone print.

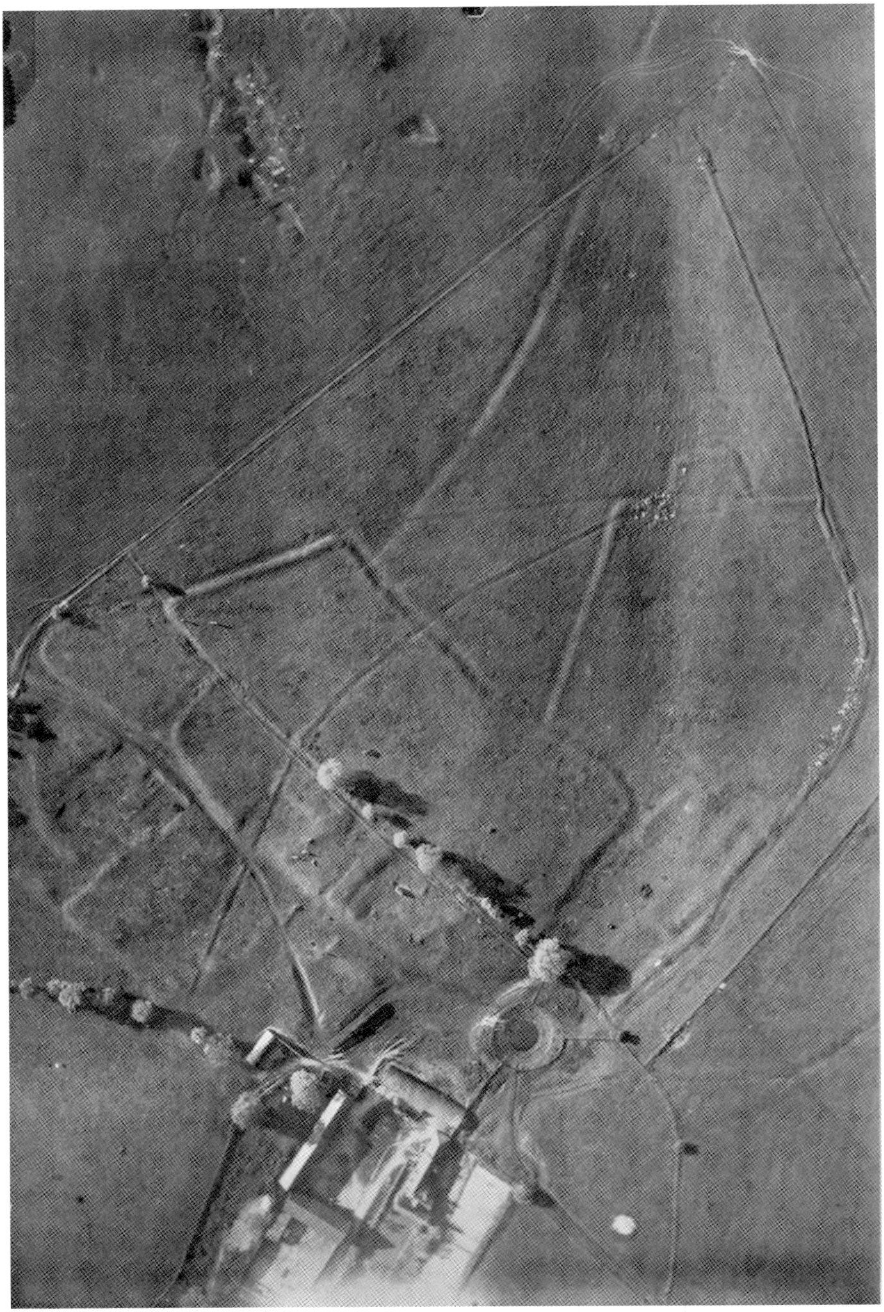

46 O.G.S. Crawford, 'Barbury Farm', in *Wessex from the Air*, p. 242, plate XLVI, halftone print.

is that of the master physiognomist, assessing what lies in the depths by scrutinizing often minute surface traces. Yet it also diminishes, or perhaps takes for granted, the rise of this entire technique of surveillance technologies in practices of war, and demands for the mastery of the landscape. This too, however, enters obliquely into Crawford's rhetoric, as in his claim that aerial observation empowers the eye beyond previous limits, so that 'archaeology can now circumvent annihilation by the plough'. Characteristically, though, he adds a tinge of nostalgic appeal in the face of modernity, that 'even air photography cannot recover what is hidden between coal tips and garden cities'.[13]

Yet while the rise of aerial archaeology was certainly enabled by the interested, and hardly benign, demands of military operation, there are also historical points of resistance to this development. The French photographer Nadar had been a pioneer in making the photographic camera airborne. The contemporary caricarturist Daumier portrayed him at work in the gondola of a balloon, above a city gone mad for photography, his top hat blown off and garments undignifiedly flowing, with the sarcastic title 'Nadar Elevating Photography to the Height of Art' (illus. 47).

47 Honoré Daumier, 'Nadar Elevating Photography to the Height of Art', 1862, lithograph.

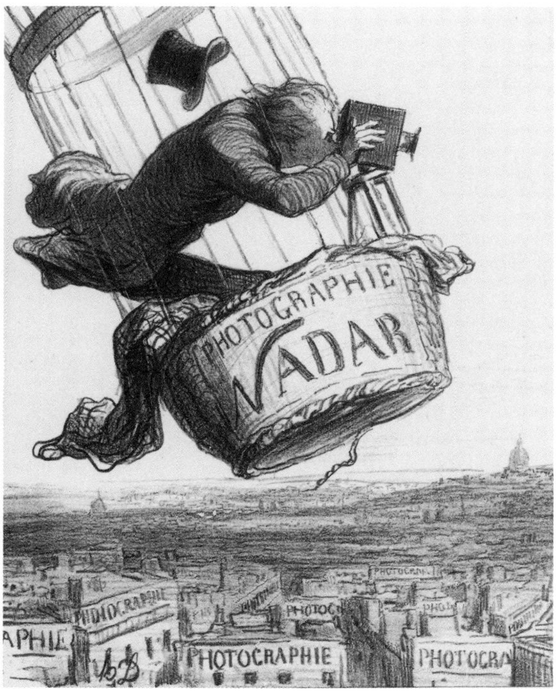


In actuality, Nadar was also a resolute pacifist who refused to turn over his technique to the French army for use in aerial surveillance during the Franco–Prussian war. Perhaps this was even a factor in France's decisive loss. In any case, aerial archaeological photography is hardly only a continuation of military work but rather a branching off from its limitations to explore with the camera the possibilities of a new way of gaining knowledge of the physical world, not just for archaeology.

Thus a new kind and remarkable variety of imagery proliferated through the global employment of aerial photography. When leaving densely forested or cultivated landscape areas like Crawford's Europe, from Middle Eastern deserts to Asian steppes, and far beyond, aerial photography in unrelieved locales of stone or desert proved even more direct and visually dramatic.

In 1931, for instance, Robert Shippee and George Johnson embarked upon the first aerial survey devoted to examine the prehistoric ruins of Peru. It garnered the first photographic traces of the ancient wall, more than 60 km (37 miles) long, that runs throughout the country's Santa valley: in photos a vast raised scar hugging the complex topography of hills and valleys. What was hitherto known only from the ground, in portions, was first really seen as a single object from the aeroplane's privileged viewpoint

Remarkable in another way are the aerial photographs of Chan Chan, remains of the ancient capital of the Chimor people (illus. 48). Raked in the same delicate dusk/dawn light as Crawford's photos, the

48 Robert Shippee and George Johnson, 'Chan Chan, Peru', 1931, gelatin silver print.

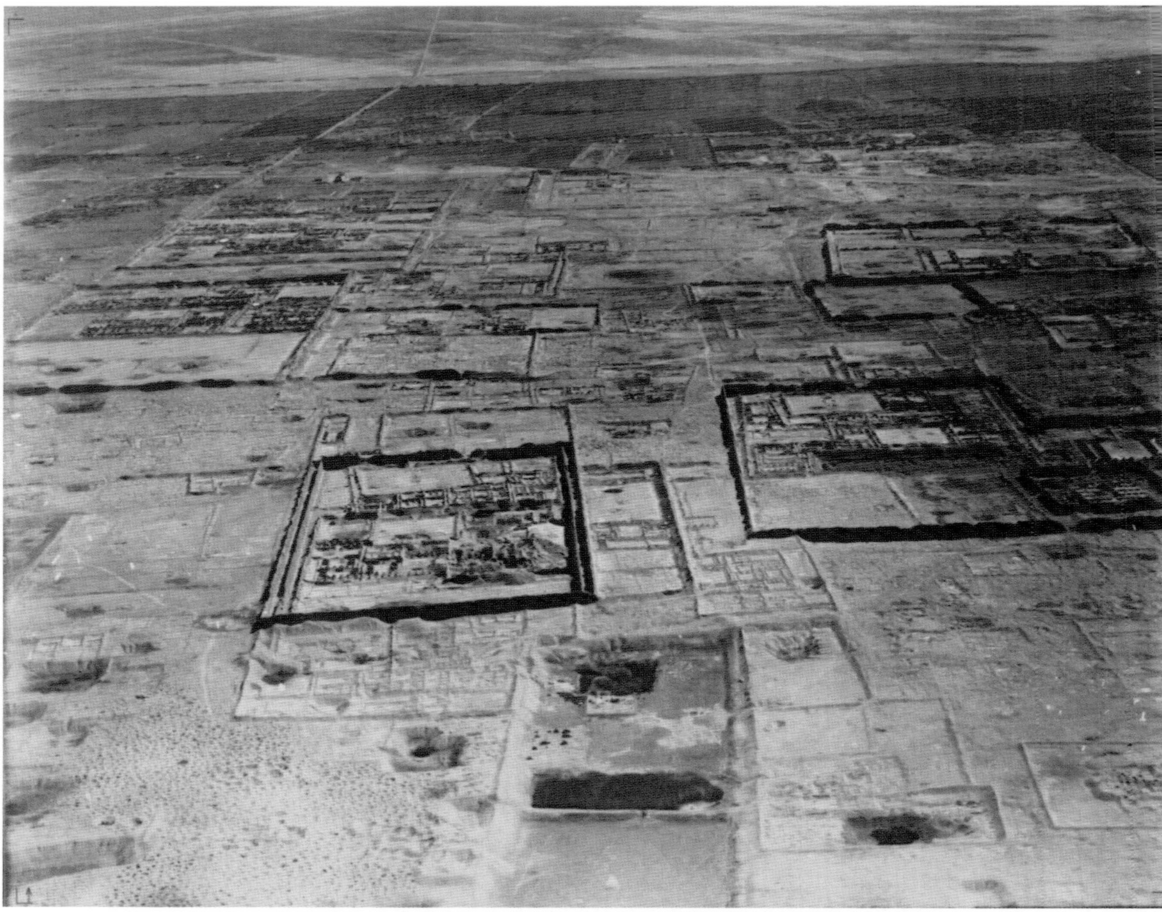

Shippee-Johnson photos present a series of grids within grids, their relative heights and relation to each other marked by the size of enclosing shadows. This is a site that comes close to replicating in photography its schematic drawing, a rare unity of physiognomic and anatomic representational modes.

A year before the survey began, Johnson explained: 'From an airplane, or, better still, in an aerial photograph (for the camera catches and records much that the eye cannot grasp in the rapid flight of the plane) one sees the whole scene spread out in a single unhindered panorama in which the broader features and relationships are lifted clear and unmistakable from the details that conceal them on the ground.'[14] Unlike Crawford's emphasis on the human interpreter as central figure, Johnson acknowledges the technological root of archaeological vision. The camera's ability to arrest time so it is not subject to the flow of lived experience and constant intrusion of the senses uniquely allowed the researcher to find the information sought. Photography was thus also diametrically opposed to the filmic recording of aerial observance that was also soon attempted (and which still plays a lesser role in archaeology).

The viewpoint of aerial photography is a sort of archaeological space, in a way comparable to the concept of 'archaeological time'. Archaeological time refers to a kind of deep time, taking the long view of history and in the process revealing new relationships. The spaces portrayed in aerial archaeological photography offer a similar grander-than-usual scale, as well as a parallel ability to manifest new information in forms that are not confined to conventional representational clues. While perhaps unforeseen by photography's initial promoters, it is one of the most productive and popular types of archaeological photography. Its rise in the 1920s and '30s almost provides a new impetus for photographic recording as a whole in archaeology. The revelation of a 'new world of antiquities', proclaimed by Botta when descending into the earth in the 1840s, is matched by a further new world, glimpsed by aerial archaeologists rising above the earth a century later.

Further, the full promise of aerial archaeology is perhaps only now reaching fruition, as coverage reaches saturation and access is greater than ever. 'Armchair archaeology' has burgeoned in the five years that

Google Earth has existed, making high-resolution satellite images widely available, even of locales difficult to enter for either physical or political reasons. Among the most dramatic of recent announcements is that of nearly 2,000 potential archaeological sites in Saudi Arabia, made by David Kennedy from an office in Perth, Australia.[15] Having combed areas in Jordan and elsewhere, Kennedy is an accomplished practitioner of aerial archaeology in the Middle East, but has never been in Saudi Arabia. From Perth he examined digital images of more than 1,200 sq km (463 sq miles) of the land and located a host of potential sites, including more than 1,000 stone tombs in a characteristic tear-drop shape. Photography on the ground of some selected sites later confirmed the finds. The quality and precision of available aerial imagery will only increase, but, from Crawford to Kennedy, the finds of aerial archaeology are as much the result of habits of astute viewing as technological accomplishment.

Bringing photography back down to earth, considering its practical engagements within experiencing archaeological monuments, charts a different trajectory. The painstaking business of photographing inscriptions, for instance, though central to archaeology around the globe and at the heart of its initial promise to the field, offered something quite different from the revelatory vision from aloft.

Direct photographic rendering often provided considerable distraction from the desired 'objective content' of glyphs. While questions of surface, lighting and accessibility, not to mention the accretions of centuries of grime, vandalism and decay, kept inscriptions from being extensively photographed in a useful way for scholars during the nineteenth century, these traces of the past nonetheless held a continuing allure, which opened it up to experimentation. The work of Timothy O'Sullivan, for instance, in photographing the American Southwest during the Wheeler survey of 1871–4, has been most celebrated for long, barely populated vistas of complex geological forms. Toward the end of his employment for the survey, though, O'Sullivan turned his attention toward native American cultures in the region and signs of their habitation. New Mexico's Inscription Rock, true to its name, was covered with marks of various peoples and O'Sullivan photographed several sides of it to record them. This view of the south wall

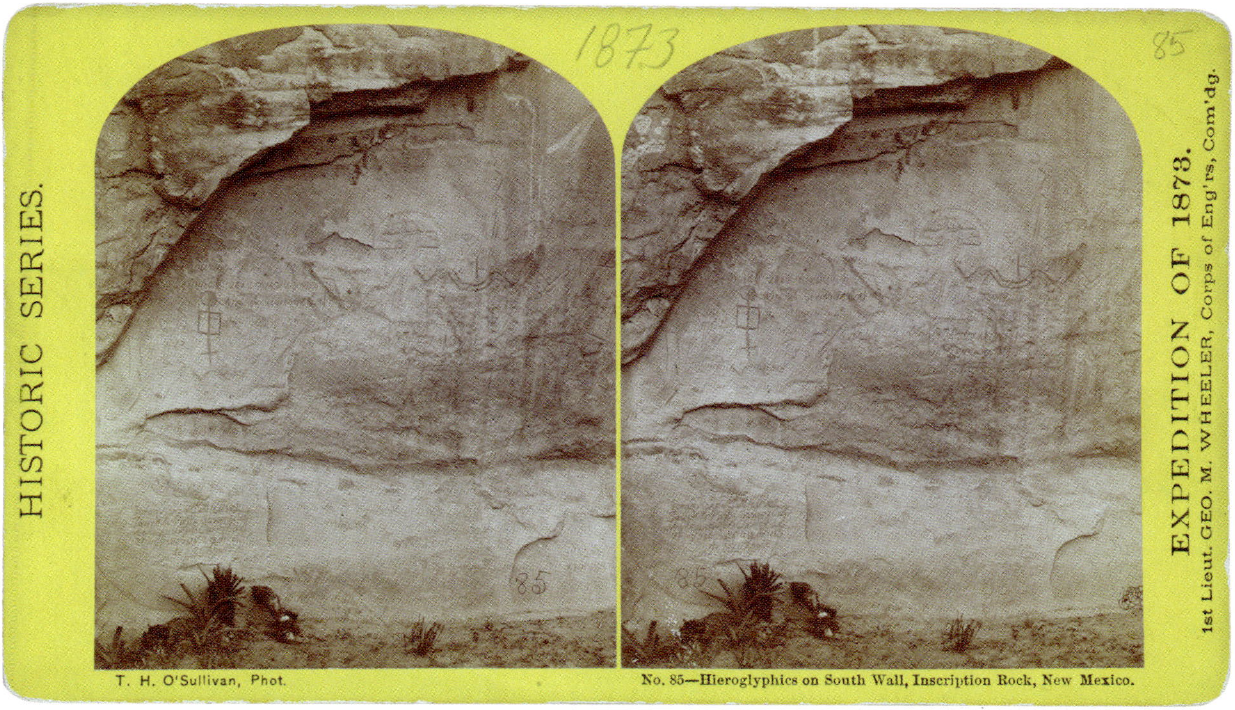


49 Timothy O'Sullivan, 'Hieroglyphics on South Wall, Inscription Rock, New Mexico', 1873, stereograph.

is a palimpsest in which Native American petroglyphs (labelled 'hieroglyphs' in the finished print) coexist with later Spanish inscriptions as well as the complex surface of the rock itself (illus. 49). While the frameless nature of the image resembles the often borderless landscape vistas of his earlier work, it also displays how a breathtaking sweep of time – the centuries between the two cultures – does not bear the same inherent visual drama as disparities of space. This particular image by O'Sullivan, though, employs a unique method, possibly for the first time, to visualize, or at least suggest, temporal disjunctures. This stereoscopic image is designed to be looked at through a viewer that enhances three-dimensional effects. In such a context, the different depths of the inscriptions do indeed inhabit different levels, and the viewer can be struck more directly by the multiple presences of the past at Inscription Rock. The entire inscription surface falls back from the rock shelf at top left, and the more deeply cut petroglyphs appear darker and more prominent than the shallow Spanish inscriptions and graffiti.

While O'Sullivan's approach is both straightforward and innovative, a more characteristic nineteenth-century approach to (and evasion of) inscription can be found in Frith's photo of a temple doorway in Kalabsha, Nubia, in Upper Egypt (illus. 50). Though it is taken up largely by inscriptions, Frith's photo revels in complexities of lighting and facts of material loss. Frith's accompanying text celebrates his being able to scramble with his heavy equipment over daunting rocks to even get this much exposed. The photograph singles out a striking vista for the armchair traveller, demoting inscription to ornament, and channelling surface into structure and image.

Both Frith's image and text play on the fundamental appeal of archaeological presence, that of entrance into and movement through a site. So much of archaeological material consists of inchoate or fragmented material that one can almost sense the relief of the photographer (anticipating that of many viewers) at this subject and its connection to experience. Images of gateways, doors and openings are a central motif in the photography of archaeological sites. They appeal in different ways to the general viewer looking for experience and the researcher concerned with original use. To look at a few, from different places and times, suggests something of the range of motivations, audiences, formats and subjects involved in archaeological photography, from the nineteenth century to recent times.

In Gustave Le Gray's photograph of the gateway of Ptolemy III at Karnak, we see through one gateway into a larger entryway further down (illus. 51). It is the same view taken earlier by Maxime Du Camp (illus. 19). But Du Camp's resolutely linear, symmetrical view is now replaced by a subtly angled path, taking in far more of the surrounding spatial context as well. As with many other views of Karnak by Le Gray, the portal is not merely a feature in its own right but also a frame whose space and shadow are used to create a compelling, abstract play of forms. It is not a place simply to pass through, but one offering an oblique path to savour and even be lost in.

Le Gray spent the last decades of his life in Egypt. His beautiful and extensive work in Egypt is a worthy conclusion to a remarkable photographic career in France. He had worked for the Mission Héliographique

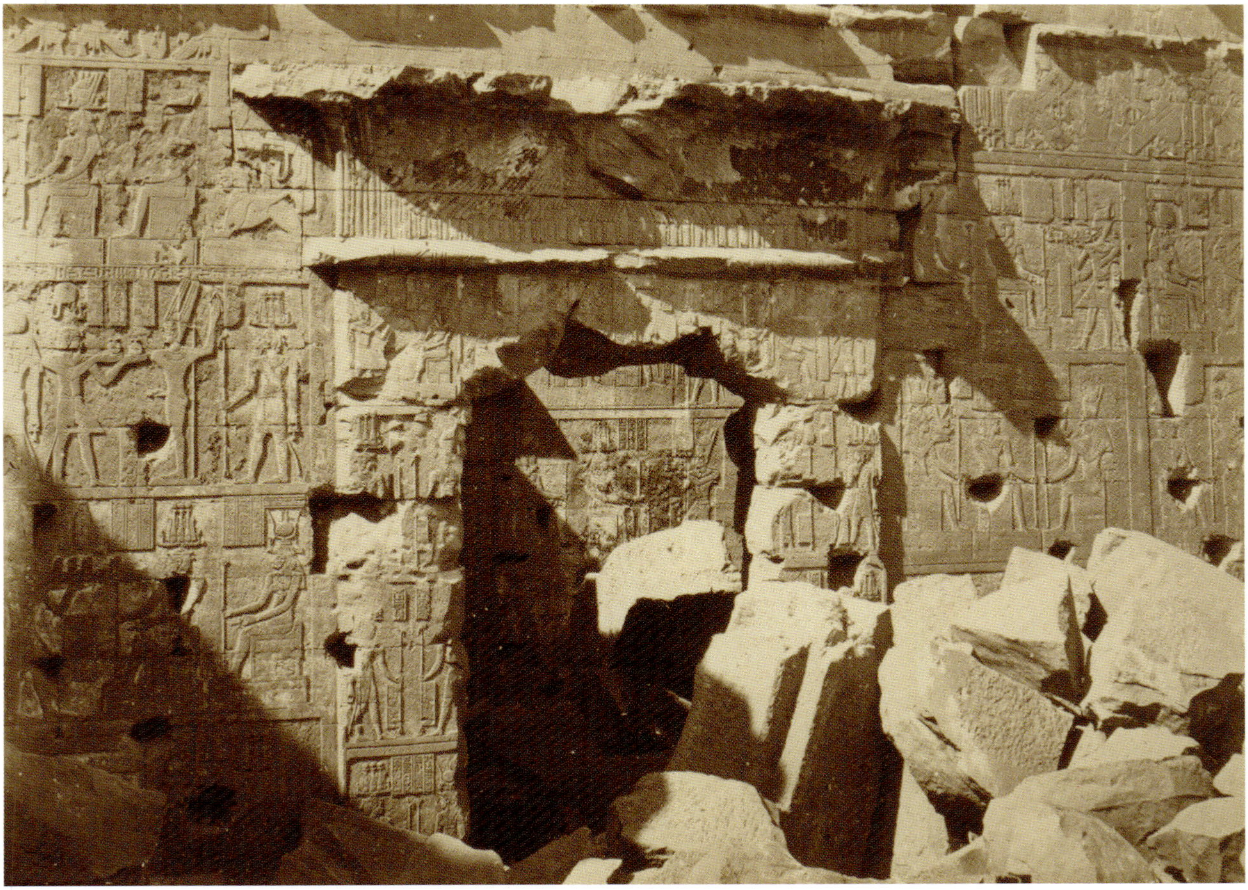

50 Francis Frith, 'Doorway in the Temple of Kalabshe', in *Upper Egypt and Ethiopia* (1862), albumen print from glass negative.

in 1851 and later specialized in landscape photography, especially marine landscapes made with extraordinary sensitivity to shading of light and an almost abstract relation of form. Le Gray commands forms on the desert just as he did on water, figures of a sublime, not quite reachable splendour, with images seen against a visible horizon. Both his marine and Egyptian subjects frequently have the sense of a compelling stage set.

Le Gray's almost Baroque vision contrasts with the coeval work of William J. Stillman, who photographed equally large and impressive antiquities in Greece. Stillman's portfolio, *The Acropolis of Athens*, first published in 1870, works to obviate distance or uncertainty between

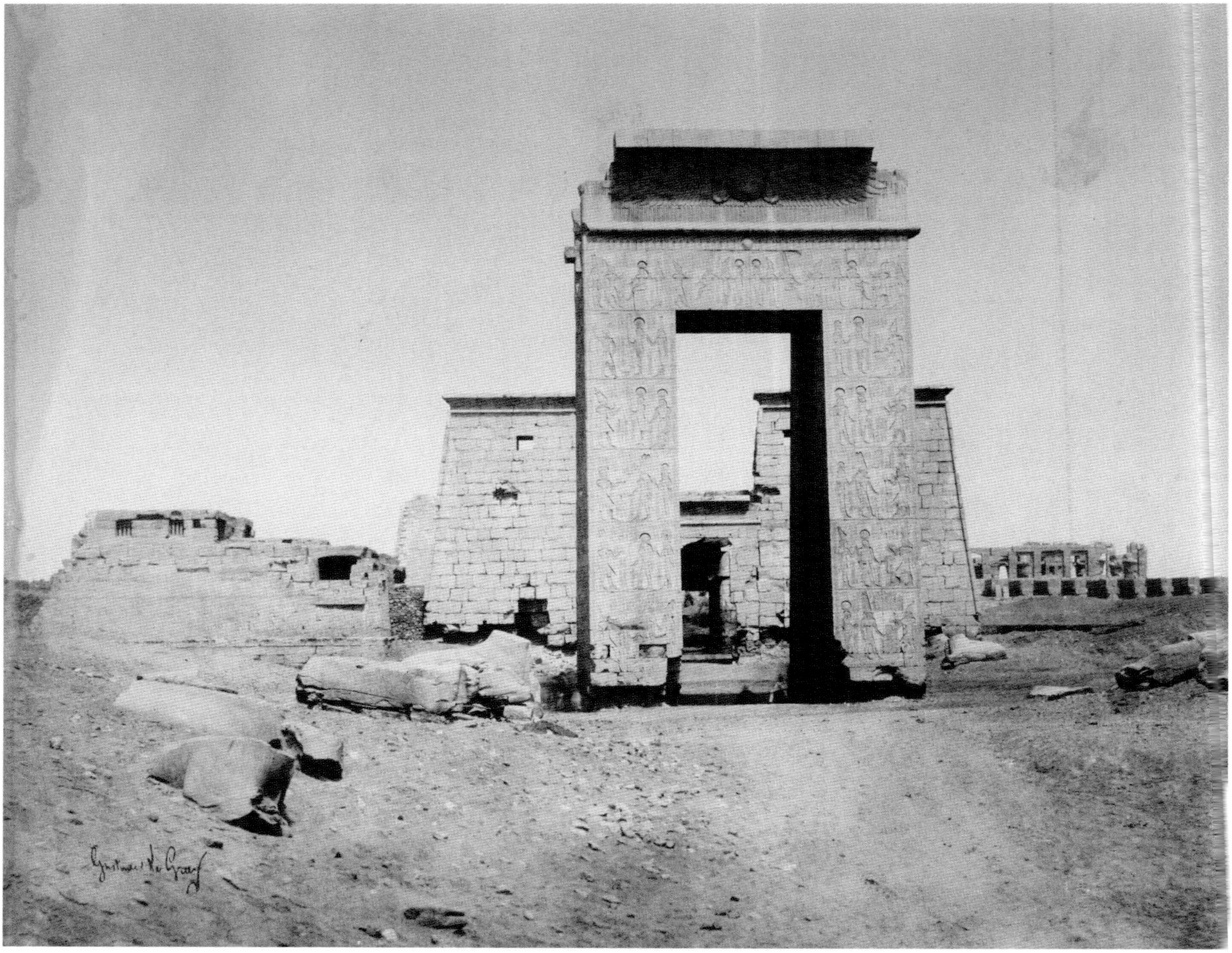

51 Gustave Le Gray, 'Gate of Ptolemy III, Karnak', after 1861, albumen print.

viewer and object, stating at its start that as much as possible its architectural photos were taken from 'points exactly equidistant from the extremities'. A compelling example is a photograph of the Pandrosion, a well-preserved portion of the Erectheion temple (illus. 52). The rectangular outer entrance stands at the precise centre of the image. Floating within it, at a point of almost precise balance, is the dark rectangle of an inner entry. This spatial logic of openings mirrors that of the structure as a whole, since the entrance is flanked by columns and a portion of pediment in a perfect symmetry to the doorway, photographed from enough distance that one can gauge perspectival diminution of the near and far columns.

Despite the astonishingly proto-modernistic appearance of his images, Stillman's interest in the site was not material or visual so much as spiritual. One of the most influential American followers of John Ruskin, and an outspoken partisan of Cretan independence from Ottoman rule, Stillman was sensitive to the symbolic significance of the site. His photograph does not document the site so much as draw the viewer into it. In fact, the next image in Stillman's sequence takes us in just the direction demanded here, now standing on the porch right before the outer entry with the inner view directly before us.

The slight disparity here of the placement of the distant opening in the nearer one (shifted a little to the left, and indicating that our viewpoint is not precisely equidistant after all) is explained by the foreground of the image. There two long beams point us directly into the distant entrance. Another beam to the right moves similarly towards an arched opening at the side. We are standing at the one spot where we can best see into both openings. The foreground ruins, not just the presence of beams but also the absence of columns before the entryways, facilitate the viewer's active probing of and entry into the structure. This process mirrors Stillman's own exploration. He wrote of the months he devoted to photographing the structures of the Acropolis:

> I studied every view in every light until I can [sic] tell the hour, the month and the weather to take any feature of that magnificent acre of earth . . . One I photographed twenty ways until I got it right . . . I think that a landscape photographer ought to haunt the field he has chosen in all hours and weathers until he has found what Nature meant when she put such land and rocks and trees together.[16]

Stillman's haunting closeness and axiality is a notable contrast to Le Gray's distance and obliquity. They present two different, but equally potent, kinds of provocations to the experience of a monument. We might call them physical versus aesthetic, both framed through openings and the invitations to entrance they offer.

Both visions, though, are based on choosing enticing paths into ancient interiors, portals to the past. The experience they put on display

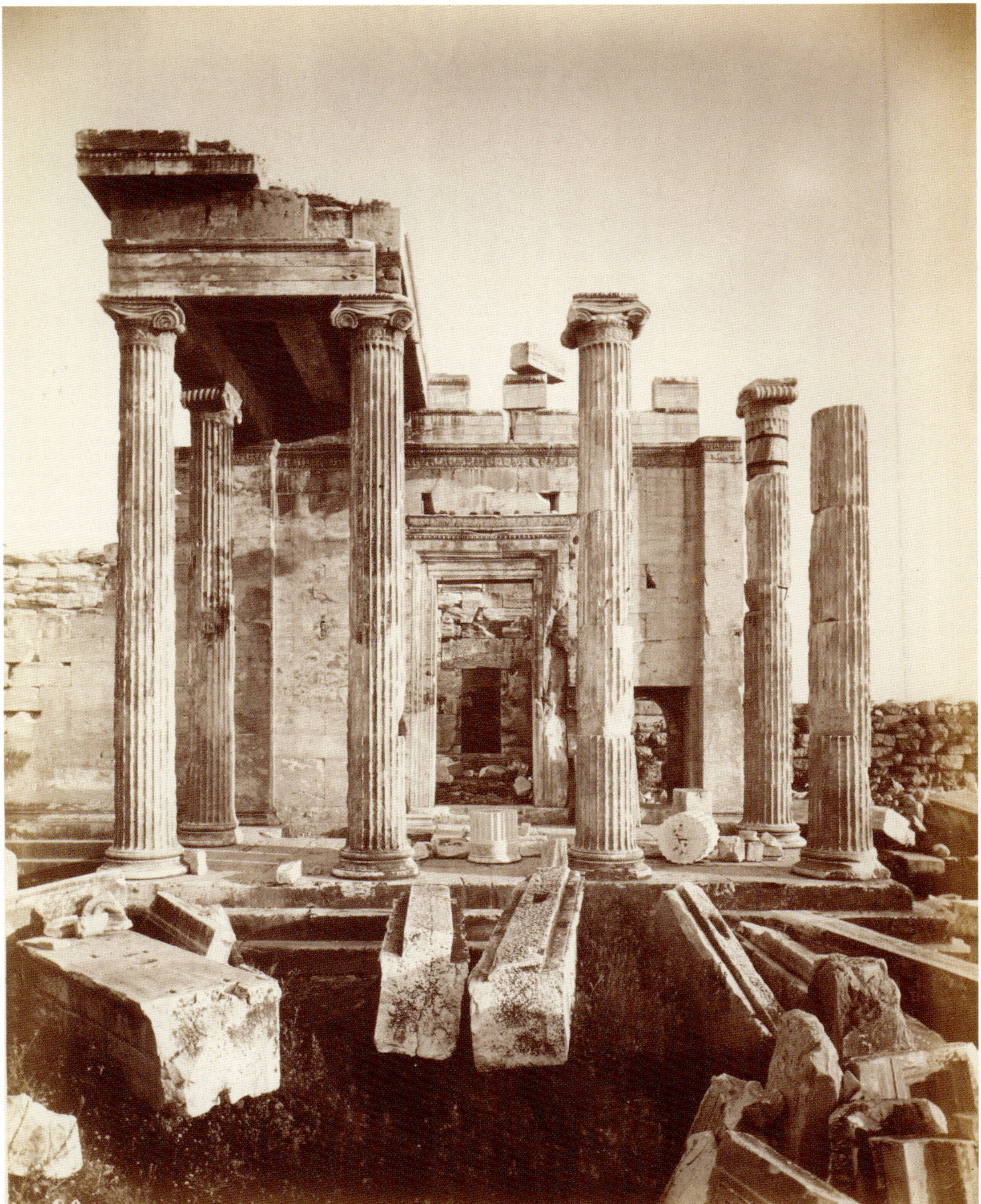
20

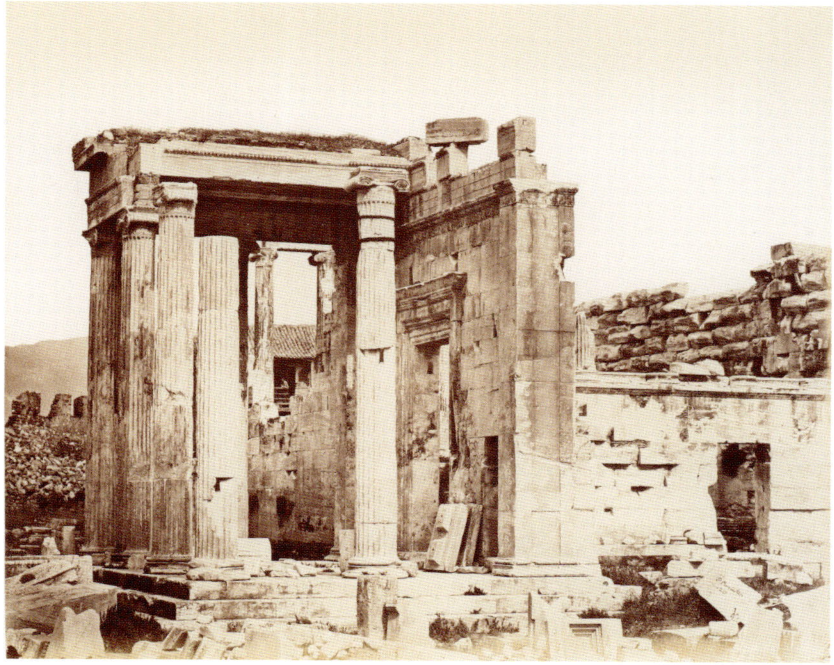

53 Petros Moraites, 'View of the Pandrosion and Surroundings', c. 1869, albumen print.

invites the viewer to participate in spaces of antiquity. This says much of Stillman and Le Gray, and their Western audiences, for whom the monuments are virtual symbols of this ancient identity, abstracted from their contemporary existence. By contrast, a signed photograph by Petros Moraites, an early Greek photographer to make images on the Acropolis, at about the same time as Stillman, chooses a different path through these same remains (illus. 53). Moraites sets the camera at what is almost a right angle to the path of Stillman's chosen view. We can still see obliquely into the Pandrosion's main opening, but the more compelling view is that which is framed by the entire colonnade: including a view of a more recent structure next to the Erectheion, beneath whose tiled roof we see a figure standing on a railed porch. Moraites's view is not as neat as that of Stillman, either compositionally or culturally. It juxtaposes paths of vision into both past and present. It instead engages with an inhabitance of the present from which Stillman, literally, looks away.

52 William J. Stillman, 'Facade of the Pandrosion', in *The Acropolis of Athens* (1870), carbon print, plate 20.

The vast, impressive aboveground monuments of places like ancient Greece and Egypt were central targets of early photographers for many reasons, ranging from their relative availability to the huge role they played in the European imagination. However, the seeming certainty and bravado present in elaborately conceived photos like those of Stillman and Le Gray is hardly the only kind of charge toward empathic viewing one can find framed within sites of movement in archaeological photography. As the permutations of archaeology grew more numerous and culturally complex in the twentieth century, as the field grew as a science and assumptions of an imperial age grew less formative, and as the photographic apparatus itself became more portable and efficient, the differing cultural resonances of archaeological photography became all the more pronounced. A pair of twentieth-century photographic treatments of ancient openings provides a case in point.

First is a photo of a drain by the 'Great Bath' at Mohenjo-Daro (illus. 54). Located in modern-day Pakistan, Mohenjo-Daro is the largest known site of the remarkable Indus valley civilization. It is comparable in size to ancient Babylon, better known in the West, and renowned for its size. It is thousands of years older than the structures of the Acropolis and many of the rest of the best-known artefacts of what was deemed the cradle of civilization. The photograph confronts us in detail with its mud brick construction, carefully vaulted at the top through corbelling. The drain, as much as any aspect of the rest of the site, testifies to a skill and imagination often surpassing that of Egyptian or Mesopotamian construction of the same or later times. This photograph appeared in a range of English publications, from *Antiquity* in 1928, where it illustrated a report of the site's latest discoveries, to a large spread the same year in *The Illustrated London News* with the caption 'Civil Engineering of a Wonderfully "Modern" Type in India 5000 Years Ago: The Vaulted Drain Through Which Water Was Drawn Off at Mohenjo-Daro.'

In an age for which modern plumbing was still new enough to be a matter of public pride, the photograph offers remarkable testimony of the advancement of a distant culture. Yet at the photograph's centre lies the empty space of the drain, and its passageway almost pushes us to the light at the other end. This is especially the case as we see at the end of the passage an Indian man in Western dress, his hat removed, most likely

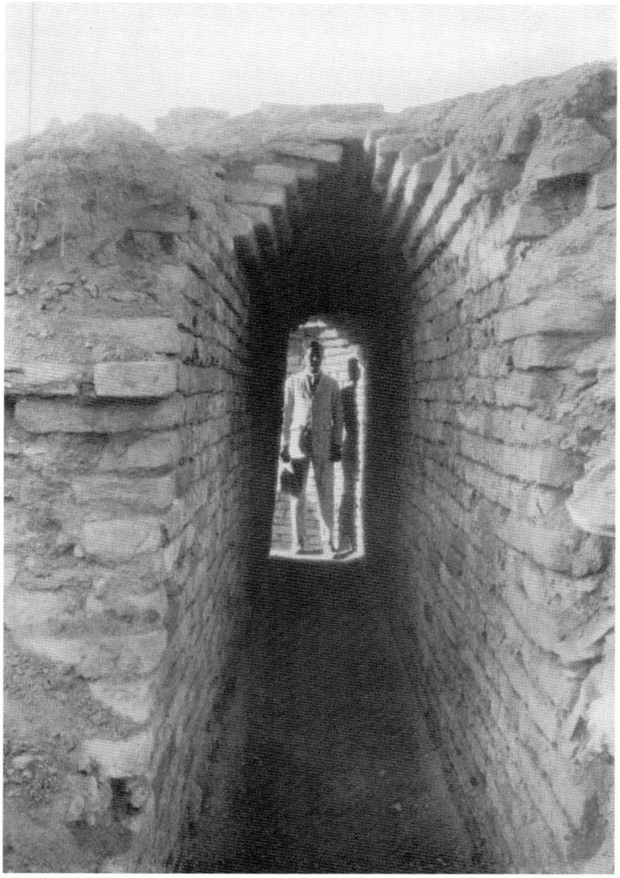

54 Devi Dayal Mathur(?), 'Vaulted Drain off of Great Bath', Mohenjo-Daro, before 1928, gelatin silver print.

one of the indigenous excavation supervisors overseen by director John Marshall, Director General of Archaeology in India. Yet despite its repeated reproduction, even in Marshall's definitive excavation report, the person at the heart of the image is never identified.[17] Such treatment is common enough for indigenous archaeological workers, used as 'staffage' to represent human scale. Here it merely attests to the observation of the excavation report that the drain is 'high enough to allow a tall man to walk through without stooping'. But in this particular case the situation is especially poignant.

The archaeological discovery of Mohenjo-Daro, like that of Great Zimbabwe or the Ohio Mounds, presented Western archaeologists with a quandary. All were remarkable monuments found in places where the ancestors of contemporary inhabitants (South African tribesmen or Native Americans) were deemed by some to be incapable of such accomplishments. Much speculation – ethnocentric, if not racist – went into convoluted historical hypotheses to explain these findings. The site of Mohenjo-Daro was actually discovered by an Indian, Rakhaldas D. Banerji, then working as an archaeologist at the Indian Museum in Calcutta. Marshall soon took over the excavation and wrote in his three-volume report of 1931, that, while he would not claim India as the new cradle of civilization, the peoples, at least of this portion of India, 'were enjoying an advanced and singularly uniform civilization of their own, closely akin but in some respects even superior to that of contemporary Mesopotamia and Egypt'.[18]

Yet the significance of this photograph also lies in its circulation, confined as it was to purely Western venues. Despite Marshall's acknowledgement of the accomplishments of the builders of the Harrapan civilization, he also sought to control information about it. Banerji and others struggled with Marshall to publicize among Indians the discovery of their past. Banerji was reproached by Marshall in 1925 for giving an interview about the finds to an Indian newspaper, while a later writer to the same newspaper asked in outrage: 'Is it a fact that the Archaeology department refused to provide local papers with copies of photographs which were first published in England, even though the Indian papers offered to pay for them?'[19]

When looked at from indigenous eyes, the situation was simpler. The discovery of Mohenjo-Daro and related sites made the vast accomplishments of the Indian past tangible, and undermined an imposed English idea of the Indian people as secondary and dependent.[20] It became a central component in the rise of an Indian national consciousness, which ultimately fed the drive for independence. The cultural interaction between directors and indigenous workers we have earlier seen represented at the excavation site is manifest in its own way in the later circulation and use of photographs themselves, here stretching directly into the political realm. The documentary charge of photography, as in many times of its history, serves as a powerful political motivator.

The most common mark of the most 'scientific' archaeological photography, the fundamental model of which has dominated archaeology since the Second World War, is that it is fraught with none of the weight of the previous photos. Aaron Levin's photograph of an archway at ancient Pompeii in 1995 brings a matter-of-factness, even banality, in which the minute material revelation of archaeology most thrives (illus. 55). As science is designed to wall out personal interests, so this image, made very early in the day before tourists were allowed on the site, excludes as much as possible the drama and complexity of inherited ideology, quite unlike some earlier, more spectacularized treatment (see p. 164)

Precisely opposite to the distilled essence apparent with Stillman, in which hundreds of images are winnowed to 25 exemplars of a locale, Levin's goal is to take as many different views as possible, to add to the archive of what might one day prove useful to a researcher in retrospect.[21] This is a fundamental principle of photography in modern archaeological excavation, and it has considerable effect on the nature of the images produced. The images are designed from the start to function within an

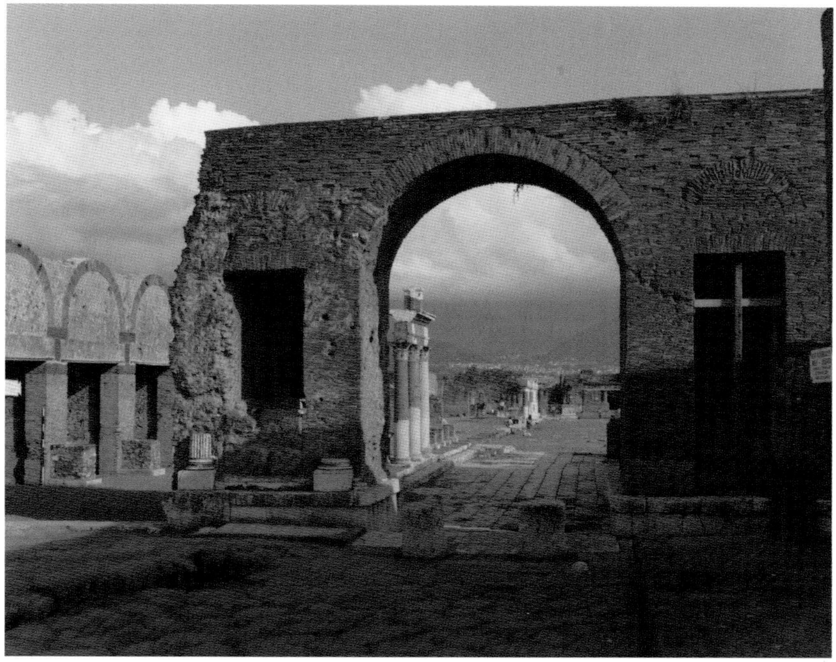

55 Aaron Levin, 'Pompeii, Forum, Northeast Arch, from North', 1995, resin-coated silver print.

archive, whose total effect emerges as an ensemble. This is not the only image of the arch. Most of all, though, these are images deemed to be as close as possible to pure documentation, deliberately eschewing traces of artistic invention.

The photo, that is, is conceived as much as a means of information as a visual image. A shadow washes across the arch surface, but it does not measurably add or detract from its display of wall surface or construction. The viewpoint is neither precisely central to the opening, nor dramatically oblique (in a manner often used by Michele Amodio, Giorgio Sommer and others in previous photographs of Pompeii). Instead, it is dictated by the spatial nature of the site and information required. Levin locates the camera almost directly in front of the right jamb of the arch, in order to offer a view through the arch, while also to most fully reveal the surface of the left jamb. The image offers scale without the complexity of human presence, by means of a standard measuring stick perched discreetly by a pillar at left. The right edge lines up precisely with an adjoining wall, displaying just enough to show us there is no more to see of the arch from this vantage point. In the logic of scientific archaeology, and more generally the reductive logic of science itself, the site can be best articulated, and reproduced, via a reduction to parts. The diminishment of the colonnade to the left draws the eye through the archway into the forum itself, which is itself documented in further photographs. A glimpse of the mountains in the distant Sorrentine peninsula and the complex pattern of clouds offers further spatial orientation, as well as a picturesque, active sense of nature.

Looking over the historical span of archaeological photography, Keith F. Davis notes: 'What has been lost in the last hundred years is the sense of individuality in image making; technology and corporate action have, by necessity, displaced the personality of the independent, self-reliant photographer.'[22] The nineteenth and twentieth century photographs we've compared certainly confirm this general observation. But it might be more accurate to say that it is no historical inevitability at work (indeed exceptions abound in both centuries), but rather the spread of a depersonalized gaze and rise of an organized, hierarchical archaeological worksite, so that a photographer's individual approach disappears to the extent that his work is controlled by someone else. Levin states flatly that 'It's the photographer's task to "see" what the archaeologist wants to say.'[23] This suggests not only the displacement of control, but also a move away from visual to documentary criteria. Moving from 'seeing' to 'saying' is, literally, moving toward a more prosaic understanding of remains.

Haynes's work at Nippur in the nineteenth century (see p. 50) under the direct control of an excavation director, who was hostile to his individual, aesthetic preferences, now appears as a crucial moment of the rise of this same 'impersonality'. The change over time confronts us with the visual implication of the rise to dominance of professional archaeology. At the same time, as we shall see in the next chapter, scientific uses of archaeology led photography into realms that utilized its recording functions in new and remarkable ways.

three

# Meaning, or the Archive

The sheer number of archaeological photographs existing today is staggering to contemplate. The shift we have seen at the end of the last chapter from the discerning photographic process of William J. Stillman in the nineteenth century to the more prolific one of Aaron Levin in the twentieth mirrors the progression of photographic technology – from metal to paper or glass negatives to roll film to digital photography – each of which makes it simpler and faster to produce a photograph and supports an ever accelerating production. But as this burgeoning corpus grows ever more vast, organization becomes equally more crucial as a way to render it intelligible for archaeological purposes.

Four years after Eugène Viollet-le-Duc wrote his introduction to Desiré Charnay's volume of Central American monuments, he wrote, in an essay on restoration, that photography 'has the advantage of making possible an exact and irrefutable presentation of a building in any given state'. 'Irrefutable' is the key word here. The scientific discourse of photography, once past its wonder at the medium's promise of objectivity, rapidly took up the rhetorical advantages of photography for historical research and argumentation. The principle was put most succinctly by the photographer Auguste Salzmann, who stated in 1856 that: 'Photographs are more than accounts (*récits*), they are facts endowed with a conclusive brute force (*une brutalité concluante*).'[1] Salzmann, as we shall see in chapter Four, was in the very thick of archaeological controversy, and photography was a tool on his side.

The essential point here is that photographic objectivity itself can be paradoxical. The 'brute force' within photographic evidence makes it difficult to confine the photograph to a documentary, second-order status. Viollet-le-Duc himself goes on to state that 'very often one discovers on a photographic proof some feature that went unnoticed on the building itself'.[2] Thus for the inquiring viewer, looking through photographs can thus take on a function virtually superior to sustained inspection of the actual object of inquiry. This chapter will explore the remarkable flux of rhetorical and evidentiary functions that can be obtained when photographs are delivered into the researcher's gaze, gathered in groups and treated as primary artefacts.

The invention of photography fostered not just a new way of imaging the world but also of organizing it. In fact, Joan Schwartz has shown how the modern archive derives from precisely the same 'defining moment' as photography itself.[3] Photography's ability not just to distil concrete imagery out of momentary vision but also to allow for infinitely varied compilations and juxtapositions of images is at the heart of its usefulness, particularly in a scientific context. Archiving allows images to be construed in new kinds of relations, which in turn cultivate new kinds of visual experience. The type of series chosen, the nature of the archive, has the ability to remake, subtly or profoundly, the meaning of the images composing the series.

The earliest monument of such reframing is the *Excursions Daguerriennes* published by Noël Paymal Lerebours. It first appeared as a volume in 1842, but portions were issued in fascicule as early as 1840, the very year after the announcement of photography. The first, and most successful, volume featured 60 images, many of them ancient monuments. But much as the book drew its appeal from the truth of photography, given the nature of the particular process, it could not directly present the daguerreotypes it named in the title and from which it drew its unique claim to credibility. The *Excursions Dauguerriennes* instead featured steel engravings drawn after daguerreotypes. A typical example is an image from Baalbek, in what was then Syria, now Lebanon (illus. 56). A dramatic view of a portion of a large classical temple complex, it also embellishes the scene with Arab horsemen riding across the landscape, typical Orientalist subjects that would hardly have been still enough for the early camera.

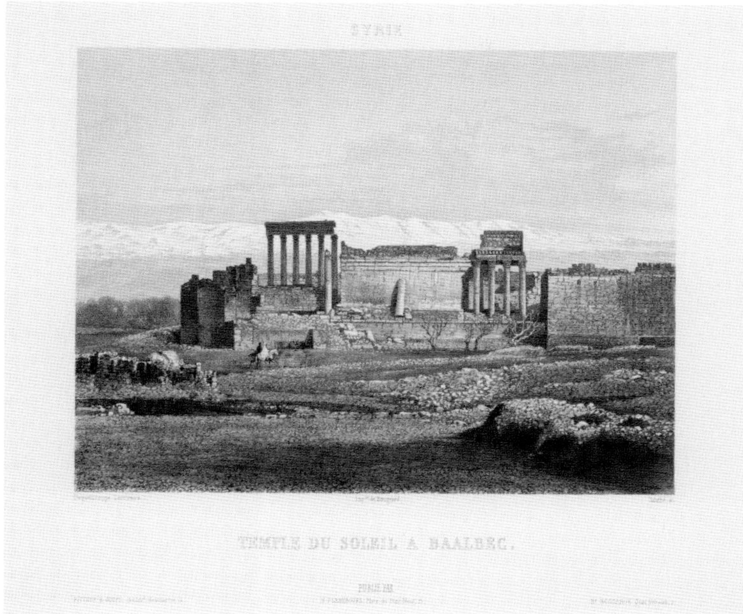


56 Noël Paymal Lerebours, 'Temple of the Sun, Baalbek,' in *Excursions Daguerriennes* (1842), plate 56 engraving after daguerreotype.

In retrospect, it is remarkable that the prestige of photography immediately led people to trust images that were clearly not photographs. But even at the time there is evidence of anxiety about access, of working to deliver the actual photographic material to the viewer's gaze. In 1852 Pierre Tremaux's *Voyages au Soudan Oriental* attempted to obviate this problem by including actual photographic prints made from paper negatives. They soon faded, a common occurrence of the time. Tremaux reverted to the established solution, and issued later editions of the same images in lithographs drawn after the photographs, sometimes even tipped in over the originals. Tremaux's later book, his *Exploration Archéologique en Asie Mineur* of 1862, was even further mixed, adding photolithographs to the combination of photographs and lithographs.[4] The drive to codify, to archive and perhaps most of all simply to see the far away as it actually was thus continually consecrated photography as its privileged medium and refused to be confined by its limitations, even mixing media in order to suture the information of the fragile but trusted photographic print to more durable print processes.

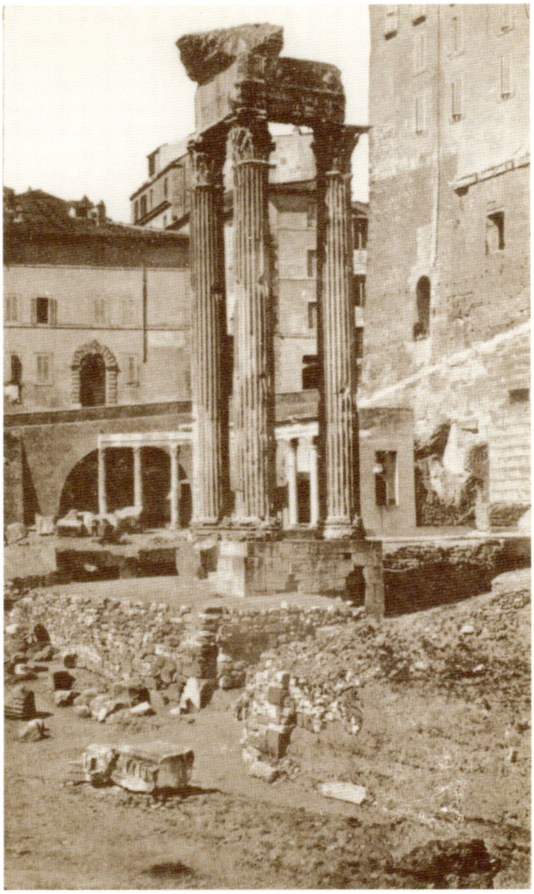

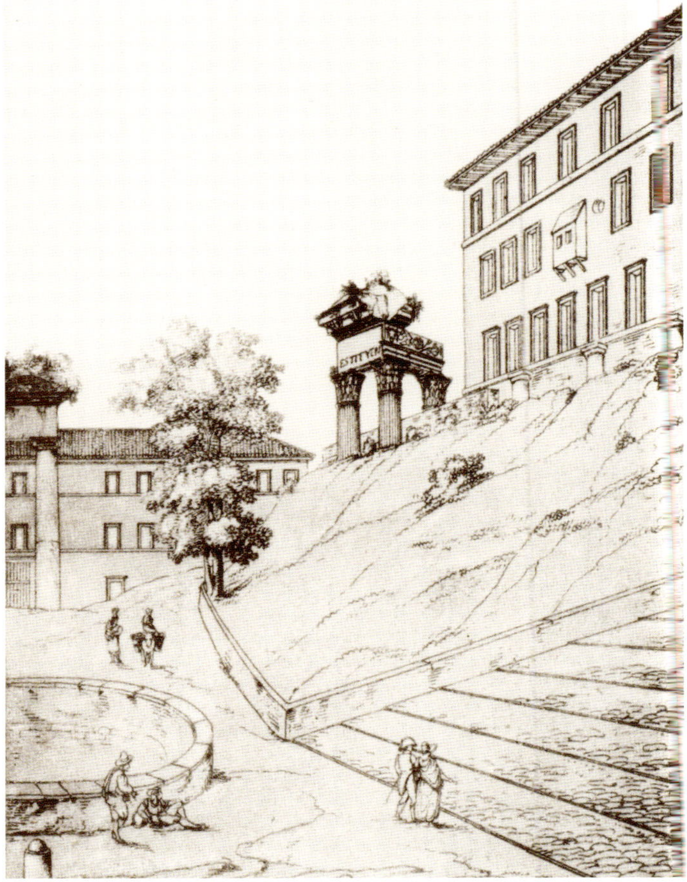

57 'Temple of Saturn in 1874', in John Henry Parker, *The Forum Romanum* (1876), plate 7, albumen print from glass negative.

58 'The Temple of Saturn in 1810', in John Henry Parker, *The Forum Romanum*, plate 6, engraving.

The drive both to see and collect sights is evident in another way, even more fundamental to archiving. The images of the *Excursions Daguerriennes* are not organized spatially or temporally within the book, in the manner of an actual excursion and the early travel literature that described it. Rather, they are bound and indexed in alphabetical order of country, from Algeria to Syria. Here, then, is one of the earliest effects of an archive, re-filing photographic imagery so as to be at the behest of the viewer. The same alphabetizing scheme remains common to photographic repertories, especially those designated for specialists, such as Ernest Nash's vast *Pictorial Dictionary of Ancient Rome.* More encyclopedia than novel, in the archive the trace of authorial expression or experience cedes importance to multiple possibilities for a user's retrieval.

Unlike much experimental science, archaeological photography largely presents images in a human scale – neither macro nor micro. But it pictures this activity in a larger temporal and spatial dimension, since a vast site can be covered first with a panoramic view and later detailed piece by piece, while the same locations can be progressively photographed over time to reveal changes and discoveries. In this way, each individual aspect of any given site can be compared to others, can be seen in a way inaccessible to the photographically unaided observer. Spaces, materials and artefacts take on new identities in new sequences.

What is most striking is how quickly and consciously the project was taken up, how immediately evident it was that archaeology was not just aided by but also in a sense functioned through photography. One of the earliest advocates of a systematic traffic in archaeological photography was John Henry Parker, a pioneer in the archaeological investigation of ancient Rome. In 1874 Parker began publishing a book series entitled *The Archaeology of Rome*, illustrated with numerous visual aids including autotype prints of key sites. This volume is among the first that we might recognize as modern archaeological discourse, simply and lucidly juxtaposing image and text.

A typical example is a plate of the remains of the Temple of Saturn in the volume dedicated to the Roman Forum (illus. 57). The angle chosen shows at lower right an ancient entrance into the even more ancient Capitolium temple, a key fact for Parker's reconstruction, while also detailing architectural structure (and distinguishing previous restorations from more ancient portions remaining). Moreover, this entire discussion contrasts with that of the previous plate, an engraving showing the same site in 1810, with barely the tops of the columns visible above a slant of soil (illus. 58). Once again, the reader/viewer can participate in the uncovering process that constitutes archaeology by turning the pages of a volume (see pp. 14 and 16). But now, the transit from an age when 'this part of Rome had been entirely neglected and despised'[5] into the present moment of archaeological awareness represented by Parker is also a movement into the age of photography.

In the first volume of the series, Parker stated:

> It appears to me better to refer to a photograph, which is easily to be obtained, or to be seen at a public library, than to the objects themselves from which the photograph is taken, as the readers cannot be expected to go to Rome to see each object on which they have any doubt, but may be expected to look at a photograph of it.[6]

Through ready availability of photographic archives, the discourse Parker wished to initiate could be widely dispersed while still anchored in actuality. This is hardly as populist as it sounds, as the 'public library' he means were the likes of Oxford's Bodleian, the British Museum and the Ashmolean Museum at Oxford, where he served as keeper.

A few years earlier, in the process of justifying the museum to its public supporters, Parker described precisely how such archives could work:

> It is by comparing small remains in one place with more perfect remains of the same kind and of the same period in other places, that we learn to understand the smaller remains. To carry on this study formerly required the power of travelling far and wide but the art of Photography enables us to pursue this study by our own fireside, and sometimes even better than we could do by travelling, because we can place the objects side by side, and not have to trust to memory or to drawings, which are not always to be depended on.

Parker's own researches were produced with heavy reliance on this nascent archive, no doubt consulted at his own fireside. Parker's photography functions as a means of comparative typology, deemed more dependable than memory or drawing. Such typology was a hallmark of the scientific archaeology that was then emerging.

Yet as Parker went on with his praise of the modern invention, he then somewhat disengaged it from its moorings in objectivity. As he continues: 'At first sight, indeed, it may appear absurd to say that in this small building the general History of Architecture can be illustrated. But the art of Photography enables us to do many things that were impossible before.'[7] Parker's view of photography, then, gives it a certain double stance toward objective perception. It both buttresses and challenges the researcher's acquaintance, helping in comparison but also putting on display a general concept that was hitherto unseeable. Parker's ideal of the working of the photographic archive is one that offers both incremental and qualitatively different improvements over those previously achievable, in ways he admits are both readily conceivable and seemingly unthinkable.[8]

Each of these two functions corresponds to a pragmatic feature performed in an archive: comparison and classification. Where comparison is local and individual, classification is universal and global. The backbone of an archive is its classification system, which in large, multi-user contexts can be as elaborate and articulated as that of any library. But the photographic archive of an excavation is often a less formal affair, kept in boxes or folders in a designated place, together with the notebooks, ledgers or other documentation used for retrieval. The point of archiving is to situate the information of a given photograph within a larger totality. Thus a photograph of an artefact from the University of Pennsylvania Nippur excavation bears the description on its verso 'Primitive burnt brick showing impression of a palm leaf' (illus. 59). It also bears the number of the negative, the photograph itself and the particular excavation year, all products of a recent, systematic cataloging project (illus. 60). But the archival function can work just as easily, or even at the same time, to otherwise interpret imagery. Thus another photograph from the same year of the same excavation states on its back simply 'Temple Library, Time of Abraham' (illus. 61, 62). The written hand now is a far older one, quite possibly dating back to the original excavation. The Nippur excavation was directed by a clergyman, John Peters, and clearly aimed at exploring the Near East to elaborate on biblical accounts. Here the act of archiving assigns a very different value, based on information derived far from the image itself. The annotations on these two Nippur photographs were certainly not made by a single cataloguer, and indeed do not belong to a common archival scheme. Instead, they underscore the contingency or impurity in markings that can surround any archive, all of which in some sense work to interpret as much as transmit archaeological findings. This is a particularly extreme

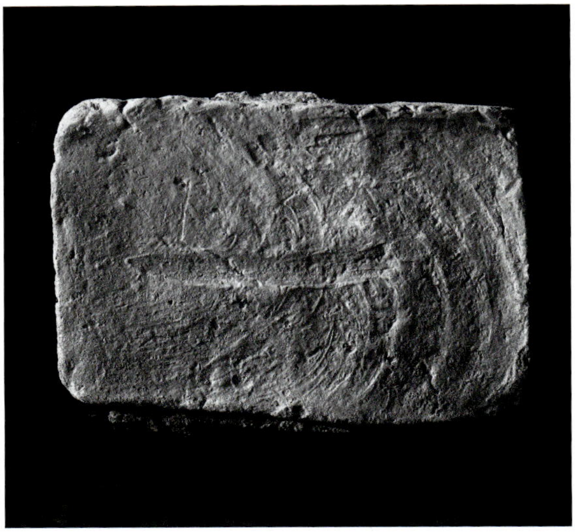

Expedition IV
Negno 6000
Photo 218
- Primitive burnt brick showing impression of a palm leaf

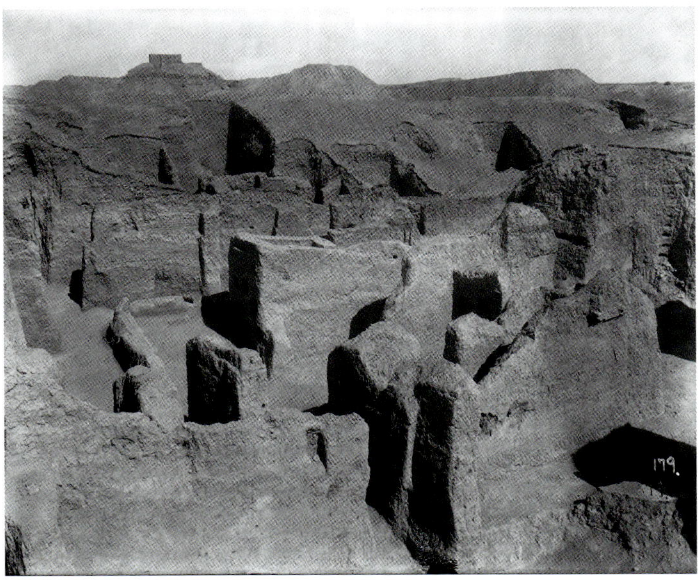
179.

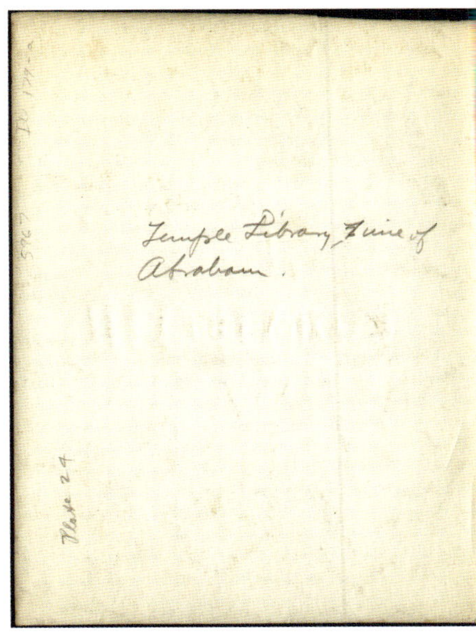
Temple Library, Time of Abraham.
Plate 24

59 John Henry Haynes, 'Nippur, Burnt Brick', 1893–1900, albumen print.

60 Reverse of 'Nippur, Burnt Brick'.

example of tension between different interpretive criteria, but is hardly anomalous in archival collections. A look at one of the most resolutely scientific excavations of its time offers its own object lesson in how photographic archiving almost always takes on something of the ideological coloration of its users.

The German excavations at Olympia, begun in 1875, are a watershed in the history of national archaeology. Sponsored by the new German government, under the Kaiser's personal guidance, and shepherded by the great classicist Ernst Curtius, later known as the 'victor of Olympia', it was a grand-scale excavation employing at its height more than 500 workers.[9] The ultimate report of the Olympia excavations consists of five vast text volumes, edited by Curtius, and an accompaniment of almost as many volumes of illustrations and maps. The text begins with praise for the enlightened German Reich, celebrating its triumph as the greatest wish of Curtius's life, as well as a realization of the cherished dream of J. J. Winckelmann.[10] Yet the very involvement of a dream brings imaginative investments that cloud the presentation of material evidence.

The excavation at Olympia was among the earliest devoted to full, systematic scientific treatment of its entire site, rather than the 'treasure hunting' of earlier archaeology, largely attuned to finding impressive objects to export. As such it uncovered a huge number of artefacts. But, just as predictably, only a tiny percentage of them were the impressive art objects, to rival national collections in France and England, which some of its governmental backers had hoped for. Perhaps the greatest single sculptural find of the excavation was a figure of a Nike, a Greek original signed by Paionios of Mende. In a sort of compensation, this figure alone is treated to the greatest number of full-page reproductions in the Olympia album, detailing views from a number of angles and, more strikingly, juxtaposing artefacts thought part of a whole, notably the head and right wrist, through purely photographic means, without visible means of support (illus. 63). The task not only recreates an artefact of antiquity as a structural whole, but also produces a proper image satisfying to modern viewers. Photography is not only a guarantor of authenticity but also a medium of an imaginative charge. Indeed, this particular artefact, uniquely among the objects detailed in the Olympia

61 John Henry Haynes, 'Temple Library, Time of Abraham', 1893–1900, albumen print.

62 Reverse of 'Temple Library, Time of Abraham'.

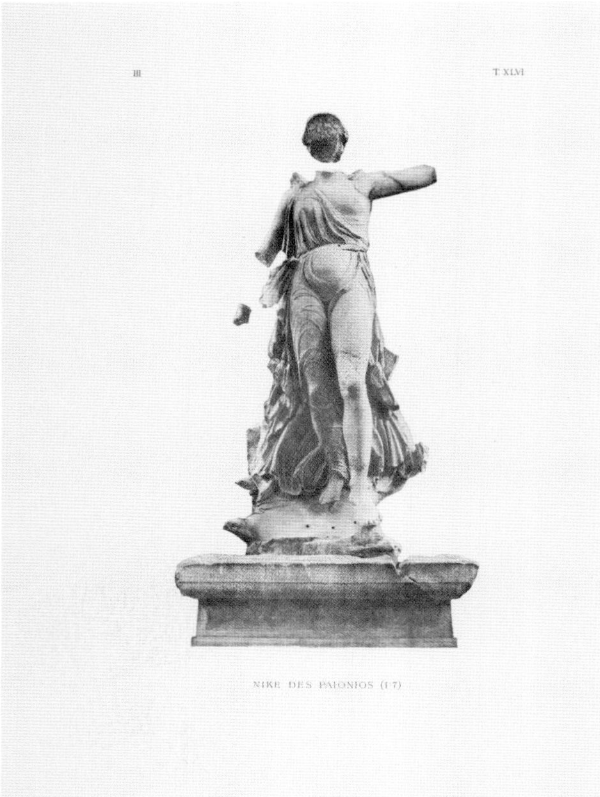


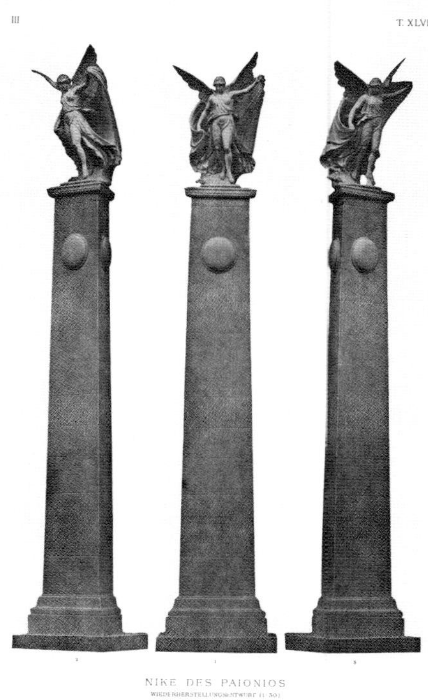


album, is the object of the excavator's contemporary attention. A third folio page of the album was also dedicated to the Nike, recreating it through photographs as a reconstructed object (illus. 64). The plinth is notably larger in relation to the statue (and of a different shape) than the archaeological evidence supports,[11] but for just that reason it might be said to bear evidence of another formative contemporary model, Berlin's own modern victory image: the Victory Column (Siegessäule), unveiled in the heart of Berlin, in 1873, at just about the same time as the Olympia excavations had begun, and with an even more extenuated proportion between base and figure (illus. 65). This remaking of a Victory unearthed by Germans in Olympia, that is, bears a visual relation to a central monument to Germany's victories in the Franco–Prussian wars,

63 Constantine and Aristotelis Romaides, 'Nike of Paionios', in *Olympia: Die Ergebnisse der von dem deutschen Reich veranstalteten Ausgrabung* (1890–7), vol. III, plate 46, photomechanical print.

64 Constantine and Aristotelis Romaides, 'Nike of Paionios, Reconstruction Design', in *Olympia*, vol. III, plate 48, photographic collage.

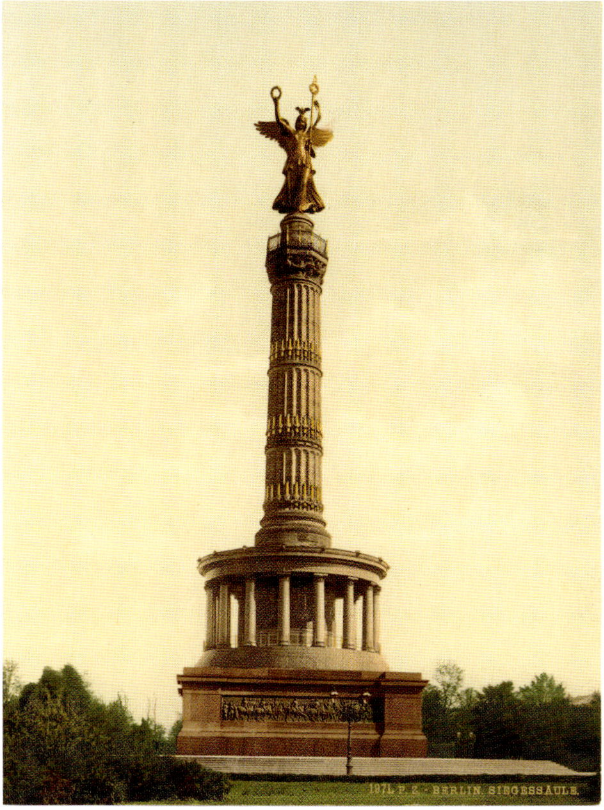


65 Detroit Photographic Company 'Berlin, Siegessäule', c. 1890–1900, photomechanical colour print.

and the founding regime that both erected the modern monument and sponsored the excavation of the ancient one. Photography in this book underwrites, and testifies to, contemporary Germany's claim to classical inheritance, as much as it dispassionately documents a scientific inquiry. Notably, the Olympia monument's unsigned photographic reinvention completely isolates it from its ancient surroundings, making imaginative comparison that much easier, and physical scale that much harder to envisage. By contrast, a series of engraved reconstructions of Olympia by Friedrich Adler at the very end of the report places the monument among others situated nearby, where it hardly stands out at all.

This is just the start of the representational fortune, the fundamental remaking, of the Nike through photography. We will revisit it in the following chapter in the context of full-blown art photography. But here the effect is articulated through the presentation of a sequence of images, each dependent on the others. This embodies the activity of the photographic archive, construing an object through an artfully arranged series of images.

Modern archaeology arose in a culture of positivistic realism. Thus Prosper Mérimée, a central figure behind the initial drive to inventory historic monuments in France, stated flatly that 'prohibiting the imagination is the archaeologist's first duty'.[12] Mérimée conceived of archaeology as a science focused solely on objective fact, one whose historical suppositions were confined to what could be proved or disproved through the physical evidence of what is now called 'the archaeological record'. Photography in such a context works to enforce this fundamentally prohibitive role, confining discussion to the objective evidence it provides, and guarding against the subjective and imaginary constructs that might be introduced by the researcher's memory or the artist's sketch.

Mérimée's conception is fundamental, as he served as Inspecteur Général des Monuments Historiques to the French government, under whose aegis took place the first systematic governmental attempt to use photography to amass a comprehensive visual archive of material traces of the past: the Mission Héliographique of 1851. The Mission Héliographique sent five photographers throughout France to document a wide variety of architectural monuments.[13]

Mérimée's post had been created in 1830, as part of a larger movement in France concerned with the preservation of French national patrimony, in response both to the horrifying destructions of the French Revolution and a new rise of interest in the Middle Ages, the 'Gothic Revival', which put a new light on France's remarkable Gothic architecture. As this interest stretched into the age of photography, it seemed prudent to turn the camera's mechanical recording capability to the Herculean task of documenting the nation's existing remains.

The Mission Héliographique was thus designed as a photographic documentary and salvage project. In about five months, its photographers produced around 300 images, which were mostly deposited in a governmental archive without elaborate exhibition or publication.

The photographers of the Mission Héliographique worked largely using the calotype process. Compared to the metal daguerreotype, the calotype, using paper for both negative and positive, produced a more delicate image with a greater sensitivity to atmospheric effects and gradations of lighting. This deliberate choice of medium was appropriate to the emphasis on artful effect, not just recording of subject-matter, with which the images were not just produced but also received. A reviewer of Gustave Le Gray's photographs of the Chateau of Blois wrote in reverie:

> Photography has attained a magic feeling that neither drawing nor painting could have reached, especially with regard to Gothic structures . . . Whereas engraving aggrandizes the Greek or Roman construction and shrinks those of the Middle Ages, photography, by profusely aerating everything, by softening the swarming details without obliterating the contours, presents to the delighted eye monuments as great as their counterparts in reality, and sometimes even greater.[14]

The extraordinary effect of the photographs is of course inflected by French national pride, but it is striking that this praise for photography works exactly against the medium's promise of objectivity, stating rather that photography is ideal for allowing Gothic art to grow in effect against the classical, to be more than it was otherwise. In this it well succeeded.

Yet the more properly archaeological dimension of the photographs of the Mission Héliographique presents them at a different sort of distance from objectivity. While the project focused largely on medieval and later monuments, a rare photo of a structure from antiquity highlights its working method, a foil to that of conventional positivist archaeology.

Édouard Baldus photographed the main and lateral facades of the ancient Roman temple of Augustus and Livia in the town of Vienne, on the Rhône in southeastern France (illus. 66). The temple had long ago been converted into a church, and a considerable portion had fallen into disuse. While one can clearly make out a row of Corinthian capitals holding up a classical entablature, a Gothic tracery, as well as later walls, windows and even a dormer in the roof, have been added.

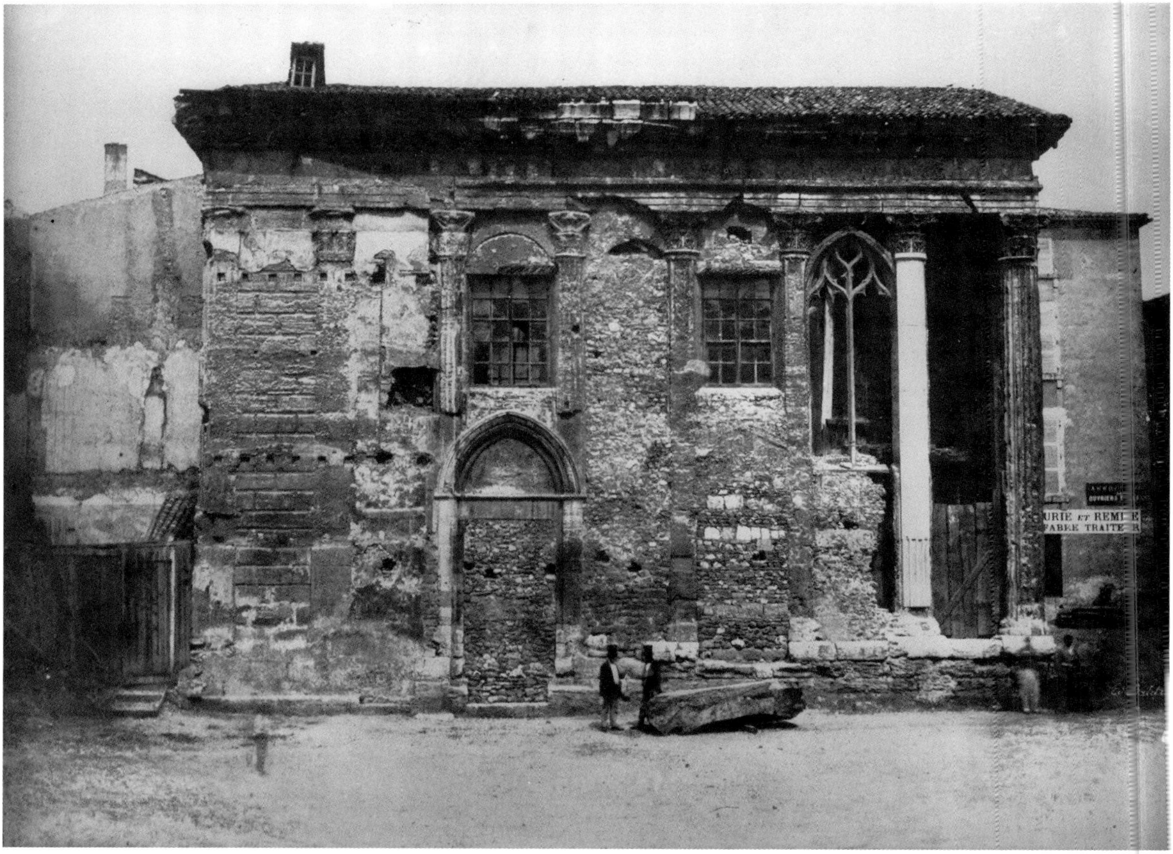

66 Édouard Baldus, 'Church of Notre Dame de Vie (Former Temple of Augustus and Livia), Vienne, Rhône-Alpes, France', 1851, salt print.

Like many other images by the Mission Héliographique photographers, focusing on churches partly hidden behind shops, or monuments within ruined streets, this one displays the tangled conditions under which the distant past could be discerned in nineteenth-century France. In fact, the monument at Vienne today has been 'restored' to its ancient state as a temple. The project was first proposed and undertaken by Mérimée himself, thus excavating a particular portion of the past while excising the rest. But the photograph itself does not support the archaeologist's intention, as it bears no trace of a motivation to isolate a single past (by singling out particular details). Instead, via the camera's insistent registration of all that is before it, it presents a document of the complex intermingling of pasts and afterlife of antiquity: a challenge to unitary identity, and testament to the work of historical imagination and adaptation, not a reductive vision of a single, pristine object. Still, the temple/church fits capaciously within the task of the Mission Héliographique, witness to the country's long and continuing historical past. The image, of a monument fully marked by its past lives, is here inflected by the archive that produces it, presenting not only given past moments, but also the long train of historical process.

This openness towards a monument's past has considerable significance for the architectural present. From the Mission Héliographique, photography could offer a repertory of imaginative possibilities, a pattern-book made of real buildings, which could serve an archaeological project on principles directly opposed to those of the positivist Mérimée. Thus Mérimée's colleague, and sometime antagonist, Viollet-le-Duc used photography as an aid not to memory so much as to imagination, as in his 'restoration' work of Notre Dame in Paris. For Viollet, 'a photograph . . . was an auxiliary to imagination and enabled the archaeologist to restore a structure to a state that may never have existed'.[15]

Just for the paradox of this formulation, it well embodies the representational flux and competing motivations in which photography was, and still is, utilized. More is collected in a photographic archive than any one director can control. Virtually from its origin, photography has had a double action that does as much to create anew as record what is pre-existent.

'History resembles photography in that it is, among other things, a means of alienation.'[16] This maxim of Siegfried Kracauer gives us a broader sense of what is at stake. Even as photography serves as a link to an external reality and common history on which a project of recovery and restoration can be based, it accomplishes its representation only by isolating one portion from the otherwise organic and continuous visual world. This act of isolation is indeed, in Kracauer's term, one of alienation. Inserting appearance into what Mary Price calls the 'strange, confined space' of the photograph, it is decontextualized, now raw material for re-use and change, such as Viollet-le-Duc's imaginative reconstructions.[17] The unique is now reproducible, and the architectural source can be difficult to discern in what it is later used to inspire. Underlying this is a second effect in which visual reality is in the process alienated from itself. That is, the previously undifferentiated field of vision becomes a penetrable, hierarchical ground for photographic investigation, a place to be carved up by the imposition of frames rather than a frameless plenum, matter from which to make scholarly suppositions, or architectural reconstructions.

This is the archive's very task. A characteristic example of its employment for scientific purposes is the photographic documentation produced by archaeologist John Garstang in his treatment of the many hundreds of photographs he took during his excavations at Jericho, begun in 1930. Garstang created a series of albums devoted to particular themes of interest, an idiosyncratic listing of the site encompassing both locations and objects: kilns, palace storerooms, pottery, 'special objects', sealings on pots and the city's famed walls. In each album, photographs are dry-mounted onto pages, hand-captioned and often accompanied by a site map. A typical example, part of a section devoted to storerooms, is meticulously made, devoted to a collection of details of two particular rooms (illus. 67). Just two rooms present much more as a whole than seven detailed photographs can, especially as two photos are devoted to the same feature at different distances. As Reisner states (see p. 23), looking through an archaeologist's eyes provides significant details, but only for the sensibility already attuned to the site as a whole. This photographic documentation is thus highly selective, anything but a stand-in for the site.

But the photographic archive can carve up archaeological experience in other ways as well, on behalf of popular as much as scholarly audiences. The world of stereographs, like that of postcards, is a vast photographic archive in its own right, aimed at a beholder whose inclinations are less purely scientific. Popular stereographs often presented ancient monuments in connection with contemporary life around them, such as images of zeppelins over the pyramids, or pilgrims at the church of the Holy Sepulchre. Unlike in more avowedly scientific archaeological photography, here the realm of the contemporary viewer is not withheld from the image but rather is present to orient the viewer. As a result, the photograph's message is not confined to, or even much focused on, the rarefied specifics of historical deduction from artefacts, but rather the poignant, contemporary human drama of confronting the past.

A stereograph of 1915 by Underwood & Underwood, the largest single producer of its time, provides an example (illus. 68). It takes the viewer to Hisarlik, the site first identified and excavated by Heinrich Schliemann as that of ancient Troy. The image turns away from contemporary debate on the subject, shutting down collective discourse for individual reverie, replacing information with experience. A traditionally dressed Turk

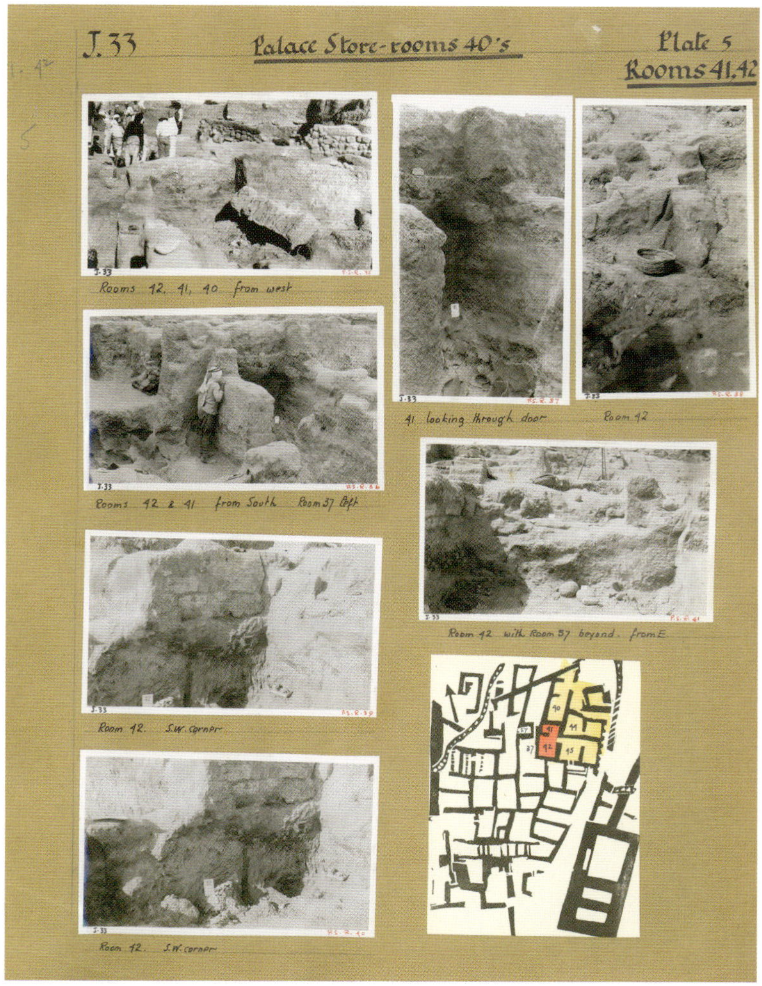


67 John Garstang, 'Palace Store rooms 40s', page from the *Jericho* photographic documentation album, 1933, gelatin silver prints.

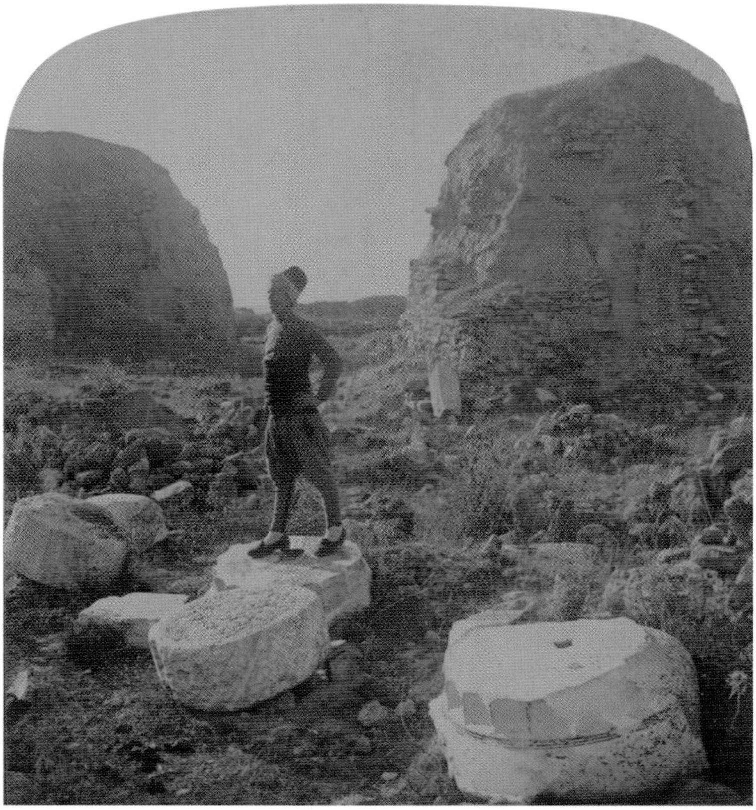

68 Underwood & Underwood, 'Storied remains of one time magnificence centre of Ancient Troy', c. 1915, portion of a stereograph.

stands elevated on a column drum placed between two mounds. His head juts above the horizon line. The image's caption states: 'Storied remains of one-time magnificence – centre of ancient Troy.' The figure's identity as Turk presents the scene as a kind of ethnographic incident, a pan-Turkish communing between an ancient and modern identity of a sort found in much racial theory of the time. In this context it is also a comment on degeneration, on the greater past than present of the country then known as 'the Sick Man of Europe'. Yet it is also an invitation to the Western viewer as archaeological spectator, a way to imaginatively participate in the project of archaeology.

In fact, each of these points is elaborated in an article that appeared in *National Geographic* in the same year, including an illustration, credited to Underwood & Underwood, which clearly featured the very same figure and setting. Jacob E. Conner's 'Homer's Troy Today' describes a tourist's visit to the site, both its imponderable present and moving past:

> Only the antiquarian can see the significance of all these things as he scrambles up and down within and among these disordered piles of what was once masonry . . . From its corner overlooking the plain of Simois, an outside stairway descends toward the river, possibly a later feature. Could this have been the corner of the wall where stood the Scæan Gate: where the venerable Father Priam brought the beautiful Helen in order to show her the enemy, her own countrymen and kindred on the plain below . . . It may well have been the same, and romance at least will have it so.[18]

Conner's article grafts on to the image itself a focus on the sheer age-value of the haphazard remains, and a larger narrative of a modern visit, displacing the modern Turk with a modern Western visitor.

While the imagery of popular versus scientific archaeology may be distinct, the audiences themselves are rather less so. The archaeologists Joan Gero and Dolores Root, looking particularly at the imagery of archaeology in *National Geographic*, are struck by the similarities between the nature of the magazine and that of archaeology itself in North America. 'Both grew out of industrial capitalism and prospered with American imperialism . . . [so that] the artifact-laden past portrayed in *National Geographic Magazine* only slightly exaggerates the role of archaeology in Western industrialized society.'[19] For Gero and Root, imagery in particular shows how the popular audience for archaeology is just a larger circle concentric to the smaller and more concentrated professional one.

Between the wide general public and scientific core of the audience is a narrow but important zone. Archaeological photographers today are still familiar with 'presentation photographs' by which archaeologists promote and justify their projects to sources of funding or access. Not surprisingly, this kind of photography proliferates in countries with entrepreneurial traditions of sponsorship separate from governmental authorities, notably the United States.

Erich Schmidt was among the most productive archaeologists of his generation, not least due to his skill and innovation in using photography to secure support. Schmidt excavated at sites from the American southwest to the Middle East. He worked extensively in Iran, Iraq and Turkey, eventually taking over from Herzfeld at Persepolis in 1934, authoring three major survey volumes there as well as a book of aerial photography, *Flights Over Ancient Cities of Iran*, in 1940. His papers are full of tales of last-minute flights to Paris or Berlin to secure ever-dwindling funds to continue work.

Among Schmidt's archival remains are a series of large portfolios devoted to particular excavations, bound in cloth for earlier work at Tepe Hissar and Fara, and then in leather for the excavations at Rayy in 1934. Each could hold ten to fifteen pieces of thick cardboard stock on which were mounted finely produced photographs. They are unbound so as to allow spontaneous regrouping or exclusion depending on a client's interests. Some of the images in these promotional portfolios portray finely lit individual artefacts or picturesque ethnographic scenes. But archaeological sites themselves also appear. Notable is a view made by the photographer Stanislaw Niedzwiecki of Tepe Hissar, among the most extensively examined Bronze Age sites in Iran (illus. 69). It portrays a working excavation, with a roped grid line following a baulk, behind which workers dig in a fog of dust thrown up by their industrious activity. In the foreground one scans a variety of locations excavated to different levels of finds, including artefacts and human remains. It is a remarkable, dramatic, textured scene of archaeological activity, cropped from a larger image and toned in development, a laboriously made advertisement for its own continuation.

Reflecting the dual nature of his goals, to satisfy both scientists and donors, Schmidt employed two photographers: the workmanlike Boris Dubensky, and the artful Niedzwiecki. Dubensky worked with Schmidt for years and his work makes up the bulk of documentation of sites and objects. The interventions of Niedzwiecki proved more short-lived. Schmidt complained about his slowness and temperamental nature. The two represent a fascinating bifurcation in photographing the archaeological artefact, the main subject on which

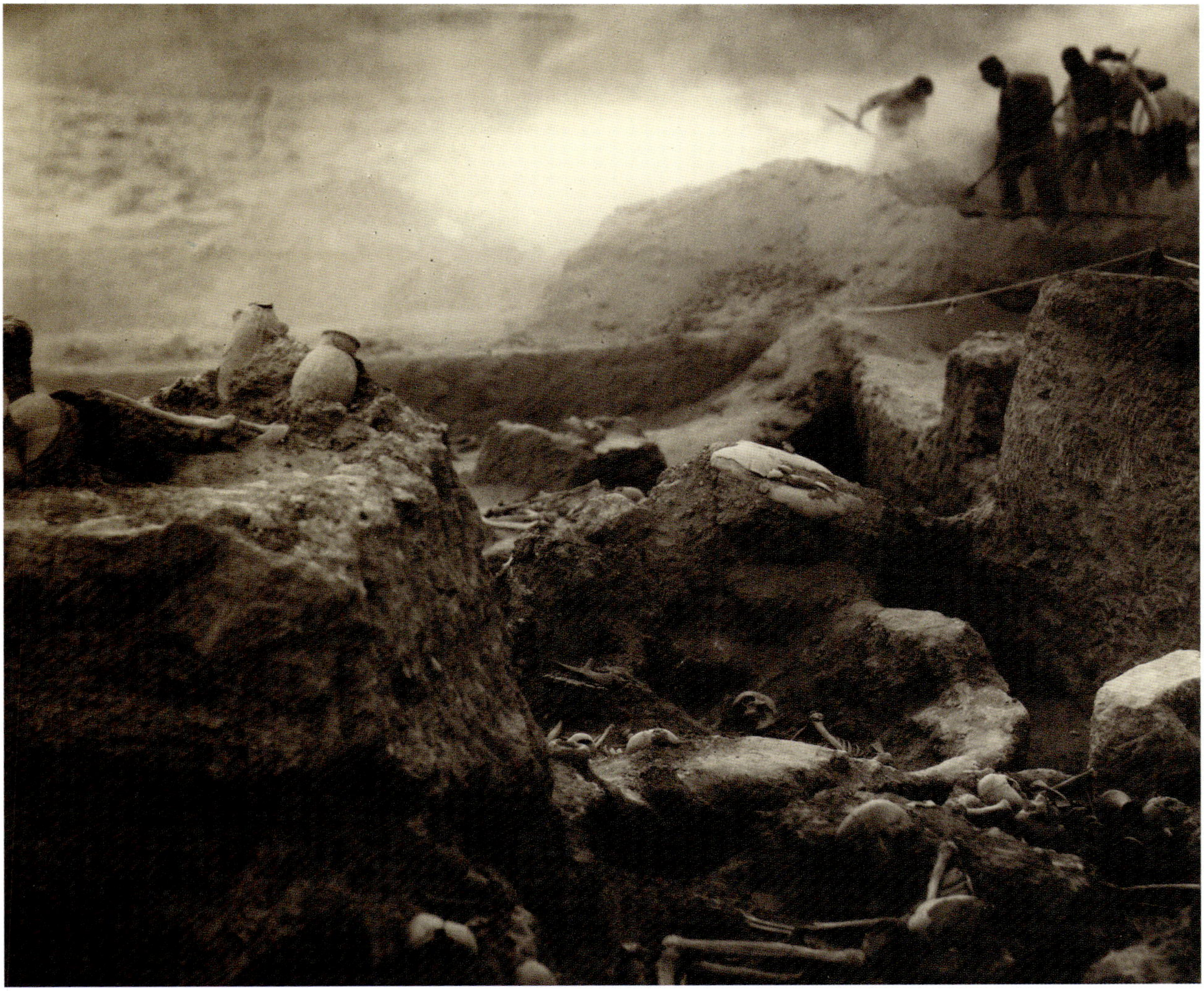

69 Stanislaw Niedzwiecki, 'Excavation at Tepe Hissar', Iran, 1931–2, toned gelatin silver print.

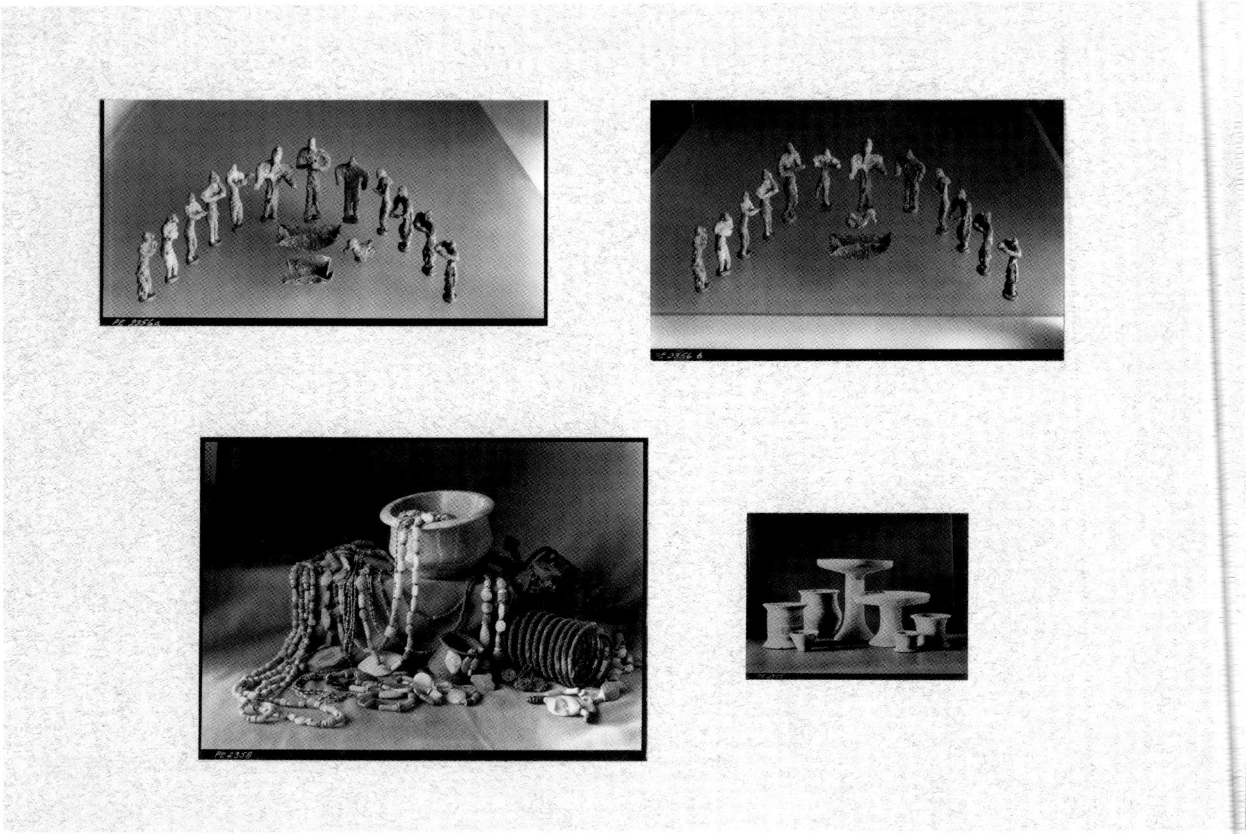

70 Erich Schmidt, *Tepe Hissar*, scientific album with four gelatin silver prints by Stanislaw Niedzwiecki (1930–32).

they both worked. Among Schmidt's comprehensive album of Tepe Hissar is a remarkable page devoted to portraying some notable objects from the site: weapons, vessels, figurines and, most notably, alabaster jewellery (illus. 70, bottom left). Whereas the rules of 'scientific' photography would treat each object individually and equally, this 'hoard' (as the label calls it) of objects of *circa* 3000 BC is turned into a single dramatic tableau. It is a sort of archaeological still-life, comparable to contemporary advertising and display imagery. A large print of this image was also present in Schmidt's presentation portfolio, and was likely a showstopper. The other prints by Niedzwiecki on the album page testify to his attempts to apply a similar eye to other objects, notably the two prints at the top, arranging a series of metal figurines in a semi-circle, and experimenting with different contrasts in printing them.

Photography for Schmidt was a mode of both documenting the look of objects for other scholars and remaking them for his own use. His images, and their packaging, are evidence of a canny, subtle eye for using photography for archaeological aims. Perhaps the most remarkable thing about Schmidt's albums is that there is more than one copy of each. Understanding that reproduction allows one to make many gifts of a single object, he presented copies of photographic albums not just to Western patrons but also to the Iranian officials who allowed his work, including the Shah himself. Photography was an instrument of archaeological diplomacy as well as recompense for support.

Given Schmidt's propensity for impressive photography, one might be surprised by his not using colour. The technology was certainly then available, as we shall see presently. Colour, however, is a vexed question in archaeological photography, as is the larger question of the aesthetic it often seems to activate. Although colours, of materials or soils for instance, are very important to document, they rarely present a picturesque image. More fundamentally, archaeology as science bears a considerable scepticism about self-consciously artistic rendering. At first glance, it might seem only proper to document a striking monument with a striking photograph. But, as we have seen as early as W. M. Flinders Petrie, the archaeological 'plain-style' distinguishes itself self-consciously from that which may activate any sense of art. A photographic encyclopedia of the 1960s makes the two approaches polar opposites, telling us: 'Archaeological photography, like scientific photography, must provide a precise and accurate representation as opposed to an artistic representation.'[20]

The early use of colour in archaeological photography implied a sort of shouting beyond the established norms of discourse. This was the case not only for aesthetic reasons, but also because the process was associated primarily with flashy, colour-saturated magazine advertising, a realm far from disinterested science. A case in point, precisely coeval with Schmidt, is the publication of Amedeo Maiuri's lavish *La Villa dei Misteri* in 1931. Director of archaeology at Pompeii, Maiuri's book offered for the first time complete documentation of the Villa of the Mysteries, discovered only two decades earlier, when its lush, compelling frescoes were first unsealed, almost two millennia after the volcano that shut them up. The

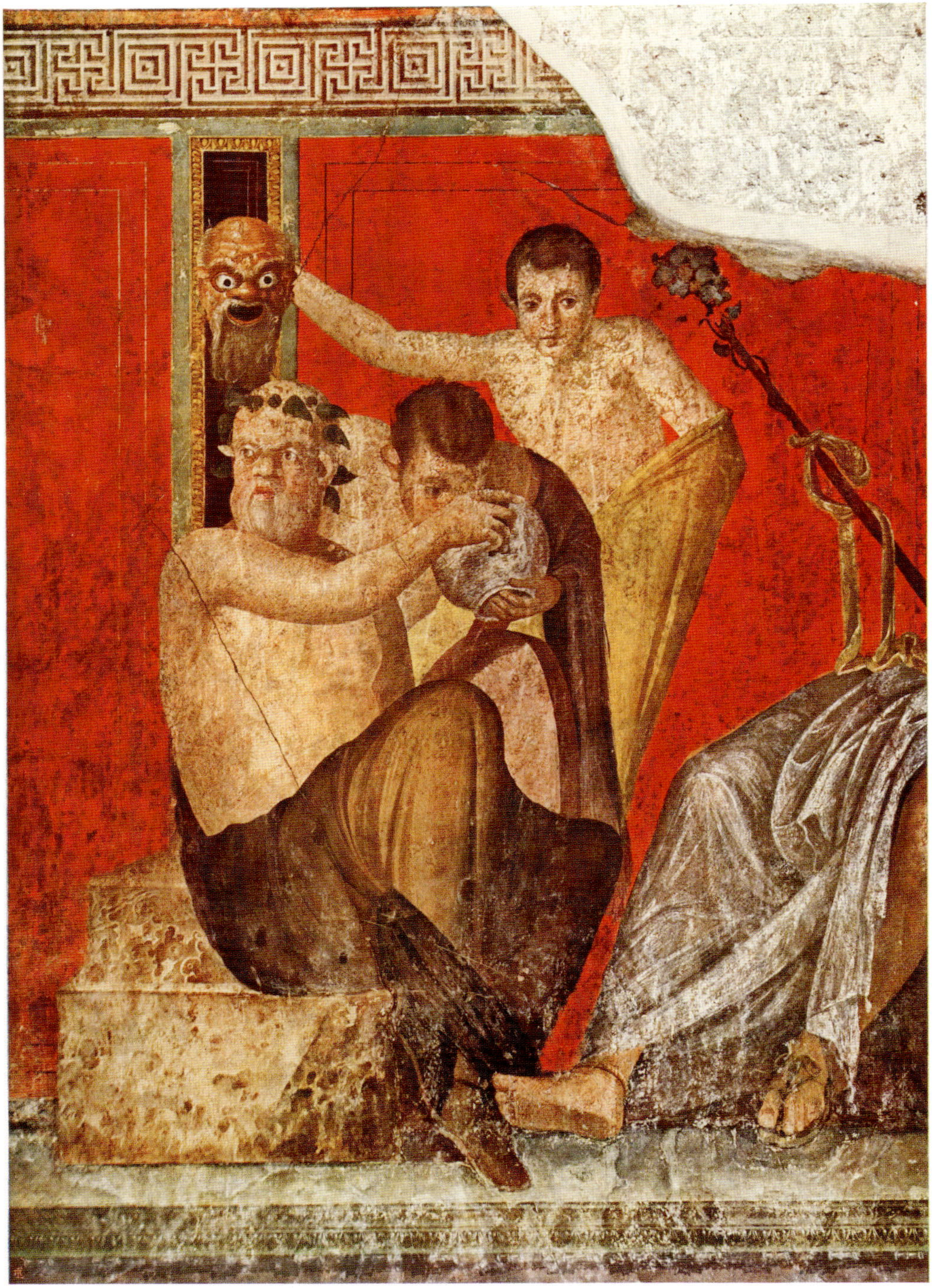

first volume took the conventional format of plans, black-and-white photographs, drawings and engravings. But its spectacular addition was a separate portfolio of framed colour plates made with the then-new tritone colour process. Maiuri succeeded not just in fixing the (ever-deteriorating) colour of the walls of the Villa, but also in making them famous, packaging them into a sought-after luxury volume. Maiuri's controversial success lay in his finding archaeological material to exercise the capabilities of modern colour technology and wide-scale luxury book distribution. But it came at a notable expense. Bettina Bergmann states that: 'The frescoes' ongoing life in photographic reproductions glosses over any breaks or discolorations resulting from nearly a century of exposure and thus perpetuates this misconception.'[21] The misconception is that the frescoes themselves live up to their photographs: as permanently intact and colourful. Moreover, in the process a continuous wall surface is fragmented into a series of framed pictures. A plate entitled 'Silenus and Satyrs' for instance, excludes an elaborate frieze above the figures heads, most likely in order to keep the viewer's attention away from the area of greatest damage to the fresco (illus. 71). Through tight cropping it is just evident (at the top right of the image). Even with such cropping, the loss area extends further into the picture plane in later images in the sequence. Thus aesthetic interest is maintained through selective attention and decontextualization.

The entire edition of *La Villa dei Misteri* sold out almost immediately, while interest remained high enough for a second edition to be printed after the war in 1947. Its example, not least its demonstration of the fame and money that can be gathered through the packaging of archaeological representation, cuts in two directions. First, it is the vanguard of large-scale colour-illustrated archaeological publications designed to go beyond a specialist audience. Perhaps the greatest practitioner of this mode was Mortimer Wheeler, the virtual face (and voice) of English archaeology in popular circles throughout the 1950s and '60s. Wheeler produced a number of large-format archaeological books with impressive colour imagery, in which he often took the role of a sort of authoritative, engaged tour guide, whose work was to gloss images (not just objects) themselves.[22] A description in Wheeler's *Roman Africa in Colour* of a photograph of the Piazza

71 'Silenus and Satyrs', in Amedio Maiuri, *La Villa dei Misteri* (1931), plate 7, trichrome colour print, depicting a portion of the East Wall of Room 5, Villa of the Mysteries, Pompeii.

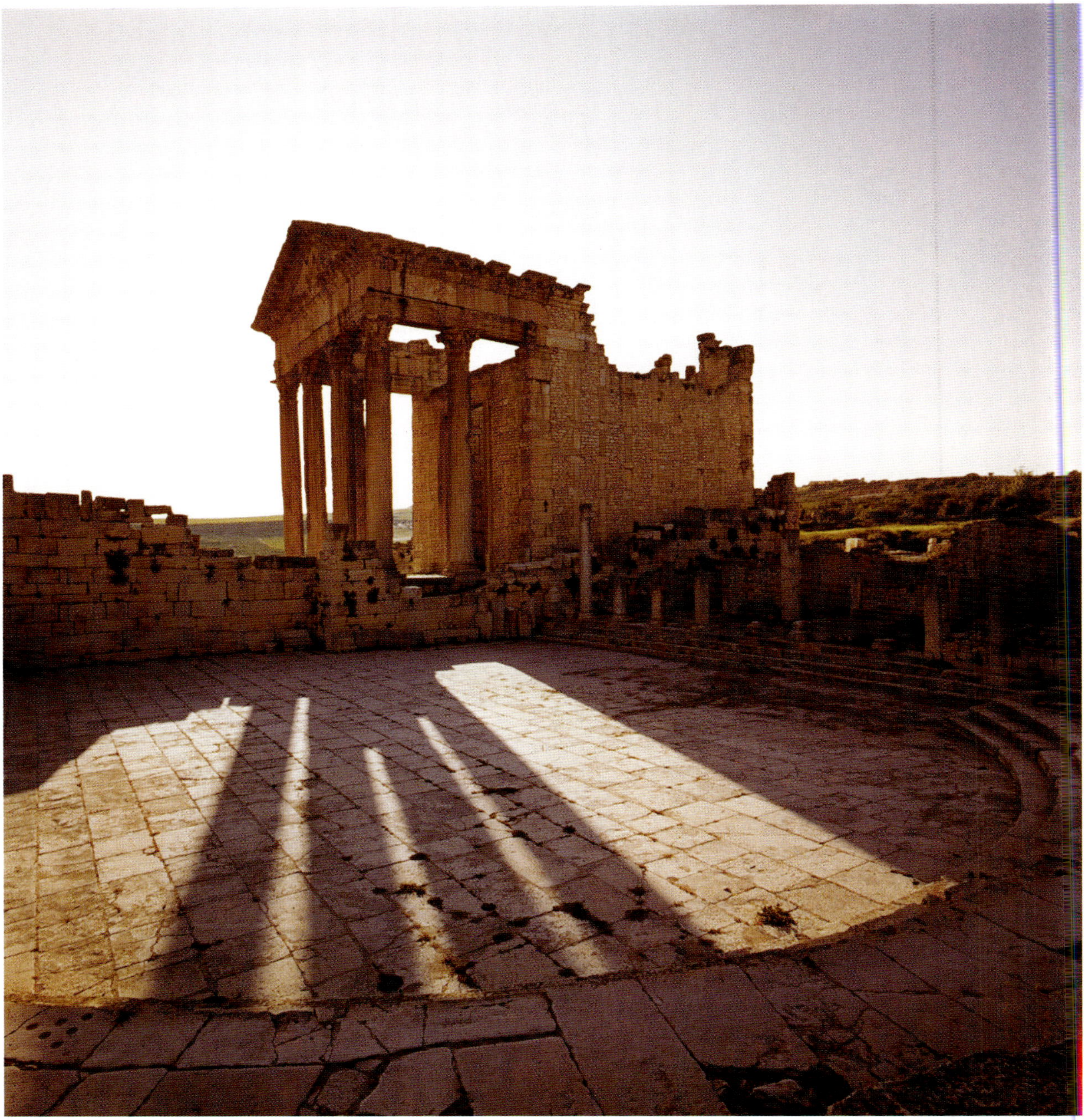

72 Roger Wood, 'Piazza of the Winds', Dugga, Tunisia, in Mortimer Wheeler, *Roman Africa in Colour* (1966), colour photograph.

of the Winds in Dugga, Tunisia, then streaked in evening shadow, begins as follows: 'The evening light brings a new range of colour to the Capitolium of Dugga and emphasizes its sedate and satisfying proportions' (illus. 72). The book's 59 colour plates exquisitely detail sites and artefacts, and Wheeler states 'the text must be regarded merely as a footnote to the photographs'.[23]

Wheeler aspired to far more than the now conventional 'coffee-table' book. Rather, he saw photography, especially colour photography, as a fundamental tool, not just in connecting archaeology to a larger audience, but also in conveying the temporality of monuments, their existence in changing physical contexts, both ancient and modern. Yet Wheeler was well aware of the limitations of such photography. In 1954, he wrote: 'The basic trouble, of course, is that the camera is an awful liar. Its inhuman eye and temperamental interpretation of colour-values combine to falsify the simplest of subjects . . . When colour-processes become the normal medium for archaeological photography, the problem will be simplified though not eliminated.'[24] Wheeler's words are here dominated by a tone of resigned scepticism. Yet even from the seasoned pragmatist, there is also a possible, though still-deferred, future for archaeological photography being fully produced in all the colours of the world.

This visionary quality takes a more radical primacy in a French photographic project of the same time. The work of André Malraux, his *Psychology of Art* (1947) followed by the three-volume *The Voices of Silence* (1951–4), is devoted to the photographic visualization of objects, particularly sculptural antiquities. Malraux's ideal, justified as a next logical step from the isolation of object from context in the art museum, was a purely photographic 'rapprochement', a sort of dialogue of and through images, largely distilled through juxtapositions between the objects reproduced on the books' two-page spreads.[25] Objects of all sorts were photographed and their reproduction elaborately attended to: lighting, cropping, choice of detail and use of framing margins all were finely calibrated to highlight particular qualities. Henri Zerner observes that: 'Like movie stars, Malraux's masterpieces have a virtual existence that can be fully realized only through their photographic reproductions.'[26]

Malraux revelled in the new possibilities of envisioning objects opened by photography. The distillation of objects to visual qualities was for him a liberating project disclosing a visible logic of form and expression, and obviating earthbound questions of material or context. As he expresses it: 'All alike – miniatures, frescoes, stained glass, tapestries, Scythian plaques, pictures, Greek vase paintings, "details" and even statuary – have become "colorplates". In the process they have lost their properties as *objects;* but, by the same token, they have gained something: the utmost significance as to *style* they can possibly acquire.'[27] Malraux's invocation of colour plates is striking. The three volumes of Malraux's *Museum Without Walls of World Sculpture* were actually made up entirely of black-and-white prints, for reasons of affordability. But his mention of colourplate is no mistake. Rather, colour stands as a metaphor of photographic modernity, a liberating ideal. It is the realm of Maiuri's Pompeii as much as the movie stars mentioned by Zerner. Malraux's work did indeed raise each object through photography to a hypostatisized level of exemplar. Each was not an image so much as a 'moment', in Malraux's term, in a totalizing history of stylistic articulation, an event, like a starlet's entrance to the Oscars.

Malraux's reliance on photography tellingly recalls an observation made by Adolf Michaelis, a German classical scholar, almost 50 years earlier. In his book of 1906, *Die Archäologischen Entdeckungen des neunzehnten Jahrhunderls,* among the earliest extended analytical treatments of the emergent archaeological methodology, Michaelis repeatedly hailed the new use of photography. At one point he states excitedly that: 'With the help of photography we have learned to see anew, and it is not the least part of the influence of photography that all modern archaeology has taken up consideration of stylistic analysis and valuation.'[28] The optimistic, almost visionary tone itself seems to presage Malraux. Michaelis goes on to note the related connection of art history with archaeology, bringing the 'stylistic, artistic viewpoint into the foreground'.

Michaelis may particularly have had in mind the example of Alexander Conze, whose archaeological album of his excavations at Samothrace, published in 1875–80, was illustrated with finely printed photos made by Wilhelm Burger. Michaelis had worked with Conze, and even dedicated the volume to him (see illus. 23). Photography here gives

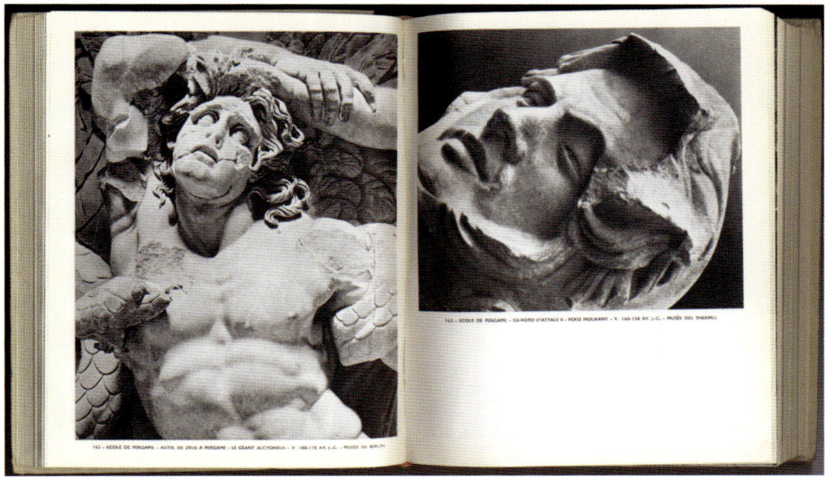

73 André Malraux, spread from *The Museum Without Walls of World Sculpture* (1952).

archaeology a heightened means to participate in the questions of style then animating the new art history associated with Alois Riegl and the Vienna School of art history. The works of 'Hellenistic Baroque' brought to museums in Paris and Berlin under Conze's aegis – notably the Louvre's Winged Victory and Berlin's Pergamon Altar – are pictured by Malraux and are among the most photogenic of the volume.

These huge, visually daunting artefacts are thus distilled into photographs. For instance, with a complex play of light on deep reliefs, faces tilted within swirling compositions, and the head fragment at right in a slightly gauzy focus, the details of the Pergamon Altar illustrated by Malraux become satisfying and deeply expressive photographic images (illus. 73). These acquisitions, both with places of pride in their respective museums, are products of an archaeology itself formed through a stylistically attuned photographic vision and, with Malraux, set out for an equally photographically oriented audience.

Archaeologists, just like art historians, or perhaps anyone who deals in detail with disparate objects, know objects through their photographs, and may well come to prefer, if only for practical reasons, the photographs to the 'real' things. Thus the archaeologist Elmer Harp wrote in 1975: 'Even in one's own laboratory it will sometimes be easier to work analytically from a batch of photographs than it is to manipulate a collection of

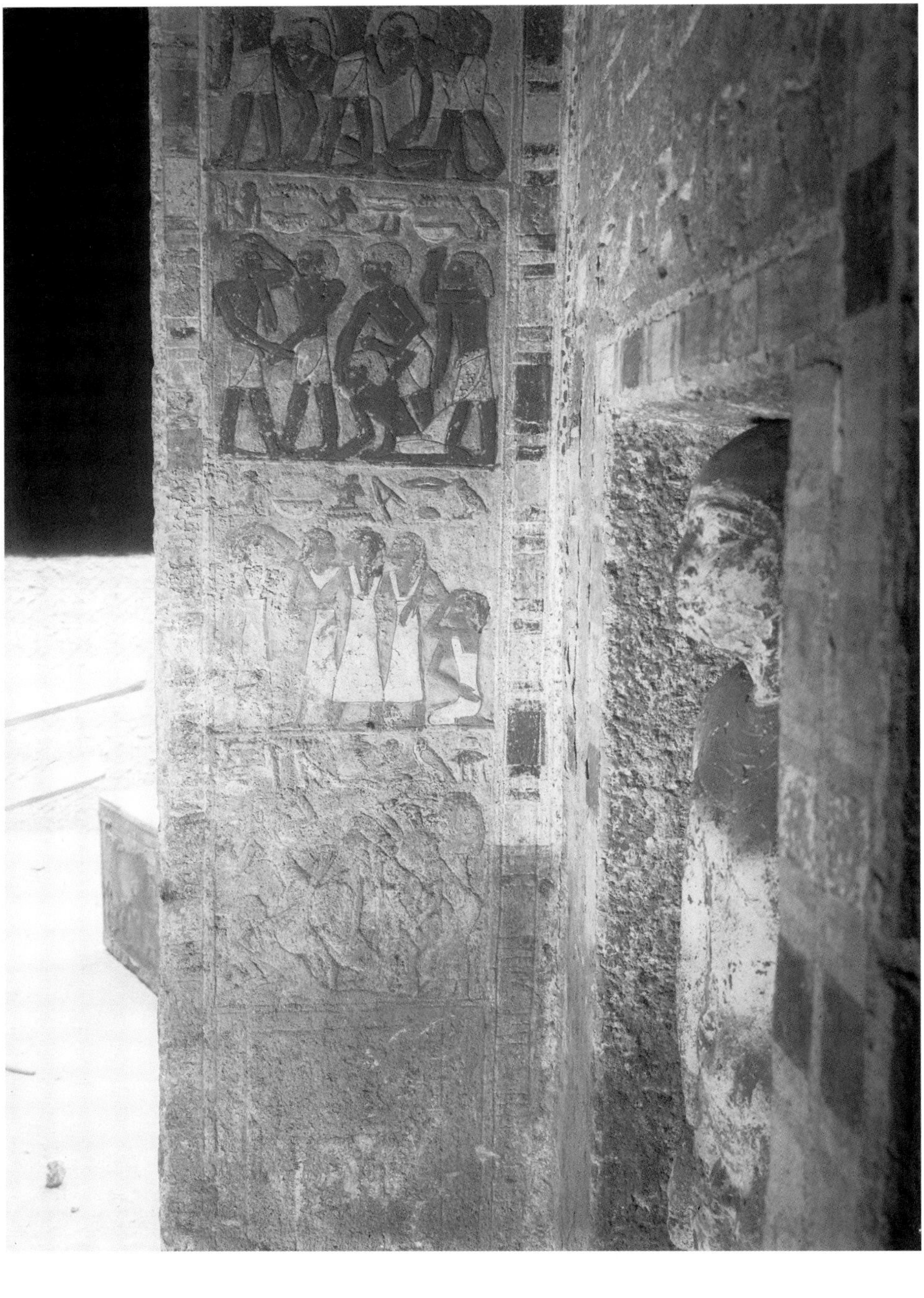

specimens.'[29] Even when artefacts are extant, they can thus virtually become their photographs. Photography emerges as the fundamental medium of archaeological exchange, keeping artefacts themselves safely ensconced in museum vaults.

The 'alienation' that Kracauer found endemic to both photography and history is acted out most dramatically in another genre of archaeological photography, that of inscription photography. Here not only is the photograph distilled reductively from the object, but it is also then reduced even from itself. The problem might be articulated by a photograph of an inscription in the Mastaba of Idu, a tomb in the great Eastern Cemetery at Giza, taken in 1925 by a Harvard/MFA team (illus. 74). It is part of a systematic survey, and presented in a strict locative taxonomy, specifying that it shows the middle registers of a relief on the portion of the north wall to the east of the entrance. Yet the precision of the labelling is hardly matched by the visual information of the image. In this constrained space the photographer does not have room to step back to take in the entire sequence, leading to an idiosyncratic cropping of the tomb's visually continuous information. Further, the sequence is progressively more damaged toward the bottom, like a length of film that suddenly becomes unintelligible, so to the unaided eye the documentation is of little use.

Petrie's manual, of 1904, provided the fundamental precedent for disentangling inscription from slab. In an essay from over 60 years later, the Egyptologist Bernard Bothmer describes a meeting of an archaeologist and a philologist, called A. and P., interested in obtaining inscriptions, in which the quest continues. 'P. and A. meet in Cairo only every five years or so, and there has not been a competent photographer available to either of them in Egypt for a long time.' They take it upon themselves to do the work, and directly improve upon one of the tricks of Petrie. 'In the old days, scholars and photographers, in unholy alliance, used to sprinkle flour or white powder into such poorly visible inscriptions, which, in part, made them more visible, but also blurred most of the details' (see illus. 44).[30] Bothmer's technique is less invasive, a light wipe with a slightly moist cloth. Pages are devoted to the details of equipment, setting, lighting and technique required. But the climax is quite simple:

74 Mohammedani Ibrahim, 'Giza, Eastern Cemetery, Cemetery G7102, Idu Chapel. N wall, E of entrance, middle registers of relief, looking N', 1925, gelatin silver print.

greater progress in the same project. 'The greatest recompense is, however, when P. admits that he can see a detail of an inscription better on the photograph than on the original.'[31] Photography has made new progress in a project we have seen begun by Fox Talbot himself, now fully snatching ideational content from its material vault. It does not merely capture but actually improves upon the hieroglyphic inscription itself.

More innovative is the philological activity pictured in the *Biologia Centrali-Americana* of Alfred P. Maudslay, published in parts between 1889 and 1902. Considerable advances in reading glyphs had taken place since the age of Charnay, and Maudslay's title, like his work, reflects his more purely scientific, analytical interests, not least in compiling one of the first significant corpuses of Mayan inscriptions. A plate devoted to two piers in the Temple of Inscriptions at Palenque confronts us with

75 Alfred Percival Maudslay, 'Temple of Inscriptions', in *Biologia Centrali-Americana* (1889–1902), vol. IV, plate 53, combined photograph and engraving.

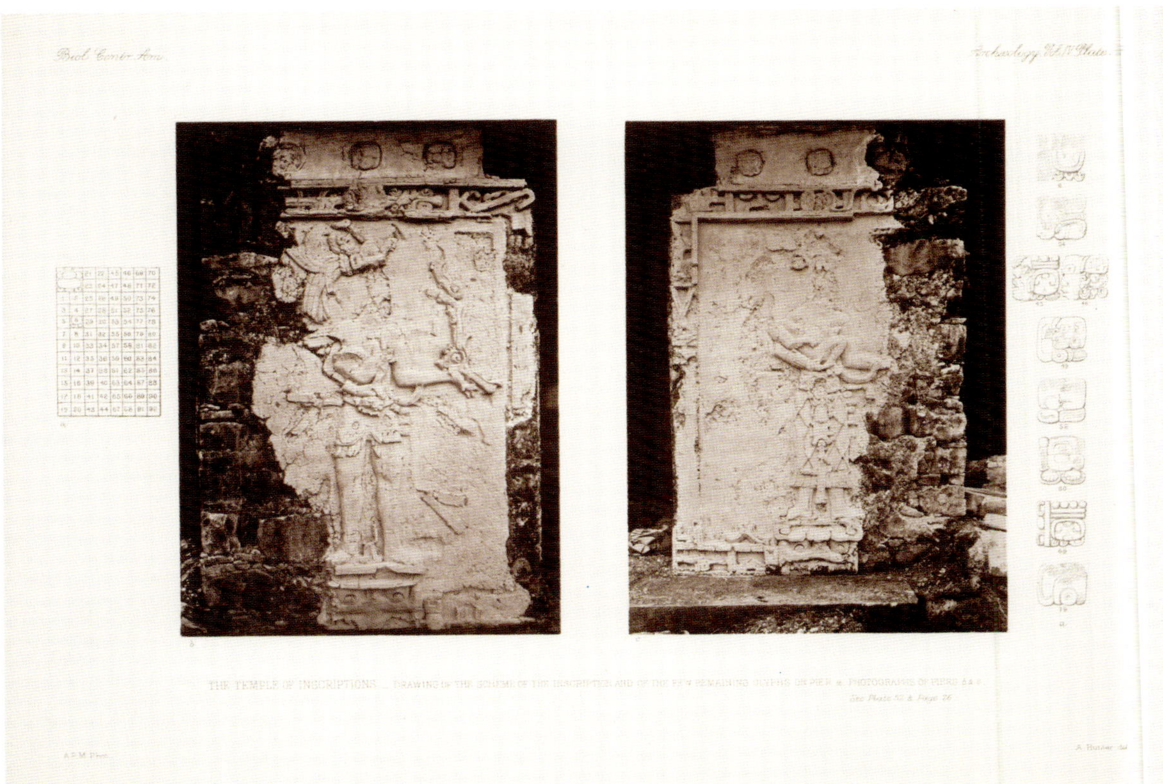

photographs of the considerably damaged monuments, but by their side are engraved glyphs, to be orientated in the plane of the monuments according to a numerical grid shown to the left (illus. 75). The writing signs are not depicted *in situ* so much as harvested or delivered from their ruined locale. Other plates in the book reproduce with greater clarity large fields of Mayan writing, but they are photographed from casts rather than from their less forthcoming original source. In both cases, photography's value to the epigrapher is not to make the monument available in its current state, but to coax linguistic signifiers from *beyond* their material condition.

Yet this is just the beginning of the scientific filtering of appearance enacted in hieroglyphic study. In the early twentieth century a new technique emerged, involving direct drawing over photographs, in effect re-recording the photographic record.[32] This method was taken up and systematized by James Henry Breasted. Trained in the German philological tradition of hieroglyphic scholarship, in a direct line from Lepsius, Breasted founded the University of Chicago's Oriental Institute as a centre for applying rigorous scientific method to archaeological endeavour throughout the Middle East. Breasted devoted decades to what is now generally known as the Chicago Epigraphic Survey. Founded in 1924 and based in Luxor, its fundamental mission is 'to produce photographs and precise line drawings of the inscriptions and relief scenes on major temples and tombs at Luxor for publication'.[33] Modern Luxor contains ancient Thebes as well as Karnak, two of the very sites on Arago's list of what a single camera could speedily accomplish. Far from being quickly done, today, more than 80 years after its founding, the task is hardly completed.

But the progress of the Chicago Epigraphic Survey illustrates something far more striking than the actual size of the project. It says much about the efficacy now accorded to photography to achieve it. As Maria Golia well notes: 'So painstaking is the process that it has taken longer to copy the inscriptions, even with the camera's help, then it did to carve them in the first place.'[34] Breasted's initial method was to take images in a room with a large-format camera, together with a trained epigrapher. The negative would be developed and printed on the spot, after which it would be 'corrected' by the epigrapher to fill in any gaps. Yet over time, as Jeffrey Abt has shown, the role of the epigrapher expanded against that of the camera. While the role of photography could never disappear, it was distinctly constrained.

By 1933, Breasted wrote, in a tone of resignation that is perhaps now familiar: 'However valuable the camera may be, the current impression that a mechanical photographic record is sufficient is fundamentally incorrect.'[35] He then went on to list its many failings in not capturing what is evident to the trained eye. By this time, well into the working of the Epigraphic Survey, Breasted had codified what is now known as the Chicago House Method. It is an elaborate process involving the collaboration of a photographer, an artist and several epigraphers, described by Breasted in fourteen separate steps. Strikingly, the photographer is both the enabler and the least prominent part of the process.

The recording begins with a photographer making a print on site, and a draftsman holding it up against the original and pencilling in all that he sees over it, especially any portion of the original not evident in the photograph. Back in the studio, the pencil lines are then inked, including adding a series of conventions of line thicknesses to show different dimensions in the relief and all signs of damage. Following this inking, and perhaps the most remarkable step, the photograph is placed into a chemical bath which bleaches away the entire photographic emulsion, leaving an inked line drawing. All signs of photographic registration are thus effaced. Only at this point, the fifth of Breasted's fourteen steps, do trained epigraphers become involved. From the (now) drawing, 'collation sheets' are made, ordinary blueprints which Egyptologists (always more than one, to avoid subjective idiosyncrasy) read, compare with any related known inscriptions, then take back to the original site to further refine and correct. Only after a full consensus is the resultant image deemed correct, and sent back to Chicago for processing and publication as part of an authoritative, large-format folio.

Among a volume devoted to the Theban tomb of Kheruf, for instance, one finds a treatment of an inscription of King Amenhotep III found on a wall surface (illus. 76). The particular placement of the inscription allows it to be clearly photographed in a way not always available in

76 Charles S. Nims and Reginald H. Coleman, 'Inscription of Amenhotep III dated to Year Thirty, Second Month of Third Season, Day Twenty-Seven', in *The Tomb of Kheruf, Theban Tomb 192* (1980), plates 27 and 28, gelatin silver print and halftone print.

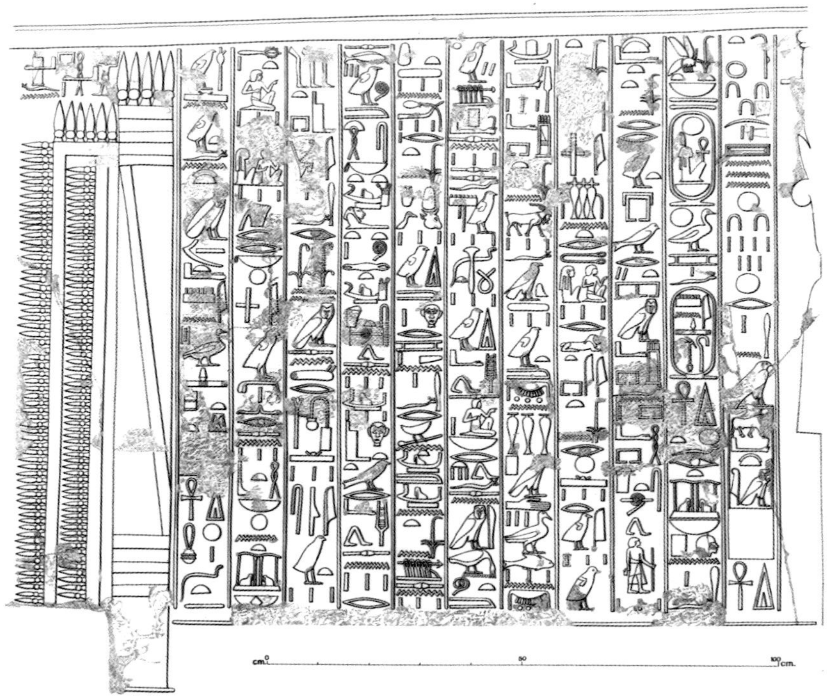
cm 0
50
100 cm

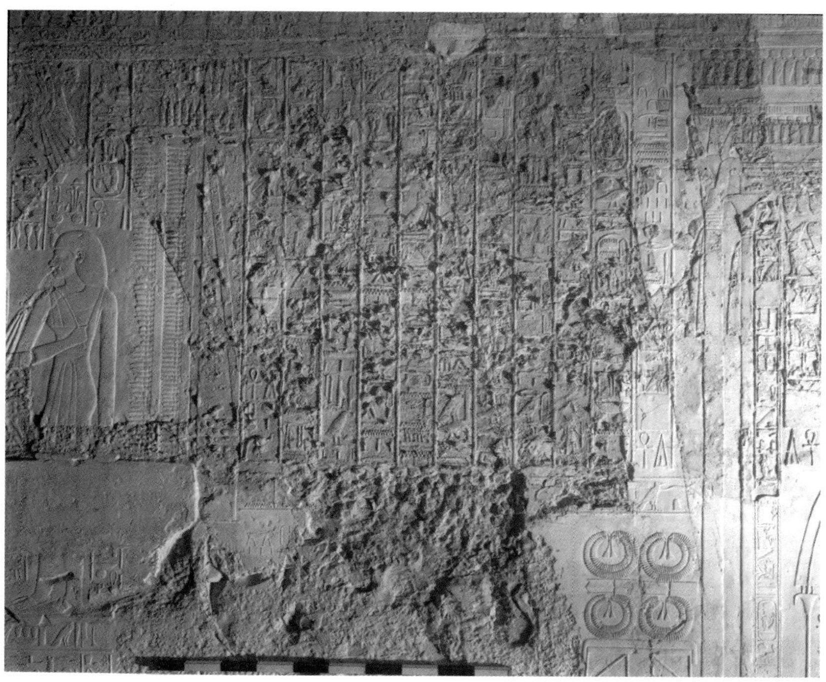

ancient Egyptian settings (see also illus. 74). But the inscription in the photograph is unclear for another reason, namely the levels of decomposition and spots of material accretion of the wall surface, which attack its decoration and interfere with the raking light set up to illuminate the raised inscription. From the initial, barely legible, photograph to the final, seemingly pristine, engraving is a remarkable jump, which notably removes the inscription from the rest of the wall surface in which it is embedded.

Breasted's method, among the most concerted ever applied to recording inscriptions, certainly exemplifies the rigorous scientific method he espoused. It is reductive rather than accretive. While it depends on photography, it actually accomplishes its goal by filtering out, or working against, the photographic component. While inconceivable without photography, it works to redeem the photograph from its photographic-ness, easing its transition from product of an individual viewpoint to a viewer-less, immaterial objectivity. Only thus is it compiled into the many folio volumes that constitute its archive for philologists.

In an archaeology in which artefacts are construed through photography, they are never far from being construed as art. Yet for just that reason, as we have already seen, a boundary between the two is continually maintained. Hieroglyphic recording is photography's most dramatic retreat from itself under the aegis of archaeology. Moving in the opposite direction, crossing the very threshold of art that has been present throughout, will be the subject of our final chapter.

four

# Art, or Reframing

As we have seen repeatedly, over a span of more than a century from Mérimée to Petrie to a recent encyclopedia entry, archaeology has taken pains to characterize its photographic images as purely documentary material evidence, not products of individual imagination or aesthetic delectation. Archaeology's assertion that its images are artless, distinct from art's proper realm, can be pictured most directly by tracking one further aspect of the representational fortune of the German excavations at Olympia.

In 1882 another volume appeared on the Olympia finds, quite unlike the many ponderous and text-heavy volumes of the official excavation report. A product of the refined Berlin publisher Ernst Wasmuth, *Die Funde von Olympia* (Discoveries from Olympia) was a single thin volume whose core consisted of 40 meticulously printed images of selected objects. In light of the disappointing (to some governmental sponsors) lack of a treasure trove of museum-worthy finds, it attempts to highlight and reframe the available aspirants to masterpiece status. Text was minimal, consisting only of brief introductions to each section. Yet the section on sculpture (the largest single portion) was written by Ernst Curtius himself, the overall excavation leader, and thus retained authoritative imprimatur.

*Die Funde von Olympia* displays a very different photographic framework from that of normative, scientific archaeology. A head of Apollo is not simply masked against a blank white background, as in the official album, but rather posed on a velvety black base, its tonalities captured among the detailed shadings of the resonant, subtle image (illus. 77). Further, whereas the authorship of photographs is virtually never directly acknowledged in the earlier album, here the images bear a surfeit of credits. Many images, like this one, bear an internal credit to the photographers Constantine and Aristotelis Romaidis, while each plate is also proudly stamped as the printing work of the Dresden firm Römmler & Jonas. The Romaidis brothers were the primary photographers of the excavation, and produced most of the images in the official album as well. But conventions of artistic rendering in photography differ from those of science in allowing, indeed welcoming, acknowledgement of individual image makers, encouraging the viewer to look *at* the photograph itself, not merely *through* it to the object documented.

One of the most striking viewpoints shown in *Die Funde von Olympia* is perhaps that of the 'Nike of Paionos'. This object now appears both more palpable and more fragmented (illus. 78, see also illus. 63). It is divorced from its unconnected fragments, restricted in a frame that dramatizes it as a single, tangible object. The lighting falls over body and drapery in a way that is far more dramatic than the flat lighting of the official album. Yet this seeming drive toward materiality, focused on a single, intact object, is also mitigated by the frame. The image minimizes the figure's intact base, which is considerable, as we have seen, but is here wiped out with a straight line. These different photos of the Nike are thus occasions for articulating different conceptions of a common object, now seeing it as art object rather than historical artefact. There are both additions, of pictorial effects and background, and subtractions, of less aesthetically amenable portions of the object.

The artefacts from Olympia could thus be processed in different ways. Art and science stand for distinct modes of envisioning that are tied to distinct audiences.

Decades after the Olympia excavations, and on the other side of the globe, one finds a more extreme example of the fragmentation of archaeological vision. Like Mohenjo-Daro, it is a harbinger of the increasing political significance of archaeological finds as indigenous populations sought to stake out identities distinct from those imposed by Western modernization. In 1911 a young Yale historian, Hiram Bingham,

77 Constantine Romaidis, 'Head of Apollo, West Gable', in *Die Funde von Olympia* (1882), plate 13, photolithograph.

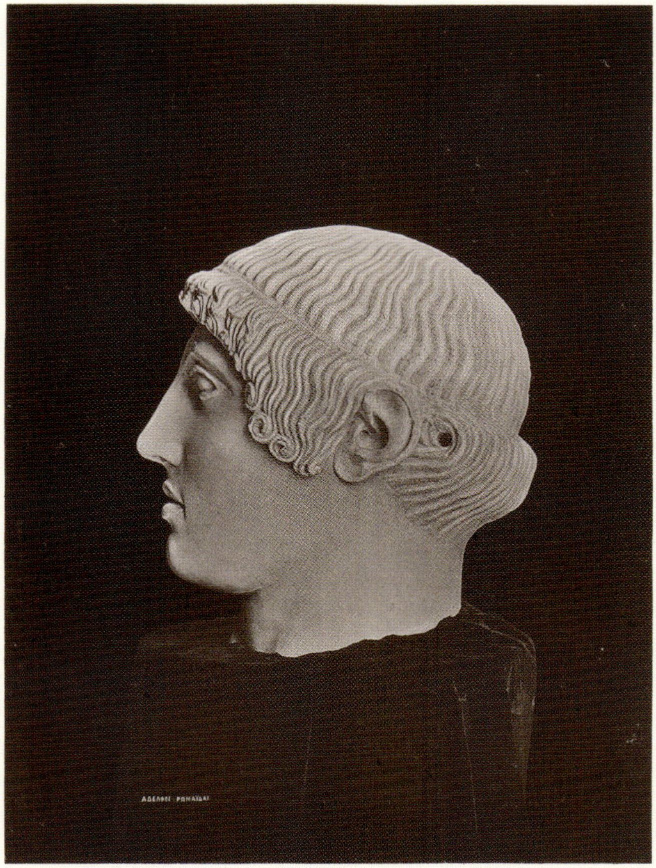

VERLAG VON ERNST WASMUTH, BERLIN. LICHTDRUCK VON RÖMMLER & JONAS, DRESDEN.

APOLLON-KOPF.

WESTGIEBEL.

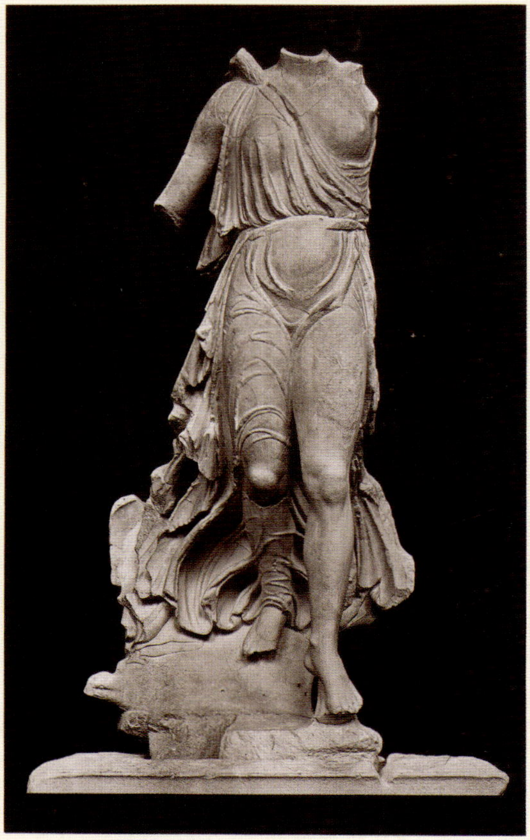

VERLAG VON ERNST WASMUTH, BERLIN. LICHTDRUCK VON RÖMMLER & JONAS, DRESDEN.

NIKE DES PAIONIOS.

rediscovered the lost Inca settlement of Machu Picchu, on a narrow saddle of rock high in the Andean mountains. Supported in his work by the magazine *National Geographic* as well as by his university, over several years he isolated its structures from dense foliage and later buildings. His 1930 report on the explorations is resolutely accessible to the organization's larger, popular audience and does not exclude lauding the beauty of his discoveries. Among his finds were what Bingham termed 'the most beautiful wall in America' while among descriptions of tomb spaces he states of the royal mausoleum, which is situated in a cave beneath a central temple, that: 'None of the other tombs found in the caves of Machu Picchu compares for a moment with this one in beauty or splendor.'[1]

While Bingham's own workmanlike photographs illustrate his volume, his vision is both aesthetically elaborated and ideologically appropriated in the photographs of Martin Chambí. An acculturated member of a Quechua-speaking family from a small Peruvian town, Chambí was meticulously trained in photography and rose to fame as a portraitist among the Cuzco elite. He was an outspoken proponent of the 'Indigenismo' movement, which demanded that indigenous peoples and their traditions be honoured and protected within the drive to modernization. Chambí's visits to Machu Picchu in the 1920s brought more than a trained photographic eye to the site. Edward Ranney notes: 'The publication of [Chambí's] photographs in the national press signaled the reclaiming of it as a national symbol.'[2]

Chambí's remarkable photograph of the interior of the royal mausoleum surely heightens Bingham's observation (illus. 79). The camera looks out from the rooms' depth, framing the entrance stonework outside with a heightened effect of light and shadow that grazes the interior stones and finely illuminates their textures, almost a trace of some immanent force within. It is a primal play of geometric forms, in which the scratches and graffiti left on its surface by centuries of visitors are also visible. Chambí, who in other images of Machu Picchu framed contemporary indigenous peoples in its archways, in a sense takes ownership of the site, settling into it on a native's behalf, just as his viewpoint literally opposes that of Bingham, reversing the archaeologist's more conventional choice of peering into the tomb from the entrance.

78 Constantine Romaidis, 'Nike of Paionios', in *Die Funde von Olympia* (1882), plate 16, photolithograph.

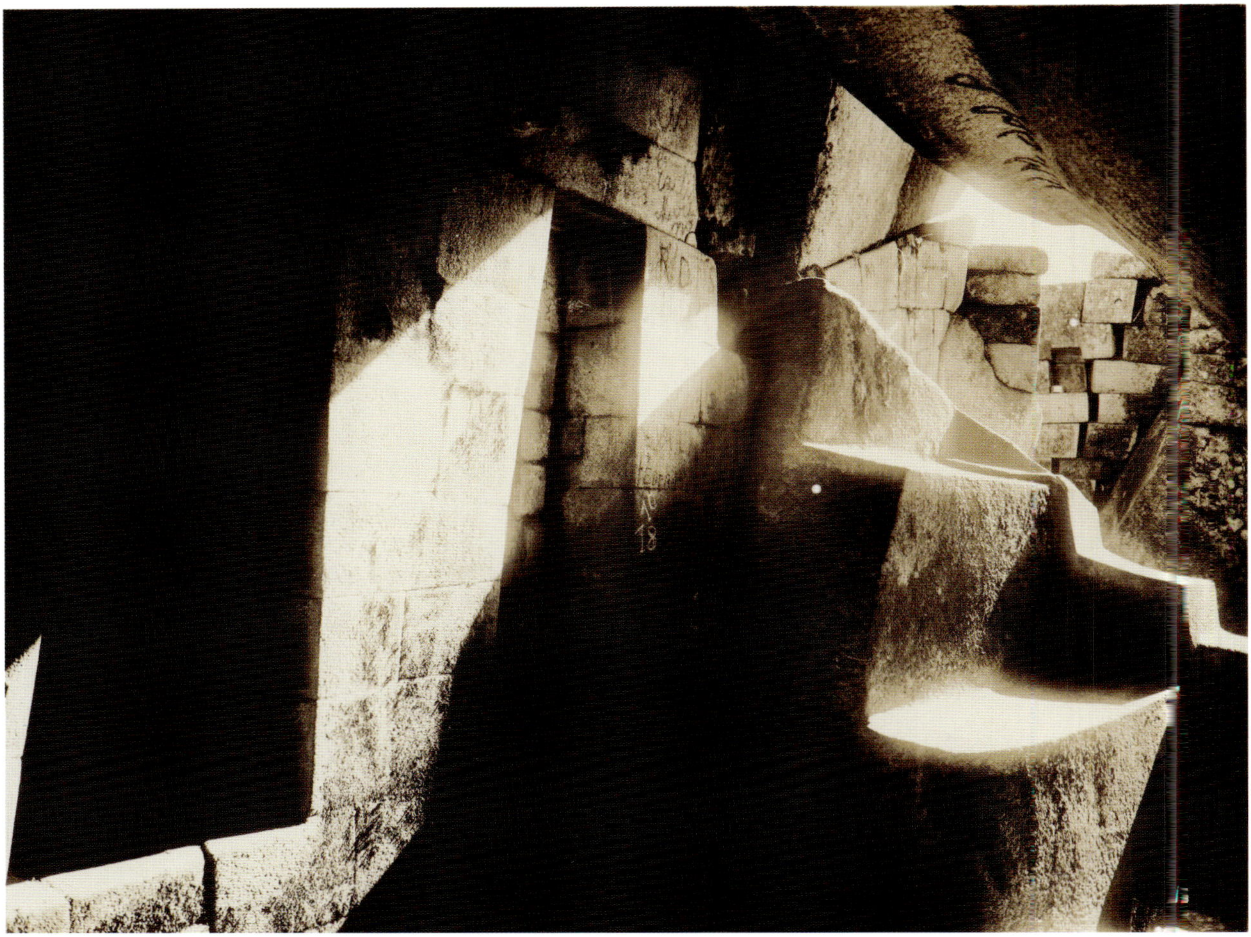

79 Martin Chambí, 'Interior View of Royal Mausoleum showing the Entrance Stonework below the Torreón, Machu Picchu, Peru', 1927, gelatin silver print.

The photographs of Chambí, like those taken of Olympia, explore (one might even say excavate) an aesthetic identity that is present but deliberately underdeveloped in archeological vision. With Chambí that vision can even be associated with a distinct political position. But art and science are not necessarily on opposite sides in archaeological representation, despite our assumption of them as 'two cultures'. Indeed, looking beyond this conventional opposition leads to some of the most striking images in archaeological photography.

The remarkable photographs in Auguste Salzmann's book *Jérusalem* (1856) have long both compelled and puzzled modern viewers. Salzmann had toured Jerusalem and related areas of Palestine on a grant from the French Ministry of Public Education, part of the same wave of state-sponsored topographical projects behind the Mission Héliographique as well as Du Camp's voyage to Egypt. Salzmann's particular charge was to provide material in connection with the historical hypothesis of the French archaeologist Félix de Saulcy. Saulcy had spent much time examining remains throughout the ancient city and, in a series of publications, had argued that they dated from the time of the ancient Hebrews rather than, as was then generally accepted, from the much more recent Byzantine past. Saulcy had published some of his own drawings in support of his thesis, but lacked the authoritative witness of the photographic camera to substantiate them. He thus hired Salzmann, whom he lauded as a 'painter, archaeologist and scholar', to aid him.[3]

In the preface to *Jérusalem*, Salzmann wrote directly of his intention to counter those who 'without getting up from their armchairs are the defenders of established opinion' by using photography 'to render a true service to science'.[4] Salzmann's text is comparable to that of other archaeological literature of the time, largely discussing Saulcy's theory in detail, especially as illuminated through particular objects. An example of Salzmann's imagery at its most evidentiary is a photograph of several cubic capitals imbedded in a wall (illus. 80). Salzmann's text identifies them as ancient Hebrew workmanship, pointing to their characteristic 'vegetal ornamentation'. Strikingly, though, Salzmann's caption to the image uses a specific term for artistic production, deeming them 'Remnants of Judaic Sculpture'.

In other images, better known today, Salzmann's work employs visual devices of artistic composition, with complex lighting, textures and cropping that often work to obscure the purely documentary function of photographic recording. A photograph of a carved stone staircase leading to a rubbish dump, for instance, moves from a light upper level downwards into a darkened pathway (illus. 81). The darkness of the lower stairs obscures the steps, which register more like light, painterly streaks on the final print. Indeed, details of surface and construction, which are so clear in the upper portion of the photo, seem systematically removed from the lower portion, almost as if by a conjuring trick, making the location of the camera itself unclear. Salzmann's photograph makes the scene tangible more than legible, indicative, as Randy Innes has written, of an 'existential investment'.[5]

A trained painter who had exhibited at the Paris Salon, Salzmann was surely as familiar with the techniques of artistic rendering as he was with contemporary archaeological debate. Modern commentators on Salzmann can be puzzled by the sometimes extraordinary beauty of his

81 Auguste Salzmann, 'Antique Stairway Carved in Rock Leading to Ancient "Porte du Fumier"', 1854, in *Jérusalem* (1856), salt print.

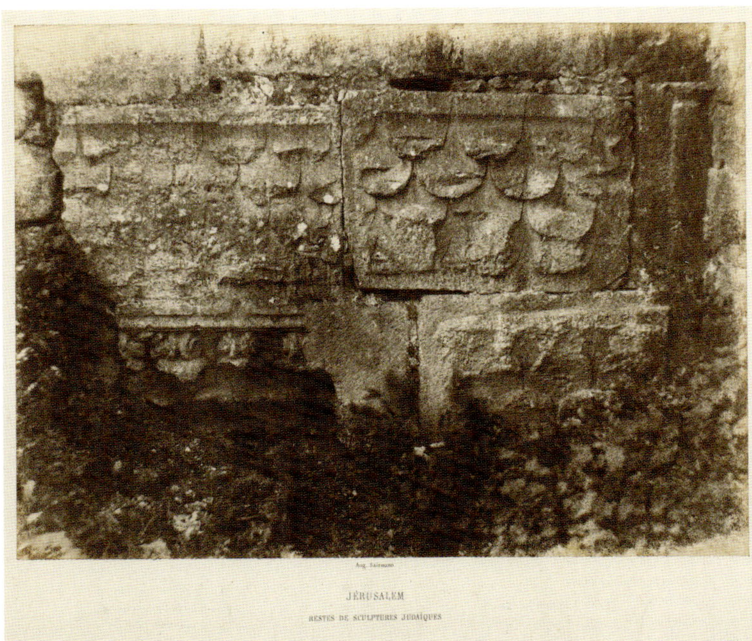


80 Auguste Salzmann, 'Remains of Judaic Sculpture', 1854, in *Jérusalem* (1856), salt print.

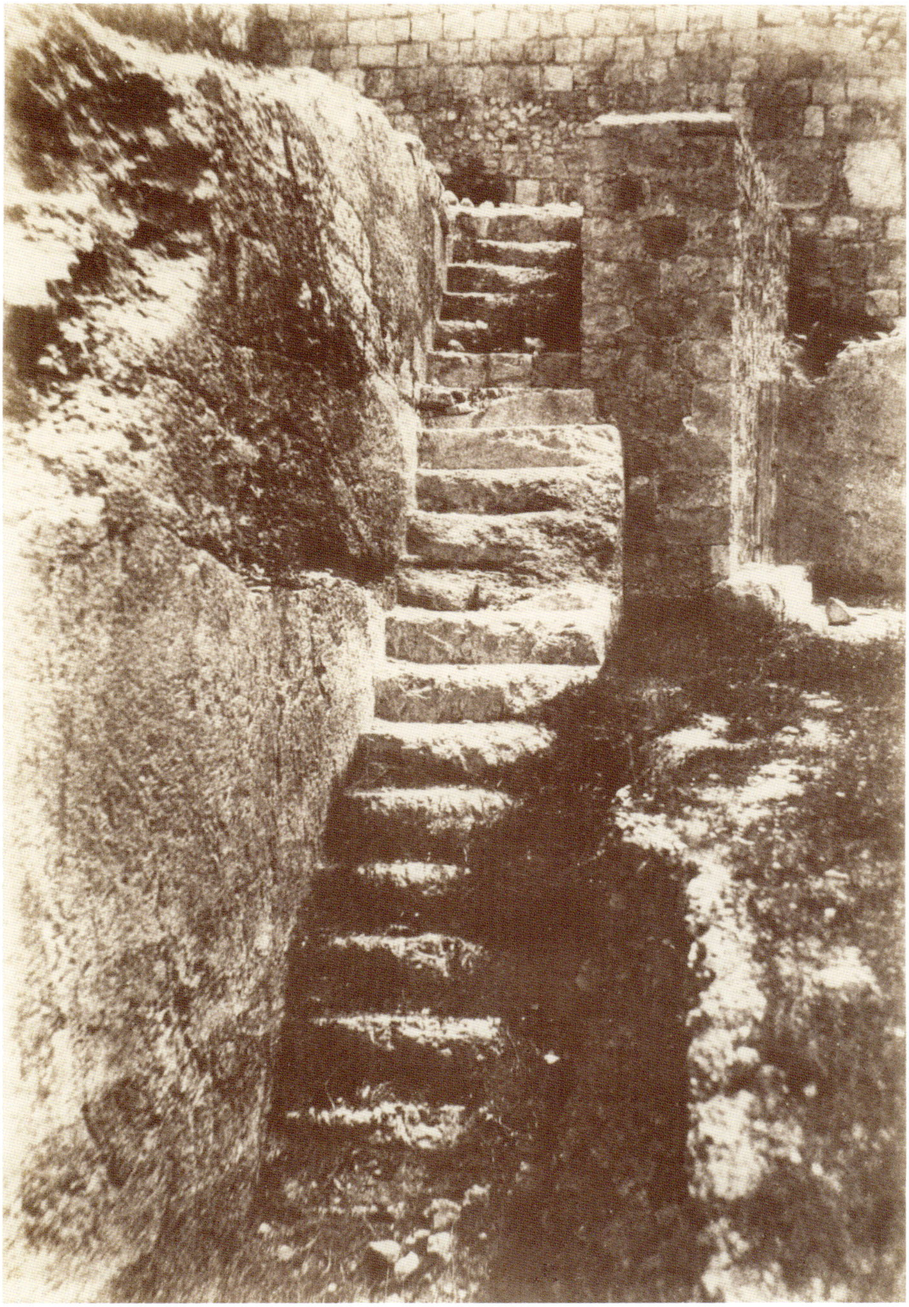

work, and often resolutely resist deeming him an artist-photographer. Thus, Abagail Solomon-Godeau states, 'this titular elevation is an ahistorical projection of contemporary attitudes and assumptions about photography'.[6] In fact, the inability to see Salzmann's photographs for what they are stems as much from an anachronistic modern assumption, not about art but the historical complexity of archaeology.

At just about the same time, Saulcy had published another work on the topic that went against established opinion, his *History of Judaic Art* (1858). In his preface, he again recounted the profound impact of viewing remains in Jerusalem nearly a decade earlier. Rather than accepting the received opinion that 'Judaic art does not exist and never has' Saulcy noted that as he accumulated sketches in his portfolio he 'acquired the certitude, with proof in hand, not only that the axiom in question was false, but that the Judaic nation had brought the arts to a very high level of perfection'.[7] Saulcy's theory on the existence and age of ancient Judaic artefacts in Jerusalem, product of the actual visual impact of the objects (and most directly offered to a reader through Salzmann's photographs), was inextricably tied to his apprehension of them as objects of art. The fusion of artistic and artefactual rendering found throughout Salzmann's photography is no anomaly, then, but a direct visual argument that, like Salzmann's choices of subjects and written text, supports Saulcy's position on the nature of Judaic antiquities.

In practice, that is, art cannot be so easily or categorically detached from archaeological vision. A notable case in point is the work of perhaps the greatest archaeological photographer of Greek antiquities in the past half-century, Alison Frantz. A Columbia PhD in classical archaeology, she directed excavations in late Antique and medieval sites as well as serving as official photographer to numerous digs in ancient Greece, working for 25 years with the Agora excavations of the American School of Classical Studies at Athens, for instance. Frantz's photography of ancient Greek sites and objects is renowned for its clarity and precision. She is among the few photographers consistently credited in her own right on the title page of scholarly monographs. Her works are perfect for the archaeological analysis they are used in, not merely in illustrating what is to be seen by the archaeologist, but also in doing the very work of seeing. The classicist Brunilde Ridgway noted that 'Frantz's use of lighting frequently rendered visible what could not be seen even when standing in front of a piece.'[8] Frantz's work was indeed commonly made with deep dramatic lighting, either sunlight or artificial, as well as complex filtering or later darkroom work. But unlike other professional photographers of Greek antiquity of the time, such as Walter Hege, Hermann Wagner or Fred Boissonas, Frantz's work does not immediately heroize the image to assert a 'style'. Rather, closer to the fashion of Clarence Kennedy, an art historian

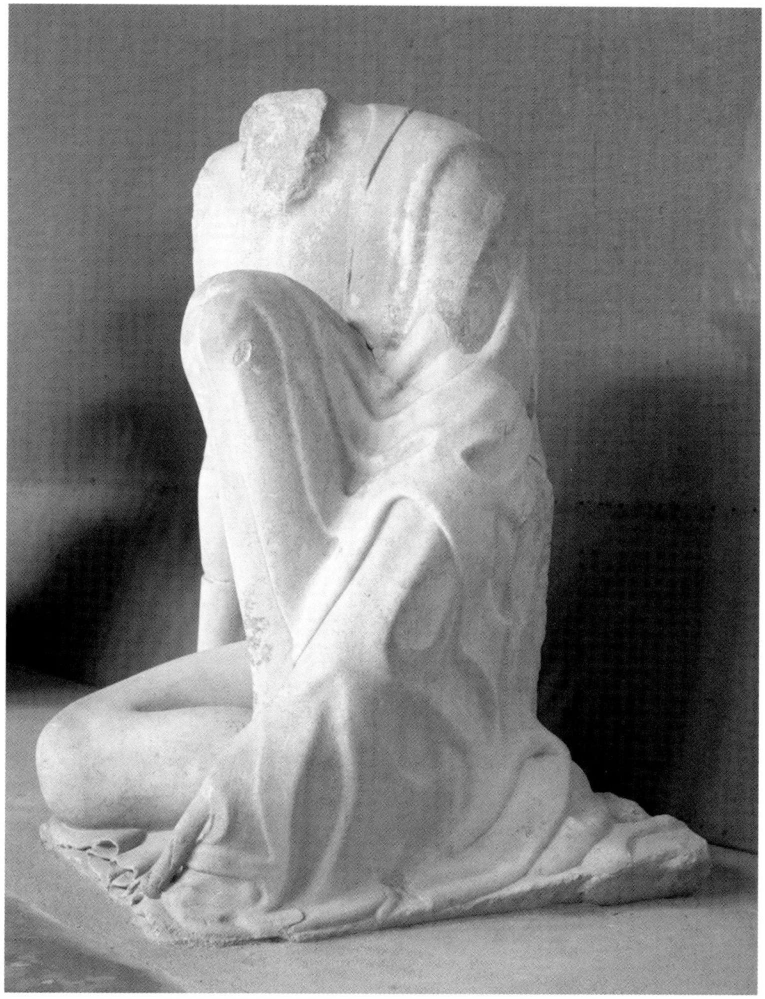

82 Alison Frantz, 'Temple of Zeus Pediment, East, Seated Boy, perhaps Arkas. Olympia, Olympia Archaeological Museum', 1964, gelatin silver print.

at Smith College when Frantz was an undergraduate, who photographed ancient and medieval sculpture, Frantz's work has an intimacy with its objects that seems almost unmediated. Yet, as Amy Papalexandrou and Marie Mauzy state: '[Frantz's] perceived "objectivity" in recording was, in fact, produced through subjective manipulation of her medium, this in large measure to support the underlying scholarly message, or "facts", of observation.'[9] Frantz's photography works most artfully to conceal its considerable art, to convince viewers that the image itself is respectfully truthful while its palpable beauty is the sole property of the object itself.

A photograph of a pedimental sculpture, a seated boy from the temple of Zeus at Olympia, confronts us with a figure covered in drapery (illus. 82). Its folds upon folds of drapery are almost like a series of cursive inscriptions written upon a body, a remarkable effect of patterning that diminishes the three-dimensionality of the figure, flattening the raised left knee against the torso. The effect is surely a product of the skill of an ancient sculptor, but it is here heightened by the oblique viewpoint and further conjured by bathing the figure in a complex chiaroscuro lighting, and presenting it against a background of varied tonality, which leads the eye by an implicit line through the shadow at the sculpture's (and body's) very centre. It is a perfect view for a student of ancient sculptural practice, but enlarges that audience to include anyone who can appreciate formal beauty.

Frantz wrote of her approach in a playful essay entitled 'Truth Before Beauty or, The Incompleat Photographer' in 1950.[10] In it she describes the various tools of her trade – photographic set-ups, lighting, use of flash, filters, backgrounds – as well as some of her experiences. Its conversational tone belies its authoritative nature. Much of Frantz's formula was based on a pre-existing idea on both how a photograph was utilized and what was to be looked for. Frantz always looked with the eyes of an archaeologist, after all, and hewed also to a certain ideal of ancient Greece. Stillman, the consummate searcher, had photographed the Acropolis throughout the day and in every season of his visit, considering every possible type of light for every shot he envisioned. Frantz, by contrast, though a long-time resident of Athens, photographed there only between May and August, and only in the harsh light of morning and midday, using heavy filters to accentuate the dramatic contrasts of the site. Hers is an art born out of a specific imaginative vision as much as a particular subject.

From the Romaidis Brothers to Auguste Salzmann, from Martin Chambí to Alison Frantz, these varieties of photographic art developed in direct connection with archaeological activity. But this is just the beginning of the reframing work of art on the subjects of archaeology. Archaeology has long been a subject that has productively impelled artists, such as Robert Smithson, Mark Dion, Charles Simonds, Nick Mangan, Cornelia Parker and Brian Conley. As this varied grouping suggests, a broader look at archaeology in modern photography, made at a greater remove from the proper realm of archaeological research, engages the techniques, material and subjects of archaeology in a far wider array of questions and contexts.

The work of Leandro Katz, an Argentinian-born photographer and filmmaker, has often taken up the near as well as distant past in Central America, particularly as embodied in its images. Perhaps the best known of Katz's works is his *Catherwood Project*, a series of 37 photographs and an installation that engage and also question the survey tour of remnants of ancient American monuments made by John L. Stephens and Frederick Catherwood at the very dawn of the photographic era (see pp. 58–61). Between 1985 and 1995 Katz followed in the footsteps of the expedition, visiting the same sites in Chiapas and Yucatán, and attempting to stand in precisely the same locations as those portrayed in Catherwood's engraved illustrations to Stephens's narrative. This is difficult not only because the sites themselves have changed in the intervening 150 years, but also because Catherwood's work, as we have seen, is not photographic but rather a rejection of photographic rendering. It was made from piecing together on-site sketches, some made with the aid of a *camera lucida*, into a later whole, a whole Catherwood deemed far truer than any photograph.

Katz made nearly 6,000 photographs during the project, and exhibited his chosen specimens in the final artwork in ways that juxtapose his vision with that of Catherwood. The most direct method is that in which he positions the camera at a given site and photographs it with an image of the book held open with his hand to Catherwood's engraving of the particular monument (illus. 83). Katz's dialogue with Catherwood in part resembles that of Chambí with Bingham, in the sense that it too

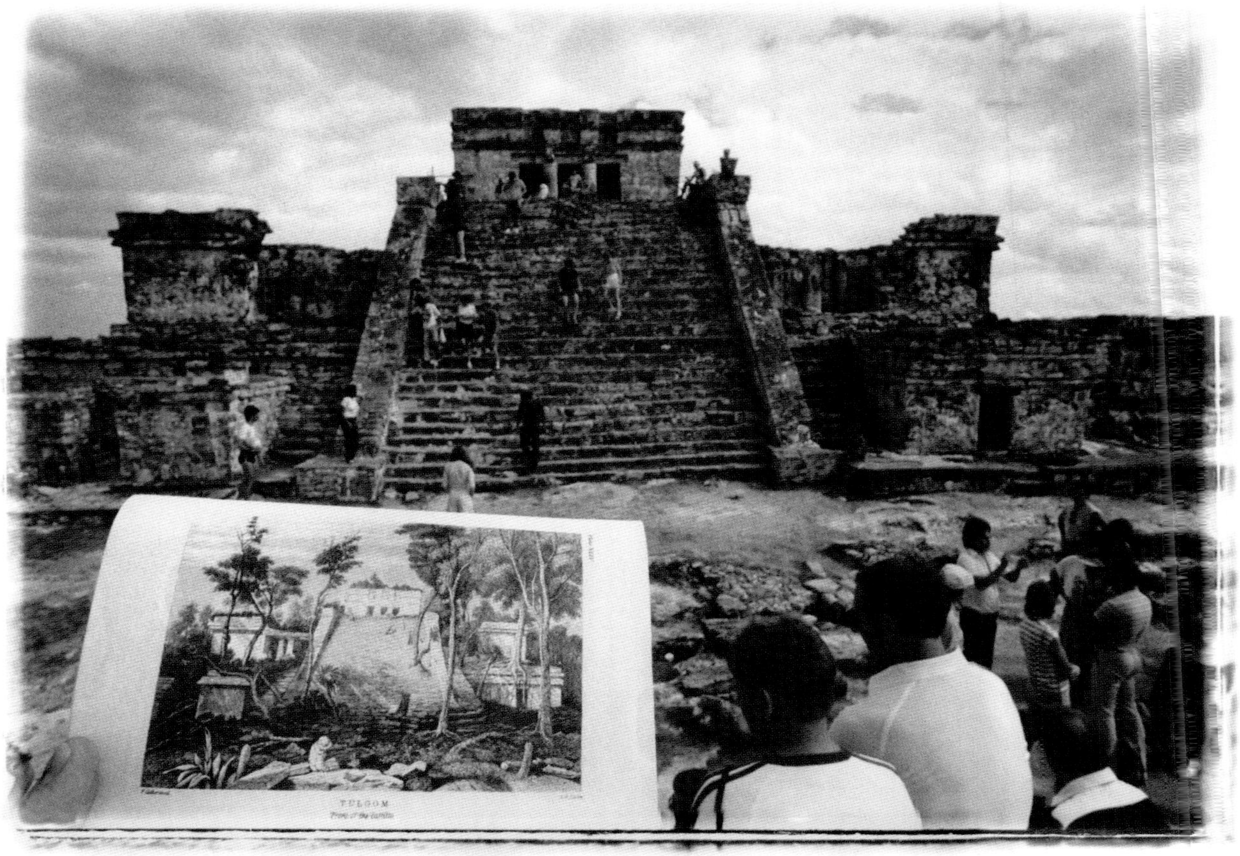

83 Leandro Katz, 'Tulúm, after Catherwood (The Castle)', 1993, from *The Catherwood Project*, 1985–95, gelatin silver print.

works to reveal the changes and power dynamics of imperialism and modernization. An image such as 'Tulúm, After Catherwood (The Castle)' seems particularly attuned to this, since it juxtaposes Catherwood's image of the monument in a secluded forest setting, viewed only by a solitary traveller seated on the rocks, with the contemporary existence of the site, now completely devoid of foliage and replete from top to bottom with tourists.

But Katz's engagement with Catherwood is also directly sympathetic to the earlier artist, open to the many complexities, from physical to cultural, involved in the making of his images. Katz states that Catherwood 'did not see in [the ancient Mexican monuments] vestiges of other cultures; he saw them as something new. And as much as his works manifest a clinical, profound accuracy, they also reveal moments of slippage and subjectivity, the result of malaria seizures perhaps, or of working in difficult locations to later reconstruct the views from sketches and memory. All these contradictions make his work even more fascinating.'[11] The Catherwood project, for Katz, is fundamentally a meditation on time, medium and culture. It traces the production of the image across time, in an object's transit from remote to familiar, and from engraving to photography. Catherwood might even have welcomed the precision of modern photographic rendering, such as the techniques Katz developed for lighting dark internal chambers.

The photography of Marilyn Bridges also takes up anew the heritage of archaeological rendering, indeed the photographic format most fundamentally associated with archaeology: aerial photography. Her purpose, however, is not so much to re-engage its history but rather to open it up beyond purely scientific documentation. Bridges's photography is a product of the experience of vision in flight, an experience as much spiritual and emotional as physical and intellectual. She began photographing from an aeroplane in Peru in 1976, recording the extraordinary 'Nazca lines'; vast, intricate geoglyphs inscribed in the desert soil by a shadowy ancient people. Bridges gave life to these forms through aerial photography, and in the process developed a distinct photographic technique. In a slow single-engine aeroplane, flying almost perilously close to earth (as low as 91 m/300 ft above surface), her photography

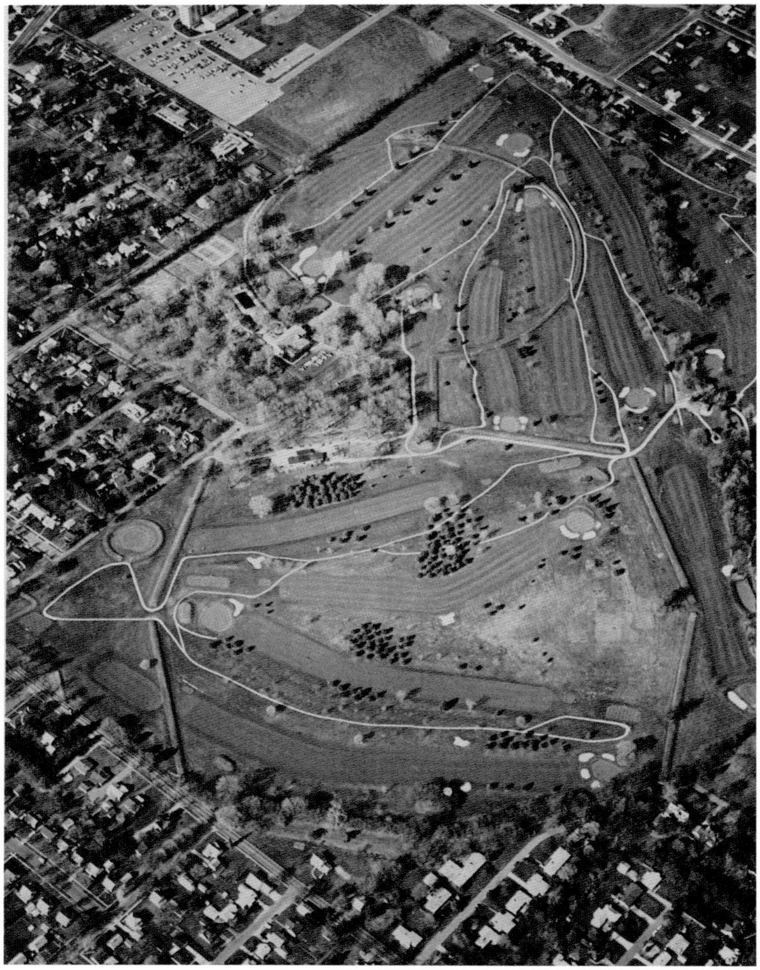

84 Marilyn Bridges, *Newark Earthworks, Hign Overview, Ohio,* 1983, gelatin silver print.

can describe an intimacy with the earth that almost goes beyond physical description. While she is perhaps best known for images of earthen formations in Europe and the Americas, Bridges has turned the same attention to man-made features such as highways, factories, skylines and railways.

Aerial photography for Bridges is a sort of social-biographical project. She notes how small are the signs of man in the vast expanse of the Americas and how melancholy the deserted sites of ancient sacred practices. But beyond this still archaeological focus for Bridges there is also the contemporary. She states: 'How we treat ourselves is visible in how we treat the landscape.'[12] Both ancient and modern are fascinatingly present, for instance, in *Newark Earthworks, High Overview, Ohio* (illus. 84). The photograph simultaneously frames remains of a ceremonial settlement of the ancient Hopewell people and a portion of the Newark Country Club golf course, both coexisting in a space hemmed in by suburban development. The ancient site, occupied from *circa* 100 BC to AD 400, largely consists of two shapes, a near exact hexagon below a perfect circle. Both are bounded by 3-m-high (10-ft-high) walls, making deeper shadows than any other physical feature. These pure geometries are, almost comically, traversed by the many irregular features of the modern golf course: greens, fairways, roughs and, most strikingly, the white pathways allowing golf carts to traverse the grounds. It is an image of what we do with our present and our past.

Even for the purely documentary-minded O.G.S. Crawford, finding the proper light was a fundamental question. For Bridges, lighting is almost a separate element to photograph. 'When I photograph', she says, 'my focus is seldom confined solely to concrete subject matter, but rather to the concrete as well as illusive matter, which is light itself . . . Often the light dictates to me the angle at which to bank the aircraft and capture both the positive and negative structure of my image. I tilt the camera at a slight downward angle as the plane bows before the subject matter. This position enables me to cheat reality and bend the light.'[13] The variety of light obtained, in some of Bridges's work almost abstracting it from the object being illuminated, can create images of which a documentary archaeological photographer would disapprove. This gesture, linking the aeroplane's own bow before the sacred with a sophisticated tracking of light and its effects, leads to a larger trend in photographing ancient remains, of a refined aesthetic whose visual traits encompass cultural or even spiritual dimensions.

Much of the photography of Laura Gilpin was dedicated to the indigenous peoples of the American Southwest, notably the Navajo. Her often delicate and subtle platinum prints document nearly 40 years of change in this culture through its people and practices. Gilpin's eye for shadowing and visual composition was also attracted by the physical dwellings of Native Americans, as at Mesa Verde or the Anasazi remains in Canyon de Chelly. Gilpin's largest foray into portraying ancient remains, though, took place on the Yucatán peninsula of Mexico. There, in effect, it combined aspects of ethnographic and archaeological observation. Though contemporary inhabitants are sometimes included, her book of 1948, *Temples in Yucatán: A Camera Chronicle of Chichén Itzá*, was devoted largely to ancient remains. Gilpin's text connects the modern people living around Chichén Itzá with classical Mayan civilization, while her images analyse the monuments for traces of that same past. Gilpin wrote: 'One difficulty in photographing these great temples is to retain their remarkable proportions and decorations and the beautiful surface qualities of the material, and at the same time retain the austere and barbaric qualities which are also present. From the practices of their religion we know that the Mayans were a barbaric people, but they had a marvelous sense of true design.'[14]

Her striking photograph of the north colonnade of the Court of the Thousand Columns, made at sunrise looking down from the Temple of Warriors, reveals the columns within a complex pattern of shadows made by a simple, rhythmic design (illus. 85). It is a powerful vista of dramatic contrasts, a sort of standing army of massive columns unadorned by anything but light. It imagines a people in the process of evoking a monument.

The distance between monument and people, as between past and present, is even further collapsed in a significant portion of photographic modernism, especially in a land such as Egypt, seen as distinctive in both past and present identity. This can be found, for example, from Lee Miller's photograph from 1938 of the shadow of the Great Pyramid at Giza projected onto modern Egyptian buildings, or from Paul Strand's almost defiantly entitled *Living Egypt* of 1969.[15] Perhaps its most remarkable monument is the book by Duane Michals, *Merveilles d'Egypte* (1978).[16] Best known is Michals's sequence of six photographs by the Giza pyramids, in which the photographer carries a dozen or so stones from beyond the frame to progressively build a pyramid from them. This pyramid, the product of an afternoon's work, ultimately takes up as much space in the frame as the real pyramid in the background. Michals's work speaks

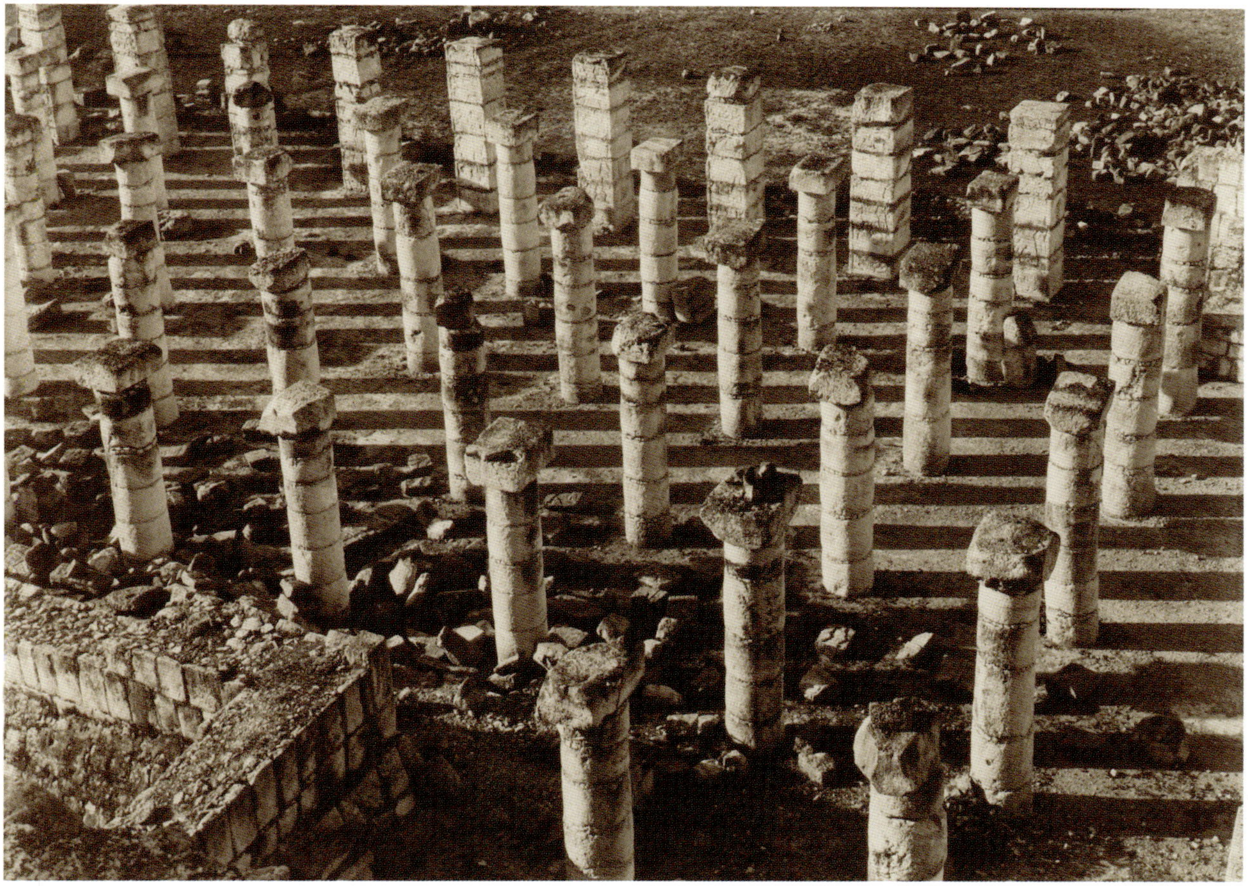

85 Laura Gilpin, *North Colonnade, Chichén Itzá*, 1932, platinum print.

of the labour involved in the ancient buildings, but also acknowledges the immense role of the pyramid (and ancient Egypt in general) in the contemporary imagination. The night before the trip Michals had watched Rex Harrison on television in *Cleopatra*, with pyramids seemingly in every background.

Much of Michals's imagery cannily plays on time, juxtaposing the eternality commonly attributed to ancient Egypt with the momentary flux of lived experience. Thus the book begins with an image of the photographer at the exact moment of his arrival at Abu Simbel, kneeling with stone colossi behind him, holding before his face a piece of paper on which is written simply: 'February 1, 1978 3:52 PM.' More barbedly absurd, a straightforward photograph of dog seated at a distance before the temple of Medinet-Habou is entitled 'the god Anubis'. Another depicts a California surfer dude in the ancient tomb of Seti I. The joke of these photos is not just the interplay between being in the present and looking for the past, but also imagining the time when that past was once present. Michals says of the surfer that it was 'as if he represented the everyday workers of antiquity'.

Photography itself is part of the past that Michals explores. The book includes four photographs of Egyptian antiquities made in 1896, purchased by the photographer at a shop in Luxor (reputedly made by the grandfather of the seller). Michals includes them since they 'add a photographic connection with the antiquities'.[17]

Michals has noted that if he had the project to do over again, he might have done it in colour, but that black and white is more appropriate because so much of the prior history of photographing Egypt is in black and white. The same preference for black and white is evident in the work of Bridges, Katz and many other archaeologically inspired contemporary photographers. Black and white has long spoken both of a seriousness (since it has long been the chosen photographic medium of archaeological science) and a visual identity: photography's own origin.

Three works from the past decade or so, however, intimate a broader range of new possibilities for photographically envisioning both the process and the experience of archaeology. For three decades, Jeff Wall has produced large-scale transparencies that are back-lit by light boxes.

Wall's work is a complex exploration of photographic representation, from that of his 'painterly' photography begun in the late 1970s to the more recent realm of 'near documentary', in which the photographer claims a less mediated stance toward the scene depicted. Significantly, archaeology enters into this latter group, notably in Wall's *Fieldwork*, an image from an archaeological excavation in British Columbia (illus. 86).

Seen from on high through a forest clearing, an American archaeologist kneels among two trenches, in the never-ending recording process of scientific archaeology. Far from a pristine site image, many accoutrements of excavation are present: orange site tags and buckets for removing soil, a trowel, brushes and different-coloured dustpans for more detailed work, plastic bags for artefacts and soil samples, the threads that define the trenches in a grid, and wooden 'mats' for the researcher to kneel without disrupting soil layers. Looking into the trench, one can make out strata of differently textured soils, and even protrusions of the remains of a former structure. As described by Wall's full title, the project of the dig is the excavation of the floor of a former dwelling built by the Sto:lo people, a First Nation group whose traces go back for millennia in what is now British Columbia. Standing and watching the kneeling archaeologist, Anthony Graesch, is Riley Lewis, a member of the contemporary Sto:lo band.

The subject of this work is the measured, calm, routine and profound work of archaeological research. It plays out in a dialogue of observation: Graesch examing the trench, Riley examining both, and, of course, the photographer/viewer looking down upon this scene from a constructed scaffolding. Wall photographed on site with the excavation for three weeks, in order, like any documentary photographer, to become as invisible as possible to his subjects. This intimate moment, a singular image of the archaeological process, is perhaps the inheritor of the photographic panoramas with which we began. While it ushers in colour, it also, like the older works, is the result of combining individual images into a larger tableau. The seemingly unmediated presence of Wall's image (nearly 2 m/6 ft wide in the original), with no trace of differences of focus or spatial distortion, is created by taking many photographs and digitally stitching them together.

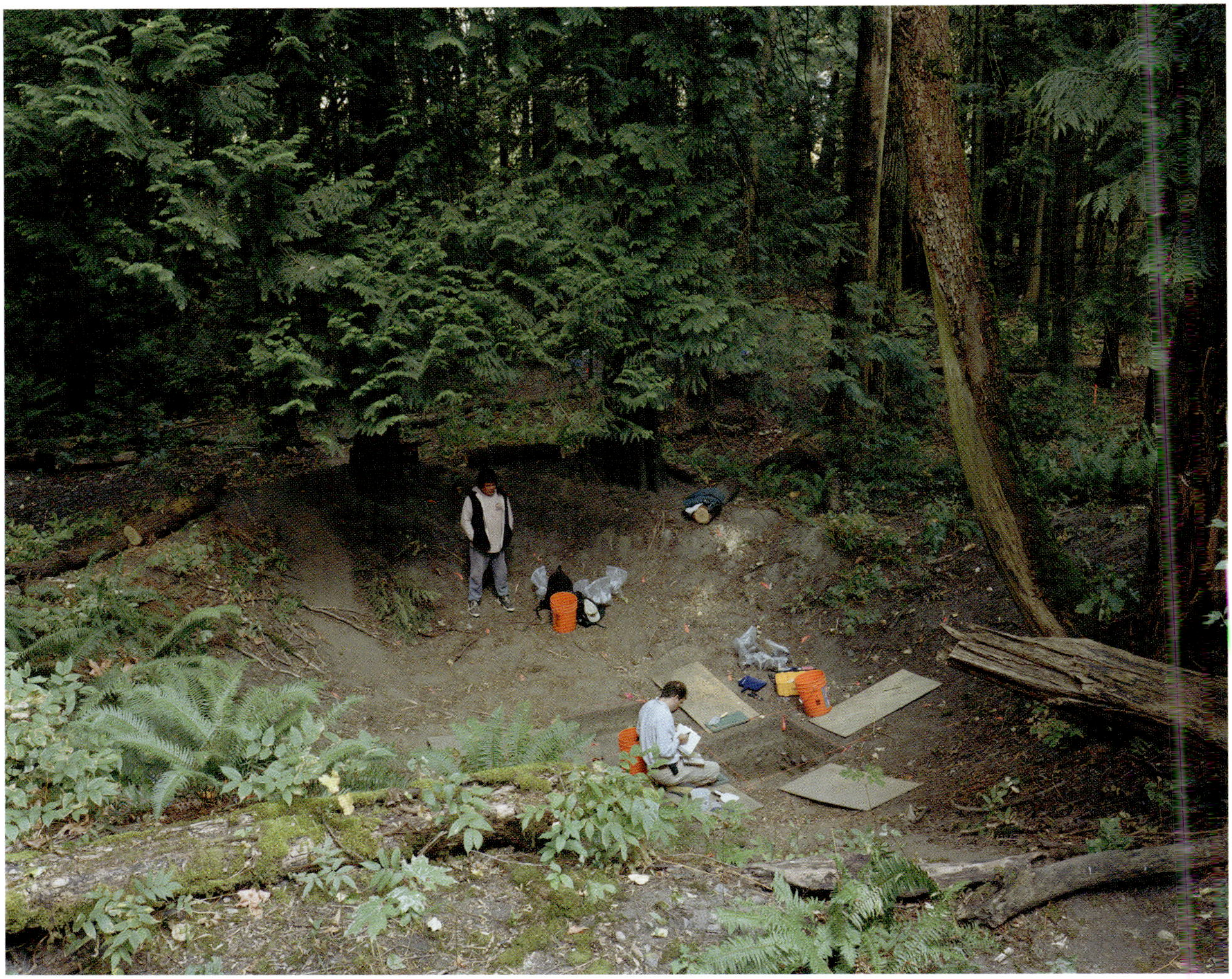

86 Jeff Wall, *Fieldwork. Excavation of the floor of a dwelling in a former Sto:lɔ nation village, Greenwood Island, Hope B. C., August, 2003. Anthony Graesch, Dept. of Anthropology, University of California at Los Angeles, working with Riley Lewis of the Sto:lɔ band, 2003*, transparency in lightbox.

Wall's single, process-centred and composedly affectless image, of past coming into the world anew, is complemented by a work by Victor Burgin which explores the afterlife of archaeology previously accomplished, and its fractured resonances for a contemporary viewer. Under the general title of *Voyage to Italy* Burgin produced three works, two photographic portfolios and one video, all triggered by a single photograph, an image made in 1864 by Carlo Fratacci of the 'Basilica' at Pompeii (illus. 87).

In Fratacci's image, the camera stares into the ruined structure. It is distanced from the initial colonnade, which includes a set of four steps that elevate the Basilican floor over the ground where the photographer has set up his camera. The camera sights a long line of column and wall fragments from which the basically rectangular outline of the structure can be made out. About one-third of the way into the distance stands a woman in contemporary dress, with a crinoline that so greatly inhabits her dress and pelerine that it makes her head and hat seem tiny, even comical, atop the vast cone of her costume.

Burgin's work takes place in the empty remains of the ancient site, but, in his own words, it is haunted by the 'midday ghost' of the woman, and a sense of her interaction with the photographer.[18] There are two photographic suites entitled *Basilica I* and *II*. *Basilica I* 'is about the relationship of the woman to that space' and consists of 24 photographs of ruined column fragments: mute, singular photographic objects which can enclose or challenge a contemporary gallery viewer as the stone objects do Fratacci's woman (illus. 88). *Basilica II* is 'prompted by the two intersecting gazes' of the woman and the photographer. It consists of eighteen more varied images that 'look around', construing alternative subjects from the given viewpoints of each figure (illus. 89). They ask the question of both tourist and photographer, 'What else is there to see here?' Impertinent as these questions may be in pure archaeology, Burgin's work insists on 'impure' subjectivity, on not repressing the present in order to apprehend the products of the past.

This becomes even clearer in the accompanying video, *Voyage to Italy*, which consists largely of a camera panning within the space of the Basilica. It connects many of the different vistas of the individual photographs, stitching them into a whole, but takes for its soundtrack something

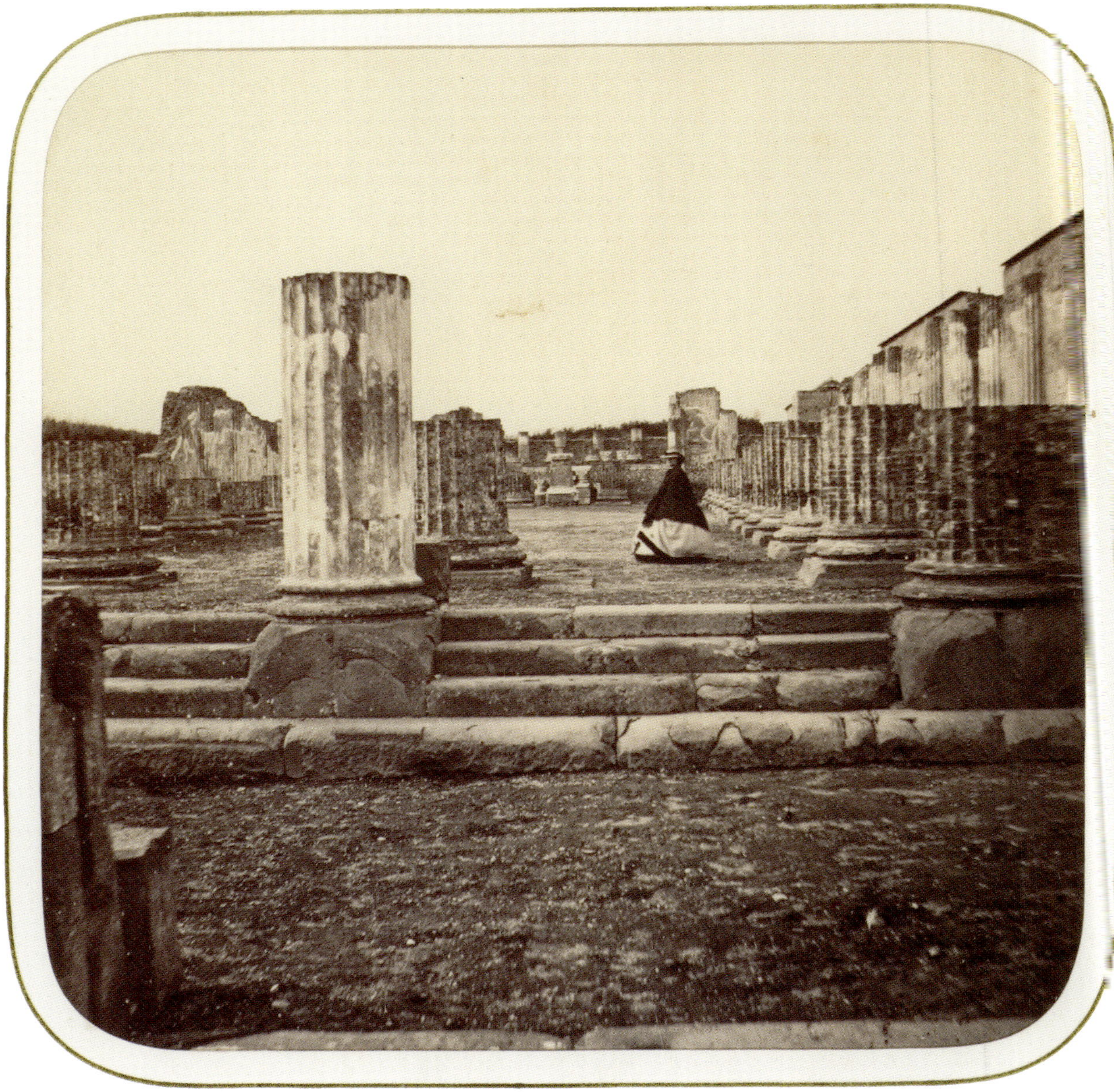

87 Carlo Fratacci, 'Basilica (Pompeii)', 1864, albumen silver print.

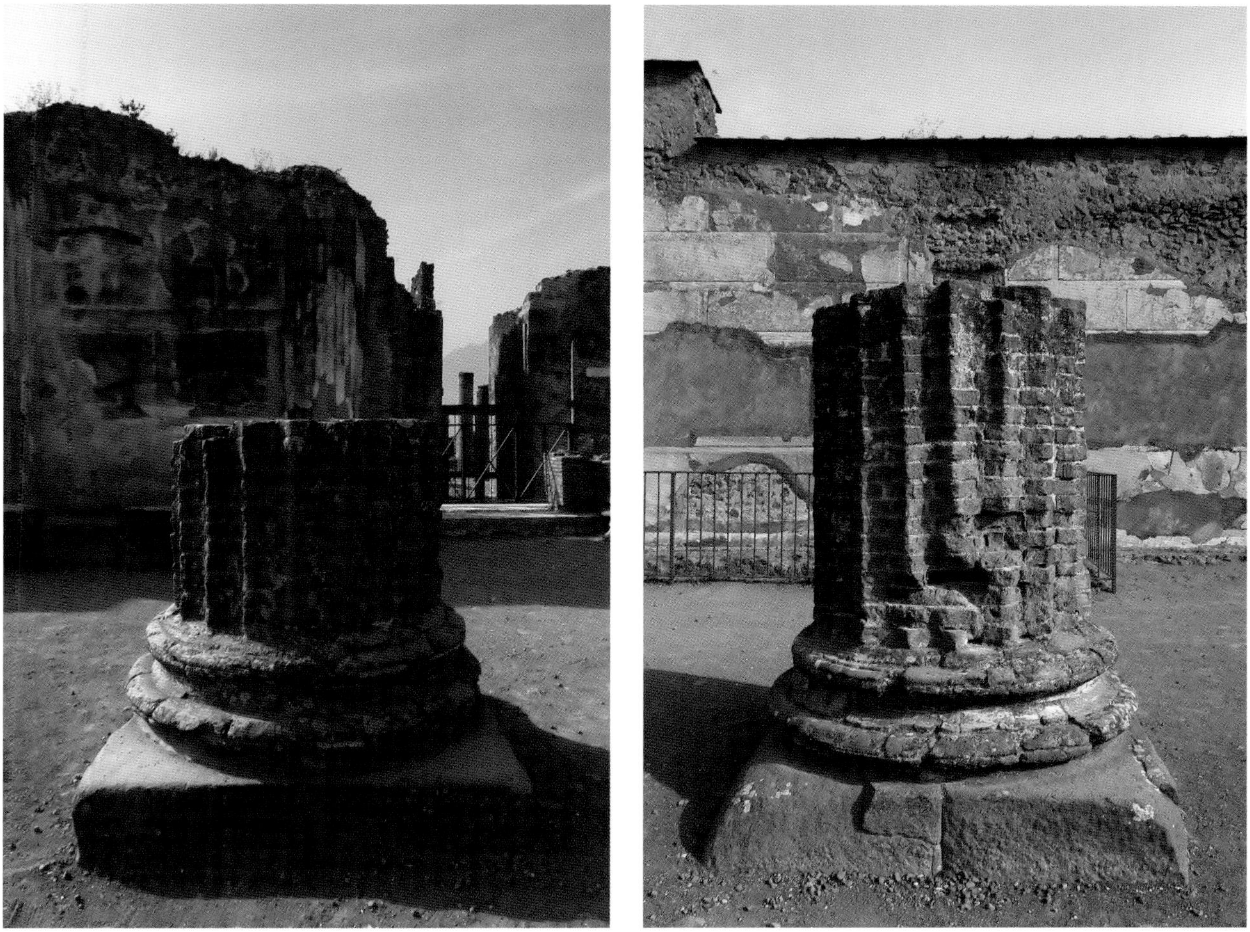

88 Victor Burgin, two prints from *Basilica I*, 2006, gelatin silver print.

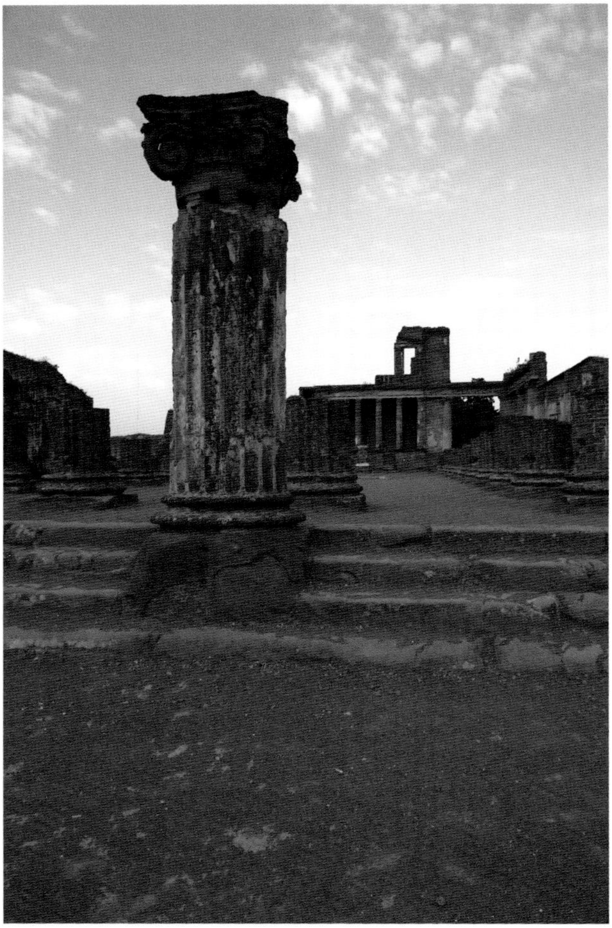

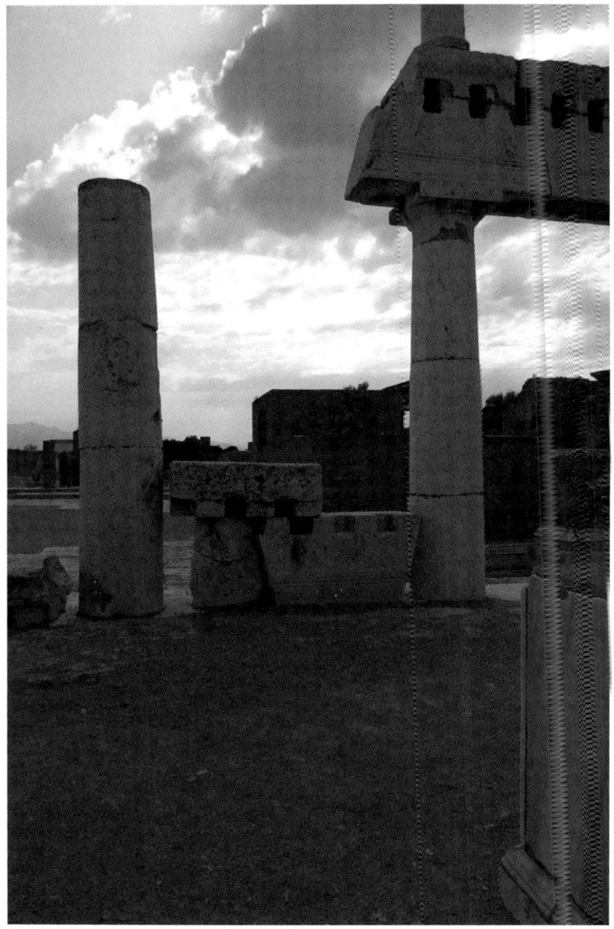

89 Victor Burgin, two prints from *Basilica II*, 2006, gelatin silver print.

almost wholly different. Burgin explains: 'As I worked, I found that the absent couple formed by Fratacci and his model became associated in my memory with another couple at Pompeii – the protagonists of Roberto Rossellini's film of 1953, *Journey to Italy*.' The video's soundtrack consists of a dialogue derived from the film, in which an unhappy English couple tour Pompeii as part of their bleak holiday, expressing their quiet hostilities to each other.

This couple are not the only ghosts perceived by Burgin, as his essay that is also a part of the piece describes many other such ghosts, other ways the past, death and Pompeii inscribe themselves in contemporary apprehension, citing works by Goethe, Théophile Gautier, Alain Resnais, Jacques Derrida, Madame de Staël, Freud and Philip K. Dick among many others. Burgin's work uses Pompeii almost as a trap to catch intertextualities. Rather than reifying a pure or originary meaning, Burgin's work collects and layers accretions of identity, like the strata of an archaeological site. The archaeological metaphor is apt here, as Burgin explicitly ties the work of photography to that of archaeology. The photograph is 'an object that tells of the loss, destruction, disappearance of "objects" . . . Every photograph is a trace of a previous state of the world, a vestige of how things were. The sum of all photographs is the ruin of the world.' Moreover, archaeological photography like that of Pompeii traces perfectly the initial imprint of its past. 'Like a photographic plate, the surface of the city has received the imprint of an event that has irreversibly transformed it . . . any photography of Pompeii is therefore the impression of an impression, the index of an index.'[19] Archaeology and photography almost subsume each other in this context, in a way that mirrors, and reflects upon, the flux from which they emerged together at their common origin.

Both Wall and Burgin work toward enlarging the spatial representation of archaeology. In this, they continue the drive toward panoramic rendering that has always been central to archaeological photography, which has ever wanted to show more than fits in the frame. Wall's unified, colour, digitally enhanced, contemporary-based 'near documentary' vision contrasts greatly with Burgin's fragmented, black-and-white (including video), historically contoured and overtly reflective investigation. They invoke different aspects of the experience of archaeology available today, and embody different perspectives on the function and practice of archaeology. For that very reason, both these innovative, knowing works of art serve as worthy monuments to accompany the knowing, reflective archaeology that is emerging in our time.

We end with a work that, in its own way, both takes up and questions the practice of archaeological photography, as well as the histories that it documents. Patrick Nagatani's remarkable *Ryoichi/Nagatani Excavations* is the record of actions pursued over a course of decades.[20] The work comprises 50 items, each consisting of one or more photographs. They claim straight-facedly to document the activities of a mysterious Japanese archaeologist, Ryoichi, with whom Nagatani began to collaborate in 1985. Ryoichi had recently received a set of maps directing him to particular locations at some of the most renowned ancient sites around the world: among them the Lascaux Caves in France, Olduvai Gorge in Tanzania, Xi'an in Shanxi Province, China, the pyramids at Moche, Peru, and Nagi Gompa in the Kathmandu Valley of Nepal. In excavations at each site his team made a similar discovery, progressively solidifying a world-changing and conventionally inconceivable history. Astoundingly, at each location Ryoichi's team discovered an automobile buried among the rubble. A 1930 Bentley was unearthed at Stonehenge, a Ferrari Testarossa at Herculaneum, a Mercedes 500 SL in the Cahokia mounds of Illinois. Ryoichi's team, we learn, covered up all evidence of its activities, and the cars were shipped to a secret warehouse in Kyoto. Nagatani's exhibition is the only extant record of the campaign. In it, together with maps and site plans, is amassed the photographic trace of these discoveries.

Among the photos displayed in the *Ryoichi/Nagatani Excavations* are several of straightforward object documentation. An array of artefact photos, for instance, hews to a representational format familiar from throughout this book (illus. 90, see also illus. 17, 27, 59, 70). In 25 gelatin silver prints, isolated against a black background, contour and surface emphasized by use of a single, consistent light source, we scan a variety of stone implements and inscribed tablets like those often found in the photographic documentation of archaeology. Yet dispersed here are more anomalous, but equally significant, artefacts for the discoverers, such as a mid-twentieth century radio, a child's etch-a-sketch, a toy (or is it part of a hood ornament?) and an automobile spark plug. This straightforward but comic tableau enunciates a version of the game of object-based historical deduction that, in a sense, constitutes archaeology.

The majority of the photographs in the *Ryoichi/Nagatani Excavations* consist of site photographs, representing an actual excavation process. For instance, a photograph of an early phase in the excavation at Chetro Ketl Kiva, one of the Anasazi 'Great Houses' in Chaco Canyon, New Mexico, built around a millennium ago, clearly shows the front grill and headlights of a BMW 535i being excavated behind a retaining wall

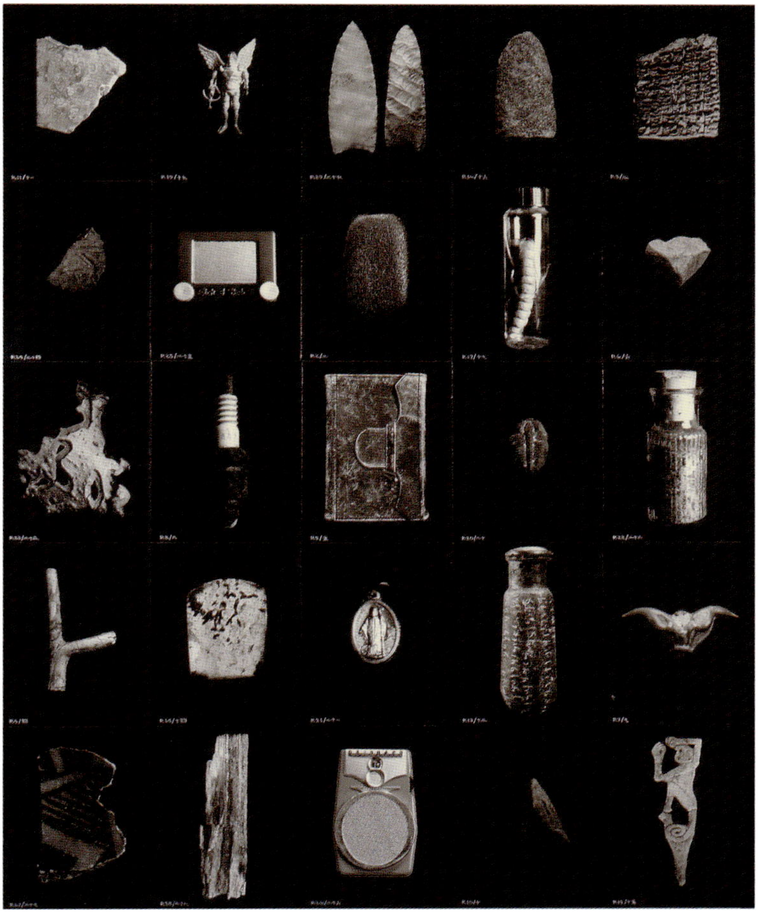

90 Patrick Nagatani, 'Excavation Artifacts', 1999, from the series *Ryoichi/Nagatani Excavations*, 1985–2001, montage of 25 gelatin silver prints.

(illus. 91). The image, like most others in the project, portrays an actual process of excavation, with ladder, shovels, hammers, pickaxes and wheelbarrows in evidence. At this site, uniquely, one finds a trace of Nagatani's camera, a large-format camera on a heavy tripod, its silver case nearby. In its general exclusion of the camera, Nagatani's work obeys the archaeological dictum we have noted throughout on suppressing the presence of the photographic apparatus for the sake of reifying its results.

The process of creating what is considered valid archaeological evidence is what is most directly on display in Nagatani's work. Playfully, but insistently, it uses the very basis of truthful, objective recording in archaeology to suggest a world history we simply cannot accept as true. As it turns out, we are not alone. Excerpts from Ryoichi's journal indicate that he was deeply shaken by these results, especially after finding that radiocarbon and dendrochronological testing indicated that the cars were actually buried in different centuries. Equally challenging was the discovery in 1998 of a car from the twenty-first century. Its documentary photography is blurry and indistinct, while the car itself was hastily reburied so as not to interfere with the future by revealing it at an improper time. Ryoichi's journal describes a sort of crisis of identity for the archaeological team itself. He states: 'We all seem to have become humanists rather than scientists.' Indeed, at the very last site, Uluru in Australia, Ryoichi's team decided not to excavate at all, but instead to leave intact a sacred dreamtime site for Aboriginal peoples. 'After all of these excavations, we have come to the realization that one aspect of what we have learned is that the quest itself has revealed to us the value of mystery and questioning. Rather than find an answer, the puzzle remains intact.'[21]

One could hardly accuse Patrick Nagatani of the falsification of external reality but rather of the wonder at the effect of scientific codification his work, both photographic and textual, creates. If one wonders if this could be true, the point is less deciding upon truth than dwelling in that wonder itself, at the nature of time, and our sense of identity. Patrick Nagatani's work, like, among others, the Hokes Archives of Beauvais Lyons, the Atlas Archive of Walid Ra'ad and David Wilson's Museum of Jurassic Technology (which is credited with lending a map to Nagatani's exhibit), uses the rhetoric of scientific discourse to play

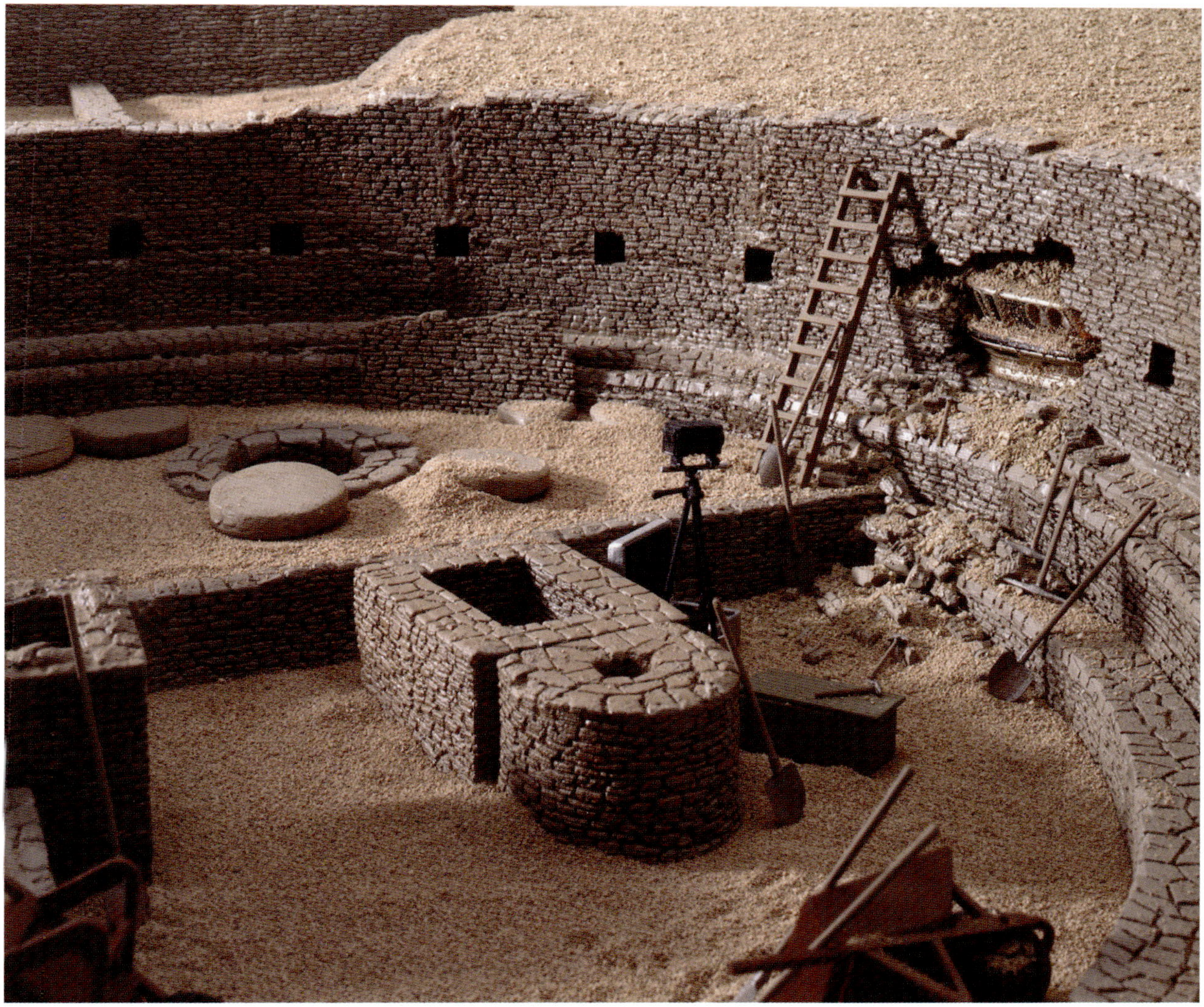

91 Patrick Nagatani, 'BMW, Chetro Ketl Kiva, Chaco Canton, New Mexico, USA' 1997–8, from the series *Ryoichi/Nagatani Excavations*, giclée print.

upon and question how we know our world. But here the process is pointed directly at archaeological photography. Nagatani himself states: 'With this project I hope to challenge us to examine the ways in which photography creates, recreates or supports a particular history . . . I am interested in how the photograph is also recognized less as a window on the "real," and far more as a malleable picture space.'

The *Ryoichi/Nagatani Excavations* are no less properly archaeological in form than any other photographic project we have considered here. With uncommon wit and invention, the piece explores the role and power of photography in not just supporting but also creating the historical narratives of archaeology. In the process, it highlights and plays on the processes and wonder of touching upon history, making the absent present, and sharing the experience with a larger audience, elements which have always been at work throughout the entwined lifetimes of photography and archaeology.

# References


## Introduction: The Image as Object

1 André Bazin, 'The Ontology of the Photographic Image', quoted in Douglas Crimp, 'The Museum's Old/The Library's New Subject', in *The Contest of Meaning: Critical Histories of Photography*, ed. Richard Bolton (Cambridge, 1989), p. 4.
2 Roland Barthes, *Camera Lucida*, trans. Richard Howard (New York, 1981), pp. 91, 93.
3 Kitty Hauser, *Shadow Sites: Photography, Archeology and the British Landscape, 1927–1955* (Oxford, 2007), p. 280.
4 Berenice Abbott, 'Introduction', in *Twenty Photographs by Eugène Atget, 1856–1927*, n.p., quoted in Judith Keller, 'Introduction' in Judith Keller and Kenneth A. Breisch, *A Victorian View of Ancient Rome: The Parker Collection of Historical Photographs in the Kelsey Museum of Archaeology* (Ann Arbor, MI, 1980), p. 11. See, for example, Herta Wolf, 'Archaeological Consciousness', in *The Photographic Paradigm*, ed. Annette W. Balkema and Henk Slager (Amsterdam, 1997), pp. 182–6, an essay on contemporary photography that never elaborates its archaeological title.
5 Walter Benjamin, *Selected Writings Volume III, 1935–38*, ed. Howard Eiland and Michael W. Jennings (Cambridge, MA, 2002), p. 108.
6 John Falconer, 'Pattern of Photographic Surveys: Joseph Lawton at Ceylon', in *Traces of India: Photography, Architecture and the Politics of Representation, 1850-1900* (New Haven, CT, 2003), pp. 164–5.
7 Michael Shanks, 'Photography and Archaeology', in *The Cultural Life of Images: Visual Representation in Archaeology*, ed. Brian Molyneaux (London, 1997), p. 80.
8 Melissa Banta and Curtis M. Hinsley, *From Site to Sight: Anthropology, Photography and the Power of Imagery* (Cambridge, MA, 1986), p. 73.
9 Marsha Hill, 'The Life and Work of Harry Burton', in Erik Hornung, *The Tomb of Pharaoh Seti I* (Zurich, 1991), p. 28.
10 Julian Thomas, *Archaeology and Modernity* (London, 2004), p. 27. See also Julian Thomas, 'Archaeology's Place in Modernity', *modernism/modernity*, XI/1 (2004), pp. 17–34.
11 Hauser, *Shadow Sites*, p. 238.
12 Alain Schnapp, *The Discovery of the Past*, trans. Ian Kinnes and Gillian Varndell (New York, 1997), pp. 275–316.
13 Peter Der Manuelian, 'George Andrew Reisner on Archaeological Photography', *Journal of the American Research Center in Egypt*, XXIX (1992), p. 20.
14 Quoted in H.V.F. Winstone, *Gertrude Bell* (London, 1978), p. 108.
15 Barthes, *Camera Lucida*, p. 93.

## one: Science, or Truth

1 OED online 'archaeology', Hood College (Maryland) database DVD (accessed 18 October 2009).
2 Dominique François Arago, 'Report', in *Classic Essays on Photography*, ed. Alan Trachtenberg (New Haven, CT, 1980), p. 17. I have slightly altered the text to better accord with the original French.
3 Lorraine Daston and Peter Galison, 'The Image of Objectivity', *Representations*, 40 (Fall 1992), pp. 81–128.
4 Pierre Bourdieu, *Photography: A Middle-brow Art* (Stanford, CA, 1990), p. 74.
5 Ricardo A. Caminos, 'The Talbotype Applied to Hieroglyphics', *The Journal of Egyptian Archaeology*, 52 (1966) pp. 65–70.
6 William Henry Fox Talbot, *Selected Texts and Bibliography*, ed. Mike Weaver (Oxford, 1992), p. 89.
7 Susan L. Taylor, 'Fox Talbot as an Artist: The "Patroclus" Series', *Bulletin of the University of Michigan Museums of Art and Archaeology*, VIII (1986–8), p. 45.
8 The most detailed history is Mogens Trolle Larsen, *The Conquest of Assyia: Excavations in an Ancient Land* (New York, 1994).
9 Mirjam Brusius, 'From Photographic Science to Scientific Photography: Photographic Experiments at the British Museum around 1850', Max Planck Institute for the History of Science, Berlin (forthcoming 2011).
10 John Hannavy, 'Roger Fenton and the British Museum', *History of Photography*, XII/3 (1988), p. 194.
11 'Notice to Members: Exchange of Positive Pictures', *Journal of the Photographic Society*, 1 (1 April 1853), quoted in Jennifer Tucker, *Nature Exposed: Photography as Eyewitness in Victorian Science* (Baltimore, MD, 2005), p. 27.
12 Paul-Émile Botta, *Monument de Ninive*, 5 vols (Paris, 1849–50), vol. V, p. 5. On the context of this passage, see Frederick N. Bohrer, *Orientalism and Visual Culture: Imagining Mesopotamia in Nineteenth-century Europe* (New York, 2003), pp. 66–84.
13 Ernest Lacan, 'La Mission de M. Place', *La Lumiére* (16 November 1851), p. 3.
14 Victor Place, *Ninive et l'Assyrie*, 3 vols (Paris, 1867–70), vol. I, p. vi. See also Elisabeth Fontan, 'Débuts de la photographie et fouilles en Assyrie: les calotypes de Gabriel Tranchand', in Elisabeth Fontan, with Nicole Chevalier, *De Khorsabad à Paris* (Paris, 1994), pp. 196–219.
15 For the tripod photo, see Fontan, *De Khorsabad à Paris*, p. 210.
16 Place, *Ninive et l'Assyrie*, vol. I, p. 84.
17 Frédéric Goupil-Fesquet, in *The Athenaeum* (London, 21 December 1839), quoted in Helmut Gernsheim, *The Origins of Photography* (New York, 1982), p. 83.

18 John Ruskin, *The Works of John Ruskin*, ed. E. T. Cook and Alexander Wedderburn, VIII (London, 1903), p. 13.
19 James Fergusson, *History of Indian and Eastern Architecture* (London, 1876), p. v.
20 Julia Ballerini observes about the book: 'His observations are commonplace, his writing a series of banal clichés, and his photographs mostly unimaginative frontal compositions.' Ballerini, 'Rewriting the Nubian Figure in the Photograph: Maxime Du Camp's "Cultural Hypochondria"', in *Colonialist Photography: Imag(in)ing Race and Place*, ed. Eleanor M. Hight and Gary D. Sampson (New York, 2002), p. 30. See also Ballerini, *The Stillness of Hajj Ishmael: Maxime Du Camp's 1850 Photographic Encounters* (Bloomington, IN, 2010).
21 Lindsey S. Stewart, 'In Perfect Order: Antiquity in the Daguerreotypes of Joseph-Philibert Girault de Prangey', in *Antiquity and Photography: Early Views of Ancient Mediterranean Sites* (Los Angeles, CA, 2005), p. 79.
22 Peter Der Manuelian, 'George Andrew Reisner on Archaeological Photography', *Journal of the American Research Center in Egypt*, XXIX (1992), p. 4.
23 John P. Peters, *Nippur, or Explorations and Adventures on the Euphrates*, 2 vols (New York, 1897), vol. II, p. 370.
24 Mortimer Wheeler, *Archaeology from the Earth* (Harmondsworth, 1954), p. 80.
25 Maria Antonella Pelizzari, 'From Stone to Paper: Photographs of Architecture and the Traces of History', in *Traces of India: Photography, Architecture, and the Politics of Representation, 1850–1900*, ed. Maria Antonella Pelizzari (Montreal, QC, and New Haven, CT, 2003), p. 34.
26 Thomas Patterson, *Toward a Social History of Archaeology in the United States* (New York, 1995) p. 12. Cited in Tripp Evans, *Romancing the Maya* (Austin, TX, 2004) p. 163.
27 At diglib.lib.utk.edu (accessed 23 November 2009), digital id#fhm 01275. This text appears to have been subsequently removed from the site.
28 Senta C. German, 'Photography and Fiction: The Publication of the Excavations at the Palace of Minos at Knossos', *Journal of Mediterranean Archaeology*, XVIII/2 (2005), pp. 209–230.
29 John Lloyd Stephens, 'Preface', *Incidents of Travel in Yucatán*, I (New York, 1963), p. v.
30 Ibid., p. 100.
31 Evans, *Romancing the Maya*, pp. 23–43.
32 Eugene Emmanuel Viollet-le-Duc, 'Preface', in Desiré Charnay, *Cités et Ruines Americaines* (Paris, 1863), p. 24.
33 Marc Pollefeys et al., '3D Recording for Archaeological Fieldwork', *IEEE Computer Graphics and Applications* (May/June 2003), p. 8.
34 'Giant Pencil Traces Archaeological Finds Fast', *New Scientist* (29 July 2009), p. 19; A. R. Jiménez et al., 'A Computerized System to Determine the Provenance of Finds in Archaeological Sites Using Acoustic Signals', *Journal of Archaeological Science*, 36 (2009) pp. 2415–26.
35 Jonathan Bateman, 'Wearing Juninho's Shirt: Record and Negotiation in Excavation Photographs', in *Envisioning the Past: Archaeology and the Image*, ed. Sam Smiles and Stephanie Moser (Oxford, 2005), p. 192.
36 Yannis Hamilakis, Aris Agnostopoulos and Fotis Ifantidis, 'Postcards from the Edge of Time: Archaeology, Photography, Archaeological Ethnography (A Photo-Essay)', *Public Archaeology*, VIII/2–3 (2009), pp. 283–309.

## two: Travel, or Presence

1 Osbert Guy Stanhope Crawford, *Wessex from the Air* (Oxford, 1928) p. 112.
2 John P. Peters, *Nippur, or Explorations and Adventures on the Euphrates*, 2 vols (New York, 1897), vol. II, p. 30.
3 Francis Frith, cited in Julia van Haften and Jon E. Manchip White, *Egypt and the Holy Land: 77 Views by Francis Frith* (New York, 198[illegible]), p. xiv.
4 Mortimer Wheeler, *Archaeology from the Earth* (Baltimore, MD, 1954), p. 200.
5 At www.archdiggers.co.uk/diggers/frameset.html (accessed 14 February 2010). Communication with photographer, 16 February 2010.
6 *La redécouverte de Delphes* (Paris, 1992), p. 174.
7 John Stathatos, *Archaeologies* (Thessaloniki, 2003), pp. 22–5.
8 W. M. Flinders Petrie, *Methods and Aims in Archaeology* (London, 1904), p. 73.
9 Ibid., p. 48.
10 Aaron M. Levin, 'Excavation Photography: A Day on a Dig', *Archaeology* (January/February 1986), pp. 39, 34.
11 Denis Cosgrove and William L. Fox, *Photography and Flight* (London, 2010), p. 41.
12 O.G.S. Crawford, 'Archaeology from the Air', in *A Book of Archaeology: Seventeen Stories of Discovery*, ed. Margaret Wheeler (London, 1957), p. 88.
13 Crawford, *Wessex from the Air*, p. 8.
14 George Johnson, *Peru from the Air* (New York, 1930), p. 2.
15 David Kennedy and M. C. Bishop, 'Google Earth and the Archaeology of Saudi Arabia: A Case Study from the Jeddeh Area', *Journal of Archaeological Science*, XXXVIII/6 (June 2011), pp. 128[illegible]–93 http://dx.doi.org at marker doi:10.1016/j.jas.2011.01.003 (accessed 5 February 2011).
16 W. J. Stillman, 'Artistic Photography', *The British Journal Photographic Almanac and Photographer's Daily Companion* (1872), p. [illegible]0.
17 *Illustrated London News* (7 January 1928), p. 14; *Antiquity* (March 1928), p. 84; John Marshall, ed., *Mohenjodaro and the Indus*

*Civilization*, 3 vols (London, 1931), vol. III, pl. XXIVB.

18 Marshall, *Mohenjodaro and the Indus Civilization*, I/133, p. viii.

19 Quoted in Sudeshna Guha, 'Negotiating Evidence: History, Archaeology and the Indus Civilization', *Modern Asian Studies*, XXXIV/2 (2005), p. 419, n. 31.

20 Bruce G. Trigger, *A History of Archaeological Thought* (New York, 1989) p. 182.

21 Levin, 'Excavation Photography', p. 36.

22 Keith F. Davis, *Désiré Charnay, Expeditionary Photographer* (Albuquerque, NM, 1981), p. 9.

23 Levin, 'Excavation Photography', p. 36.

## three: Meaning, or the Archive

1 Auguste Salzmann, *Jerusalem* (Paris 1856), p. 4.

2 Quoted in M. Christine Boyer, '*La Mission Héliographique*: Architectural Photography, Collective Memory and the Patrimony of France, 1851', in *Picturing Place: Photography and the Geographical Imagination*, ed. Joan M. Schwartz and James R. Ryan (New York, 2003), pp. 34–5.

3 Joan Schwartz, '"Records of Simple Truth and Precision": Photography, Archives, and the Ilusion of Control', *Archivaria*, 50 (2000), p. 3: 'The defining moments in both the history of modern archives and in the history of photography can be traced to the same two-year period in France, 1839–1841.'

4 Jeff Rosen, 'Lithophotographie: The Art of Imitation', in *Intersections: Lithography, Photography and the Traditions of Printmaking*, ed. Kathleen Stewart Howe (Albuquerque, NM, 1998), pp. 35–6.

5 John Henry Parker, 'Forum Romanum', in *The Archaeology of Rome*, V (London, 1876) opposite plate 6.

6 John Henry Parker, 'The Primitive Fortifications', in *The Archaeology of Rome*, I (London, 1874), p. xix.

7 John Henry Parker, *The Ashmolean Museum: Its History, Present State and Prospects* (Oxford, 1870), pp. 11–12.

8 On ideologizing effects of archives, archaeology and photography, see Michael Shanks and Christopher Tilley, *Re-Constructing Archaeology: Theory and Practice*, 2nd edn (London, 1992), pp. 77–9; John Tagg, *The Burden of Representation: Essays on Photographies and Histories* (Amherst, MA, 1988), pp. 88–92.

9 On Curtius and Olympia, see especially Suzanne L. Marchand, *Down from Olympus: Archaeology and Phillhellenism in Germany, 1750–1970* (Princeton, NJ, 1996), pp. 77–91.

10 Ernst Curtius and Friedrich Adler, eds, *Olympia: Die Ergebnisse der von dem deutschen Reich veranstalteten Ausgrabung*, 5 vols (Berlin, 1890–97), vol. I, p. ix.

11 Ibid., vol. III, p. 182; Andrew Stewart, *Greek Sculpture: An Exploration*, 2 vols (New Haven, CT, 1990), vol. I, p. 89. Both indicate the pedestal was no more than triple the height of the sculpture, and that it was triangular, not trapezoidal.

12 Quoted in Paul Léon, *Mérimée et son temps* (Paris, 1962), pp. 295–6.

13 Anne de Mondenard, *La Mission héliographique: Cinq photographes parcourent la France en 1851* (Paris, 2002).

14 Francis Wey 'Des Progrés et de l'avenir de la photographie', *La Lumière* (5 October 1851), quoted in Boyer, *La Mission Héliographique*, p. 47.

15 Boyer, *La Mission Héliographique*, p. 39.

16 Siegfried Kracauer and Paul O. Kristeller, *History: The Last Things Before the First* (Princeton, NJ, 1994) p. 6.

17 Mary Price, *The Photograph: A Strange, Confined Space* (Stanford, CA, 1994).

18 Jacob E. Conner, 'Homer's Troy Today', *National Geographic Magazine*, 27 (January–June 1915), pp. 522, 525.

19 Joan Gero and Dolores Root, 'Public Presentations and Private Concerns: Archaeology in the pages of National Geographic', in *The Politics of the Past*, ed. Paul Gathercole and David Lowenthal (London, 1990), p. 35.

20 'The Focal Encyclopedia of Photography', quoted in *Photography in the Time of Archaeology: From the Collections of Sandro Oramas and the University Gallery* (Newark, DE, 1994), p. 3.

21 Bettina Bergmann, 'Seeing Women in the Villa of the Mysteries: A Modern Excavation of the Dionysiac Murals', in *Antiquity Recovered: The Legacy of Pompeii and Herculaneum*, ed. Victoria C. Gardner-Coates and Jon L. Seydl (Los Angeles, CA, 2007), p. 231.

22 For example, Mortimer Wheeler, *Roman Africa in Colour* (London, 1966); Wheeler, *Flames Over Persepolis* (London, 1968); Wheeler, *Splendours of the East: Temples, Tombs, Palaces and Fortresses of Asia* (London, 1965).

23 Wheeler, *Roman Africa in Colour*, pp. 104, 7.

24 Mortimer Wheeler 'Foreword' in Michael B. Cookson, *Photography for Archaeologists* (London 1954), p. i.

25 André Malraux, *Le Musée Imaginaire* (Paris, 1965), p. 115.

26 Henri Zerner, 'Malraux and the Power of Photography', in *Sculpture and Photography: Envisioning the Third Dimension*, ed. Geraldine A. Johnson (New York, 1998), p. 119.

27 Andre Malraux, *The Voices of Silence* (New York, 1953), p. 44.

28 Adolf Michaelis, *Die Archäeologischen Entdeckungen des Neunzehnten Jahrhunderts* (Leipzig, 1906), p. 259.

29 Elmer Harp Jr, 'The Objectives of Archaeological Photography', in *Photography in Archaeological Research*, ed. Elmer Harp Jr, (Albuquerque, NM, 1975), p. 11.

30 'A.' (Bernard Bothmer) 'Musings of an ARCE Fellow at Work', *Newsletter – American Research Center in Egypt*, 74 (July 1970), p. 17.

31 Ibid., p. 19.

32 Ricardo Caminos, 'The Recording of Inscriptions and Scenes in Tombs and Temples', in *Ancient Egyptian Epigraphy and Paleography* (New York, 1976), pp. 10–11.

33 At http://oi.uchicago.edu/research/projects/epi (accessed 22 February 2010).
34 Maria Golia, *Photography and Egypt* (London, 2010), p. 36.
35 James H. Breasted, *The Oriental Institute*, University of Chicago Survey, XII (Chicago, IL, 1933), p. 203, quoted in Jeffrey Abt, 'Drawing Over Photographs: James H. Breasted and the Scientizing of Egyptian Epigraphy, 1895–1928', *Visual Resources*, 14 (1998), p. 46.

## four: Art, or Reframing

1 Hiram Bingham, *Machu Picchu: A Citdael of the Incas* (New York, 1979), pp. 91, 90.
2 Edward Ranney, 'Images of a Sacred Geography', in *The New World's Old World*, ed. May Castleberry (Albuquerque, NM, 2003), p. 102.
3 Quoted in Abagail Solomon-Godeau, 'A Photographer in Jerusalem, 1855: Auguste Salzmann and His Times', in *Photography at the Dock: Essays on Photographic Histories, Institutions and Practices* (Minneapolis, MN, 1991), p. 155.
4 Auguste Salzmann, *Jérusalem: Étude et Reproduction Photographique des Monuments de la Ville Sainte Depuis l'Époque Judaïque Jusqu'à Nos Jours* (Paris, 1856), p. 3.
5 Randy Innes, '*Jérusalem* revisited: On Auguste Salzmann's Photo-Topography', *Art and Religion*, 15 (2011) p. 33.
6 Solomon-Godeau, 'A Photographer in Jerusalem', p. 168.
7 Félix de Saulcy, *Histoire de L'Art Judaïque* (Paris, 1858), pp. i, iii.
8 Amy Papalexandrou and Marie Mauzy, 'The Photographs of Alison Frantz: Revealing Antiquity through the Lens', *History of Photography*, XXVII/2 (Summer 2003), p. 143, note 32.
9 Ibid., p. 132.
10 Alison Frantz, 'Truth Before Beauty or, The Incompleat Photographer', *Archaeology*, III/4 (Winter 1950) pp. 202–14.
11 Leandro Katz, 'Catherwood Project': www.leandrokatz.com/Pages/Catherwood.html (accessed 12 November 2009).
12 Marilyn Bridges, *The Sacred and the Secular: A Decade of Aerial Photography* (New York, 1990), p. 52.
13 Quoted in Lucy Lippard, 'American Landscapes', in *Markings: Aerial Views of Sacred Landscapes. Photographs by Marilyn Bridges* (New York, 1986), p. 56.
14 Quoted in Martha A. Sandweiss, *Laura Gilpin: An Enduring Grace* (Forth Worth, TX, 1986) p. 61.
15 For Miller, see Maria Golia, *Photography and Egypt* (London, 2010), p. 144–5.
16 Some of the information in this discussion derives from a conversation with the photographer on 8 February 2010.
17 Duane Michals, *Merveilles d'Egypte* (Paris, 1978), p. 101.
18 Victor Burgin, 'The Shadow and the Ruin', in *Voyage to Italy* (Ostfildern, Germany, 2007), p. 79. All other Burgin quot[illegible] from this essay derive from object files on the work in the Canadian Center for Architecture, Montreal, Canada.
19 Burgin, 'The Shadow and the Ruin', pp. 86, 79
20 Some of the information in this discussion derives from a conversation with the photographer on 8 March 2011, and related documentation.
21 Michele M. Penhall, ed., *Desire for Magic. Patrick Nagatani, 1978–2008* (Albuquerque, NM, 2010), p. 235.

# Select Bibliography


Ballerini, Julia, *The Stillness of Hajj Ishmael: Maxime Du Camp's 1850 Photographic Encounters* (New York, 2010)

Banta, Melissa, and Curtis M. Hinsley, *From Site to Sight: Anthropology, Photography and the Power of Imagery* (Cambridge, MA, 1986)

Beard, Mary, 'Souvenirs of Culture: Deciphering (in) the Museum', *Art History*, XV (1992)

Biblioteca Vallicelliana, *Archeologia in posa: Dal Colosseo a Cecilia Metella nell'antica documentazione fotografica* (Milan, 1998)

Bergstein, Mary, *Mirrors of Memory: Freud, Photography, and the History of Art* (Ithaca, NY, 2010)

Bernhardsson, Magnus T., *Reclaiming a Plundered Past: Archaeology and Nation Building in Modern Iraq* (Austin, TX, 2005)

Bohrer, Frederick N., 'The Sweet Waters of Asia: Representing Difference/Differencing Representation in Nineteenth-century Istanbul', in *Edges of Empire: Orientalism and Visual Culture*, ed. Jos Hackforth-Jones and Mary Roberts (London, 2005)

Burgin, Victor, *In/Different Spaces: Place and Memory in Visual Culture* (Berkeley, CA, 1996)

Castleberry, May, ed., *The New World's Old World: Photographic Views of Ancient America* (Albuquerque, NM, 2003)

Coates, Victoria C. Gardner, and Jon L. Seydl, eds, *Antiquity Recovered: The Legacy of Pompeii and Herculaneum* (Los Angeles, CA, 2007)

Constantinou, Fani, and Aliki Tsirgialou, *Athens, 1839–1900: A Photographic Record* (Athens, 2004)

*D'après l'antique*, exh. cat., Louvre Museum, Paris (2000)

Debroise, Olivier, *Mexican Suite: A History of Photography in Mexico* (Austin, TX, 2001)

Denise, Fabrice, and Lévon Nordiguian, *Une aventure archéologique: Antoine Poidebard, photographe et aviateur* (Marseilles, 2004)

Derrida, Jacques, *Athens, Still Remains: The Photographs of Jean-François Bonhomme* (New York, 2010)

Desrochers, Brigitte, 'Giorgio Sommer's Photographs of Pompeii', *History of Photography*, XXVII (2003)

Deuel, Leo, *Flights into Yesterday: The Story of Aerial Archaeology* (New York, 1969)

Diaz-Andrieu, Margarita, *A World History of Nineteenth-century Archaeology: Nationalism, Colonialism and the Past* (Oxford, 2007)

Dorrell, Peter G., *Photography in Archaeology and Conservation* (Cambridge, 1994)

Downing, Eric, *After Images: Photography, Archaeology, and Psychoanalysis and the Tradition of Bildung* (Detroit, MI, 2006)

École francaise d'Athènes, *La redécouverte de Delphes* (Athens, 1992)

Edwards, Elizabeth, *Raw Histories: Photographs, Anthropology and Museums (Oxford, 2001)*

Evans, R. Tripp, *Romancing the Maya: Mexican Antiquity in the American Imagination, 1820–1915* (Austin, TX, 2004)

Feyler, Gabrielle, 'Contribution à l'histoire des origins de la photographie archéologique, 1839–1880', *Mélanges de L'École française de Rome Antiquité*, IC (1987)

Gere, Cathy, *Knossos and the Prophets of Modernism* (Chicago, IL, 2009)

Gerster, Georg, *The Past from Above: Aerial Photographs of Archaeological Sites* (Los Angeles, CA, 2005)

Godlewska, Anne, 'Map, Text and Image, The Mentality of Enlightened Conquerors: A New Look at the *Description de l'Egypte*', *Transactions of the Institute of British Geographers*, N.S. XX (1995)

Greenewalt, Crawford H. Jr, *The City of Sardis: Approaches in Graphic Recording*, exh. cat., Harvard University Art Museums, Cambridge, MA (2003)

Gregory, Derek, 'Scripting Egypt: Orientalism and the Cultures of Travel', in *Writes of Passage: Reading Travel Writing* (London, 1999)

Guha-Thakurta, Tapati, *Monuments, Objects, Histories: Institutions of Art in Colonial and Postcolonial India* (New York, 2004)

Gunter, Anne C., and Stefan R. Hauser, eds, *Ernst Herzfeld and the Development of Near Eastern Studies, 1900–1950* (Leiden, 2005)

Gürsan-Salzmann, Ayse, *Exploring Iran: The Photography of Eric F. Schmidt, 1930–1940* (Philadelphia, PA, 2007)

Hallote, Rachel, 'Photography and the American Contribution to Early "Biblical" Archaeology, 1870–1920', *Near Eastern Archaeology*, LXX (2007)

Hauser, Kitty, *Bloody Old Britain: O.G.S. Crawford and the Archaeology of Modern Life* (London, 2008)

——, *Shadow Sites: Photography, Archaeology and the British Landscape, 1927–1955* (Oxford, 2007)

Innes, Randy, '*Jèrusalem* Revisited: On Auguste Salzmann's Topography', *Religion and the Arts*, XV (2011)

Kennedy, David, and Robert Bewley, *Ancient Jordan from the Air* (London, 2004)

Lyons, Claire L., ed., *Antiquity and Photography: Early Views of Ancient Mediterranean Sites*, exh. cat., J. Paul Getty Museum, Los Angeles, CA (2005)

Marchand, Suzanne L., *Down from Olympus: Archaeology and Philhellenism in Germany, 1750–1970* (Princeton, NJ, 1996)

Maynard, Patrick, *The Engine of Visualization: Thinking Through Photography* (Ithaca, NY, 1997)

Mondenard, Anne de, *La Mission héliographique: Cinq photographes parcourent la France en 1851* (Paris, 2002)

Moser, Stephanie, *Wondrous Curiosities: Ancient Egypt at the British Museum* (Chicago, IL, 2006)

Nassar, Issam, 'Early Local Photography in Jerusalem: From the Imaginary to the Social Landscape', *History of Photography*, XXVII (2003)

Nordström, Alison, 'Making a Journey: The Tupper Scrapbooks and the Travel They Describe', in *Photographs, Objects, Histories: On the*

*Materiality of Images*, ed. Elizabeth Edwards and Janice Hart (New York, 2004)

Osborne, Peter D., *Traveling Light: Photography, Travel and Visual Culture* (Manchester, 2000)

Pai, Hyung-Il, 'Capturing Visions of Japan's Prehistoric Past: Torii Ryuzo's Field Photographs of "Primitive" Races and Lost Civilizations', in *Looking Modern: East Asian Visual Culture from Treaty Ports to World War II*, ed. Jennifer Purtle and Hans Bjarne Thomsen (Chicago, IL, 2009)

Papadaki, Eirini, 'Mass-produced Images of Archaeological Sites: The Case Study of Knossos on Postcards', *Visual Resources*, XX (2004)

Pelizzari, Maria Antonella, ed., *Traces of India: Photography, Architecture and the Politics of Representation, 1850–1900*, exh. cat., Canadian Center for Architecture, Montréal/Yale Center for British Art, New Haven (2003)

Piggott, Stuart, *Antiquity Depicted: Aspects of Archaeological Illustration* (New York, 1978)

Poole, Deborah, *Vision, Race and Modernity: A Visual Economy of the Andean Image World* (Princeton, NJ, 1997)

Reed, Jane Levy, and Douglas Nickel, eds, *Photography and Archaeology: A Template for Investigation, Camerawork: A Journal of the Photographic Arts*, XXIV (Fall/Winter 1997)

Renfrew, Colin, *Figuring it Out: The Parallel Visions of Artists and Archaeologists* (London, 2003)

Riley, D. N., *Air Photography and Archaeology* (London, 1987)

Schlanger, Nathan, and Jarl Nordbladh, eds, *Archives, Ancestors, Practices: Archaeology in Light of Its History* (New York 2008)

Schmidt, Erich F., *Flights Over Ancient Cities of Iran* (Chicago, IL, 1940)

Schnapp, Alain, *The Discovery of the Past* (New York, 1997)

Scott, Sarah, 'Art and the Archaeologist', *World Archaeology*, XXXVIII (2006)

Schubert, Franz, and Susanne Grunauer-von Hoerschelmann, *Archäologie und Photographie: Fünzig Beispiele zur Geschichte und Methode* (Berlin, 1978)

Schwartz, Joan, and James Ryan, eds, *Picturing Place: Photography and the Geographical Imagination* (London, 2003)

Shanks, Michael, *Experiencing the Past: On the Character of Archaeology* (London, 1992)

Smiles, Sam, and Stephanie Moser, eds, *Envisioning the Past: Archaeology and the Image* (Malden, MA, 2005)

Wallace, Jennifer, *Digging the Dirt: The Archaeological Imagination* (London, 2004)

Wigoder, Meir, 'History Begins at Home: Photography and Memory in the Writings of Siegfried Kracauer and Roland Barthes', *History and Memory*, XIII (2001)

Wood, Christopher S., 'Notation of Visual Information in the Earliest Archaeological Scholarship', *Word and Image*, XVII (2001)

# Acknowledgements

This book had a slow gestation, floating among the remarkable resources of three research centres at which I have been privileged to hold fellowship: The Clark Art Institute in Williamstown, Massachusetts, the Getty Research Institute in Los Angeles, California, and the Canadian Center for Architecture in Montreal, Canada. I am deeply indebted to the directors, staff members and fellow researchers of these institutions for innumerable discussions, questions and suggestions. I doubt this book would exist without them. My thanks go also to staff at the many other libraries and archives at which I have done research on this topic over the past decade.

Jennifer Ross read the manuscript and told me what an archaeologist thought of it, which was both challenge and relief. Joanne Lukitsh read the manuscript and told me what a photo historian thought of it. I am grateful for her thoughts, and even more for her friendship. I owe to Zainab Bahrani, Martha Bari, Laurie King, Stephanie Moser and Alan Wallach a broader intellectual debt for a continuing and stimulating conversation.

For someone who usually writes about people long dead, it has been a particular pleasure to work with the contemporary artists, archaeologists and archaeological photographers considered here, who have been almost unfailingly generous with their time and images.

My thanks to Burt Blistein, Nadine Granoff, Allan and Mary Holtzman, Dena Jacobs, Vivian Keller and Sara Williams, for many kindnesses, suggestions, support and just for listening. A special thanks to Marie-France Daigneault Bouchard who arrived at a critical period, and made amazing things happen. I am grateful also to Vivian Constantinopoulos for her steadfast support and Blanche Craig for many wise textual ministrations.

# Photo Acknowledgements

The author and publishers wish to express their thanks to the following sources of illustrative material and/or permission to reproduce it:

Courtesy of Aaron Levin and the Pompeii Forum Project: 55; Art Resource, NY: 10, 95 (Reunion des Musées Nationaux); Alison Frantz Photographic Collection, American School of Classical Studies at Athens: 151; Bibliothèque Nationale de France: 6; © The British Museum Library Board: 34 (Talbot 22(264)); Corbis: 130 (Roger Wood); © École Française d'Athènes: 74 (top), 77; Freer Gallery of Art and the Arthur M. Sackler Gallery Archives, Smithsonian Institution, Washington DC: 18–19, 80 (Ernst Herzfeld Papers. Gift of Ernst Herzfeld, 1946), 38 (bottom; Carl Whiting Bishop Papers), 79, 81 (Myron Bement Smith Collection. Gift of Katherine Dennis Smith 1973–85); Courtesy of Frank H. McClung Museum, The University of Tennessee, Knoxville: 57; Gertrude Bell Archive, University of Newcastle: 24 (Image Number K088); The J. Paul Getty Museum, Los Angeles: 32, 45, 47–8; © Marilyn Bridges 1983: 156; The Metropolitan Museum of Art, Image © The Metropolitan Museum of Art: 14–15 (Photography by the Egyptian Exhibition. Rare Books and Special Collections, McGill University Library); © Ministère de la Culture/Médiathèque du Patrimoine, Dist. RMN/Art Resource, NY: 118; Photograph © 2011 Museum of Fine Arts, Boston: 134; Photographic Collection, Miriam and Ira D. Wallach Division of Art, Prints and Photographs, The New York Public Library, Astor, Lenox and Tilden Foundations: 62; Oriental Institute, University of Chicago: 23, 55, 72, 139; Palestine Exploration Fund: 121; Courtesy of Penn Museum: 52, 112, 125–6; Rosenwald Collection. Image courtesy of the National Gallery of Art, Washington DC: 47; Science and Society Picture Library: 30, 31 (National Media Museum).

# Index

*Page numbers in italics refer to illustrations*